THE TRAGI-COMEDY OF
VICTORIAN FATHERHOOD

Examining Victorian middle-class fatherhood from the fathers' own perspective, Valerie Sanders dismantles the persistent stereotype of the nineteenth-century paterfamilias by focusing on the intimate family lives of influential public men. Beginning with Prince Albert as a high-profile patriarchal role-model, and comparing the parallel case histories of prominent Victorians such as Dickens, Darwin, Huxley and Gladstone, the book explores the strains on men in public life as they managed their private relationship with their children and found a language for the expression of their pleasure, grief and anxiety as fathers. In a context of cultural uncertainty about the legal rights and moral responsibilities of fatherhood, the study draws on a wealth of unpublished journals and letters to show how conscientious Victorian fathers in effect invented a meaningful domestic role for themselves which has been little understood.

VALERIE SANDERS is Professor of English at the University of Hull.

CAMBRIDGE STUDIES IN NINETEENTH-CENTURY LITERATURE AND CULTURE

General editor

Gillian Beer, *University of Cambridge*

Editorial board

Isobel Armstrong, *Birkbeck, University of London*
Kate Flint, *Rutgers University*
Catherine Gallagher, *University of California, Berkeley*
D. A. Miller, *University of California, Berkeley*
J. Hillis Miller, *University of California, Irvine*
Daniel Pick, *Birkbeck, University of London*
Mary Poovey, *New York University*
Sally Shuttleworth, *University of Oxford*
Herbert Tucker, *University of Virginia*

Nineteenth-century British literature and culture have been rich fields for interdisciplinary studies. Since the turn of the twentieth century, scholars and critics have tracked the intersections and tensions between Victorian literature and the visual arts, politics, social organisation, economic life, technical innovations, scientific thought – in short, culture in its broadest sense. In recent years, theoretical challenges and historiographical shifts have unsettled the assumptions of previous scholarly synthesis and called into question the terms of older debates. Whereas the tendency in much past literary critical interpretation was to use the metaphor of culture as 'background', feminist, Foucauldian and other analyses have employed more dynamic models that raise questions of power and of circulation. Such developments have reanimated the field. This series aims to accommodate and promote the most interesting work being undertaken on the frontiers of the field of nineteenth-century literary studies: work that intersects fruitfully with other fields of study such as history, or literary theory, or the history of science. Comparative as well as interdisciplinary approaches are welcomed.

A complete list of titles published will be found at the end of the book.

THE TRAGI-COMEDY OF VICTORIAN FATHERHOOD

VALERIE SANDERS

CAMBRIDGE
UNIVERSITY PRESS

CAMBRIDGE UNIVERSITY PRESS
Cambridge, New York, Melbourne, Madrid, Cape Town, Singapore, São Paulo, Delhi

Cambridge University Press
The Edinburgh Building, Cambridge CB2 8RU, UK

Published in the United States of America by Cambridge University Press, New York

www.cambridge.org
Information on this title: www.cambridge.org/9780521884785

First published 2009

Printed in the United Kingdom at the University Press, Cambridge

A catalogue record for this publication is available from the British Library

ISBN 978-0-521-88478-5 hardback

For my own father
Dr Michael Sanders

Epigraph

My eldest boy – married not particularly to my satisfaction – is in business as an Eastern Merchant in the City, and will do well if he can find continuous energy; otherwise not. My second boy, with the 42nd Highlanders in India, spends more than he gets and has cost me money and disappointed me. My third boy, a good steady fellow but not at all brilliant, is educating expensively for engineers or artillery. My fourth (this sounds like a charade), a born little sailor, is a Midshipman in H.M.S. Orlando now at Bermuda, and will make his way any where. Remaining two, at school; . . . and Francis Jeffrey (I ought to have counted him as the third boy, so we'll take him in here as No. 2 and a half) in my office, pending a vacancy in the Foreign Office. Now you have the family bill of fare.

Charles Dickens enumerating his children in 1862

Contents

Illustrations

Acknowledgments

The initial idea for this book came from a conference, *Father Figures: Gender and Paternity in the Modern Age*, held at Liverpool John Moores University in 2003, which opened up a fabulously rich field for researchers from all disciplines. The paper I gave on Kingsley, included in the book of conference essays, *Gender and Fatherhood in the Nineteenth Century* (2007), edited by Trev Lynn Broughton and Helen Rogers, has been expanded for this current book. The chapter on Dickens and Macready was given as a research paper, first at Hull University and then for a seminar at the University of Sunderland: I am grateful to colleagues past and present for their comments on each occasion. Further topics, such as the 'idle son' theme, Thomas Arnold's attempts to make his daughter curtsey to her mother, and patterns of godfathering, were prompted by other conference opportunities: the British Association for Victorian Studies in Liverpool in 2006; *Gendering the Subject*, University of Wales, Gregynog in 2004; and *The Politics of Domestic Authority in Britain* at King's College, Cambridge, in 2006. I owe much to people I met at these events, who are unaware that they had a hand in producing this book.

Among those who are, special thanks are due to Linda Bree of Cambridge University Press for her positive response to the initial proposal, and to Maartje Scheltens for guiding the finished product towards publication. Noël O'Sullivan suggested the importance of 'contingency' to the psychology of the Victorians, and an email correspondence with Martin Danahay helped develop my ideas on idle sons and masculine work. Janet Clare kindly checked the material on Macready and Shakespeare. Practical help was offered by many librarians who always had the boxes of papers ready on the day, especially Anne Barrett at Imperial College, and staff at the Flintshire Record Office. Teaching relief to begin and complete the research was provided by the University of Hull, and The Arts and Humanities Research Council (AHRC) Research Leave

Scheme gave me time to finish the project in the spring term of 2008. To the anonymous AHRC assessors and the Cambridge University Press readers I owe particular thanks for their thoughtful suggestions on how to improve the work once it was under way.

For permission to quote from unpublished manuscript material in their collections, I am grateful to the following: The Bodleian Library, Oxford; The British Library; the Brotherton Collection, University of Leeds; the Syndics of Cambridge University Library; The Trustees of the Royal Botanic Gardens, Kew; Flintshire Record Office; Sir William Gladstone and C. A. Gladstone; Trinity College, Cambridge; the Trustees of Lambeth Palace Library and the Archbishop of Canterbury; Imperial College London; Oxford University Press; St Deiniol's Library, Hawarden; and The Wordsworth Trust, Dove Cottage, Cumbria. Illustrated material appears by permission of the National Portrait Gallery; the Mary Evans Picture Library; the Flintshire Record Office; and the Shakespeare Birthplace Trust, Stratford-upon-Avon. While every attempt has been made to discover the copyright holders of manuscript papers, this has proved exceptionally difficult and confusing in some cases: I can only apologise for any unintentional oversights.

Quotations from Howard Jacobson's novel, *The Making of Henry*, are reproduced with permission of Curtis Brown Group Ltd, London, on behalf of Howard Jacobson. The epigraph quotation is from Charles Dickens, *The Letters of Charles Dickens*, ed. Madeline House *et al.*, 12 Vols. (Oxford: Clarendon Press, 1965–99), Vol. x (1862–4), ed. Graham Storey, p. 53.

Quotations from Matthew Arnold's letters are reprinted by permission of The University of Virginia Press, from Matthew Arnold, *The Letters of Matthew Arnold*, ed. Cecil Y. Lang, 6 vols. (Charlottesville and London: University of Virginia Press, 1996–2001), © The University of Virginia Press 1996–2001.

The book is dedicated to my own father, Dr Michael Sanders, who took me to my first day at school, cured me of many childhood illnesses, and still worries about my walking home alone. My mother, Patricia Sanders, like all the wise wives and mothers in this book, has provided constant support, and more hot dinners than I care to mention.

Arts & Humanities
Research Council

Introduction. Looking for the Victorian father

> The father was a stern and thinking man: 'cold and cross-grained', the neighbours called him, though what the meaning of the term 'cross-grained' may be, I will not undertake to say, as I only understand the term when applied to wood.[1]

This description of a stereotypical Victorian paterfamilias, written around 1845–50 by the adolescent Charles Lutwidge Dodgson, otherwise Lewis Carroll, future author of *Alice's Adventures in Wonderland* (1865), features in 'Sidney Hamilton', a story Dodgson serialised in the family's *Rectory Magazine*. Already displeased with his son when the story opens, Mr Hamilton 'received him with a cold and distant manner, and a brow gloomier than that which he usually wore' (p. 9), but when Sidney refuses to abandon an unsuitable friendship, the father threatens to cut him off. '"Look you here, son!" shouted he seeing that his words made little impression on his son, "obey me, or on this spot I disinherit you!"' (p. 11). So far so predictable: Dodgson's writing perfectly encapsulates the essence of the Victorian 'heavy father' of popular imagination. More surprisingly, as the story develops, the father turns out to be right: Sidney's unsuitable friend, Edmund Tracy, is exposed as a thief, and after a nightmare in which Sidney imagines his father letting him drown, Mr Hamilton – up before the magistrate on a false charge – is happily reconciled with his headstrong son. Both men have something to learn from the episode, about patience, stubbornness and trust, but the reader's sympathy is assumed to be with the romantic son as he flees domestic tyranny, and sees his father publicly shamed before the reconciliation.

Over thirty years later, F. Anstey's *Vice-Versa; or, A Lesson to Fathers* (1882) seems to expand and develop Dodgson's idea of punishing the father, while half admitting he is right, in an extended battle with his schoolboy son. In this role-swapping fantasy, Paul Bultitude is changed by a magic wishing stone into his own son Dick, while Dick sees his father off to Dr Grimstone's boarding school, and for a glorious week revels in paternal freedom and authority, though he has an entirely different way of running both business and household. He abandons his job in the city and spends most of the day at home playing soldiers with the baby in the dining-room. 'You would laugh to see him loading the cannons with real powder and shot', Paul's daughter Barbara comments (assuming she is writing to her brother at school), 'and he didn't care a bit when some of it made holes in the side-board and smashed the looking-glass'.[2] While Dick causes chaos at home, Paul has much the same effect on Dr Grimstone's school, where he is first expelled, and then threatened with a public flogging, before he makes a laborious escape back home. There father and son confront each other in their changed identities: 'It was a strange sensation on entering to see the image of what he had so lately been standing by the mantelpiece. It gave a shock to his sense of his own identity' (p. 194). What the reader gathers from this role-swap is that being the father is infinitely preferable to being the son. In Dick's eyes at least, what fatherhood consists of is 'No school, no lessons, nothing to do but amuse myself, eat and drink what I like, and lots of money' (p. 197).

Both these texts offer what is essentially a son's view of being a father. In many ways a stereotypical fantasy of power and freedom, this impression of fatherhood is created from the outside, by youths who are too young and inexperienced to know what paternal responsibilities are. Victorian literature and life-writing are full of such stern fathers who are alien and other in their children's limited understanding, created from their perspective, rather than the father's own. In fact there are few good fathers in Victorian fiction, perhaps for the obvious reason that a good father, even more than a good mother, forestalls any real plot development or initiative on the children's part. Since it was his responsibility to provide for his offspring, the existence of a sympathetic and competent father was normally sufficient guarantee of a safe destiny for his children. In fiction, this often goes wrong when the father, like Meredith's Sir Austin in *The Ordeal of Richard Feverel* (1859), becomes unduly fixated on some plan or 'system' for his son. Dickens's fathers are especially prone to such schemes, from Mr Dombey (1848) to Pip's father-substitute Magwitch in *Great Expectations* (1860–1). The most notorious is probably Samuel Butler's Mr Pontifex (1903), who thrashes his sons to suppress any signs of self-will. 'You carry so many more guns than they do that they cannot fight you', the narrator says of fathers who bully their sons into conformity.[3] Others are distracted by an external grievance, leading to revenge fantasies: Elizabeth Gaskell's John Barton (*Mary Barton*, 1848) brooding on his resentment of the factory-owners; George Eliot's Mr Tulliver (*The Mill on the Floss*, 1860) waiting for his moment to get back at Mr Wakem; or Hardy's Michael Henchard (*The Mayor of Casterbridge*, 1886), whose troubles with his wife, daughter, mistress and business rival prevent him from forming any lasting domestic relationships. In Victorian life-writing, similarly preoccupied fathers abound: Philip Gosse, the scientist and religious fanatic of Edmund Gosse's *Father and Son* (1907); the intense Edward White Benson, Archbishop of Canterbury; Sir Leslie Stephen demanding sympathy and accurate household accounting from the daughters of his dead wife Julia; and Charles Kingsley and Charles Dickens, who, to their children, seemed to be always striding about the countryside in a tornado of activity, divided between their real-life practical concerns and their swarming imaginations.

Moreover, the father is very often the only parent who figures significantly in the novel or memoir. Dickens's children rarely mention their mother in their memories of him, even though she outlived her husband; while in his novels, Mrs Dombey dies in the opening chapter, Mrs Copperfield is survived by Mr Murdstone; Mr Jarndyce of *Bleak House* can offer his charges no motherly guardian other than Esther, herself a ward; and Mr Dorrit, the 'Father of the Marshalsea', loses his wife when Little Dorrit ('Little Mother') is a child of eight. There are, of course, plenty of memorable single mothers in Dickens's novels, such as Mrs Clennam and Mrs Nickleby, but the widowed or unpartnered dominant surviving father is a much more prominent feature of Victorian writing, especially in novels by Elizabeth Gaskell (Mr Gibson, John Barton, Nicholas Higgins) and George Eliot (often foster-fathers, such as Silas Marner, Mr Brooke, and Sir Hugo Mallinger). All the negative features of the angry widowed father seem to converge in Ephraim Tellwright of Arnold Bennett's *Anna of the Five Towns* (1902): a domestic tyrant who is also a miser, refusing to let Anna control her own finances, or be late home for tea. The Victorian 'heavy father' seemingly ends the century as secure in his bullying presence as he began it.

The purpose of this study, however, is to dismantle the stereotypical image of the Victorian father, and to do so by changing the perspective from which he is viewed. Because there is such a wealth of memoirs published by traumatised children, relatively little has been written about, or from, the father's own position. This material is found less in memoirs and novels, where reticence about parenthood is common to both male and female life-writers, than in the voluminous correspondence for which the Victorians were so well known. Here Victorian men can be found writing to their children, or to friends who were also fathers, and comparing notes on every stage of their children's progress. Here, too, fathers express their feelings about fatherhood in a way that was often unguarded or outspoken: regretting superfluous births, worrying about the slow progress of unmotivated sons or mourning the loss of a favourite child. Although these letters often mention the children's mothers, it is usually to imply that the mother has a different kind of relationship with her children – a more physical, practical and domestic one – while the father feels responsible for the overall direction of the child's life and eventual destiny. If proof is needed of an involved, 'hands-on' approach to nineteenth-century fatherhood, the letters of men such as John James Ruskin, Matthew Arnold, Charles Dickens and Charles Darwin provide ample evidence, much of it so far unused for this purpose.

This approach to finding out more about Victorian fathers owes much to the pioneering scholarship of researchers who have already tackled the strange 'absent presence' of nineteenth-century fathers in social history and literature. In fact, thanks to their recent efforts, there is no longer any real need to prove that the typical Victorian father was as decent and humane as his modern counterpart. Leonore Davidoff and Catherine Hall, drawing on studies of specific families, have already shown that many late-eighteenth and early-nineteenth-century fathers were emotionally engaged with their children and closely involved in their lives.[4] Though some Victorian fathers were undoubtedly harsh and distant, we know that the majority took their responsibilities seriously and wanted to do their best by their families; they bonded well with their children and were distraught when they were ill or died. Moreover, as John Tosh and others have suggested, respect for the untouchable authority of fathers seems to have declined as the century progressed.[5] As early as 1865, *All the Year Round* claimed that the 'old patriarchal father', who was 'a sort of Jove to his children', had begun to disappear 'about the time when penny postage was adopted' (1840). 'It may be said', this reviewer concludes, drawing on political analogies suggested by the 1832 Reform Act, 'that children have compelled their autocratic fathers to give them a constitution'.[6] Twenty years later, even a reviewer for the conservative *Quarterly Review* was admitting that 'the practical domestic authority of an English Father in his own household was once vastly greater than it is now. The ceremonious forms with which he was addressed by his children and even by his wife have disappeared.' Citing a Latin term for the powers traditionally lodged with the chief of the household, he concludes that they are living in the presence of a 'decayed Patria Potestas'.[7]

Nonetheless, the bullying stereotype of the Victorian father is curiously persistent – in the popular imagination, at least – and fictional examples reappear throughout the century. It is almost as if we *want* fathers to have been monsters, in order to have someone to blame for all that was wrong with the Victorian family. Given the current critical fashion for 'problematising' norms and monoliths in cultural history, especially the middle-class patriarch, the Victorian father is the ideal problem that won't go away, the louring villain in the drawing-room preventing wives and children from fulfilling themselves in the world beyond the home. He belongs, however, to a highly complex structure of relationships with women and children, colleagues and friends. The language he uses ranges from professional jargon to the private, subdued tones of grief and intimacy. He relates awkwardly to the sentimental, which he nevertheless needs *in extremis*. Clearly fatherhood cannot be discussed apart from motherhood, the history of gender relations, or indeed the dynamics of the whole family as it began to emerge from the Industrial Revolution into something recognisably like our current structures. Nor is it easy explaining exactly how fathers related to their children in view of our dependence on incomplete or atypical written records, or the tendency of fathers to dramatise their role in correspondence with male friends. 'We know a lot less about fathers than we do about mothers', Nancy E. Dowd asserts.[8] Although she is referring to contemporary American society, her view that 'Fathers parent less than mothers', sounds like what we suspect of Victorian fathers, whose slippery social and domestic position is the focus of much current scholarship.

Following the lead of Davidoff and Hall, fatherhood specialists such as John Tosh, Trev Broughton, Helen Rogers, John Gillis and Claudia Nelson have examined in detail the anomalous condition of Victorian fathers as both central and liminal to the culture, uncomfortably aligned with its versions of middle-class masculinity as gentlemanly, well-bred, detached and self-controlled. Paternity makes men vulnerable as well as affirming their virility, especially in cases of childhood death and illness, yet as John Gillis (1996) suggests, fathers have long occupied only a threshold presence in family and domestic life. His impression is that our culture 'simply will not take paternity as seriously as maternity'.[9] This view is especially true of the Victorians, for whom motherhood is the cornerstone of the whole domestic structure, while the father's place is more often than not in the external workplace. This is in fact the central paradox of Victorian fatherhood. The traditional patriarch belongs at the head of his table or as God the Father's representative in the home, leading the family in morning and evening prayers, but his domestic role the rest of the time evades definition. The fact that many men worked from within their homes (clergymen, headmasters, authors and doctors especially) seems to have had little impact on the 'separate spheres' ideology, with the father at best relegated to his study where he worked in a tangential relationship with the rest of the household.

Social historians have now identified specific patterns of behaviour within upper- and middle-class family homes. David Roberts, for example, focusing on the memoirs of what he calls the 'Victorian Governing Classes', categorised his findings according to three characteristic fathering patterns: 'remoteness, sovereignty, and benevolence', concluding that fatherhood 'was a conservative institution in Victorian England, one that prompted continuity more than it did rebellion'.[10] More recently, John Tosh (1999) named four different fatherhood models which had become established by mid century. These were the absent, the tyrannical, the distant and the intimate father. Tosh also confirms that 'Of all the qualifications for full masculine status, fatherhood was the least talked about by the Victorians.'[11] Because of its hidden performance in the home, and the assumption that everyone knew what a father was supposed to do, much of what he actually did do – apart from his legal responsibilities – apparently went untheorised. If the details of 'mothering' have been hidden from history until relatively recently, still more have the daily emotional and domestic commitments of 'fathering', as Stuart C. Aitken has argued in a discussion of its 'awkward spaces'. Aitken claims that fathers suffer from an invisible 'identity predicament': they may be seen as co-parents with mothers, but they have always had more freedom than mothers to walk away from their children, and therefore opt out of active fatherhood. According to Aitken, this was particularly the case during and after the Industrial Revolution, which, in separating the male workplace from the home, legitimised the father's emotional disjunction from his family. Moreover, though history has also seen mothers as 'incomplete fathers' (unable to provide materially for their children), fathers fare worse as 'incomplete mothers' because, as Aitken points out, in social science research at least, 'mothers are the benchmark for norms in fathering'.[12] As 'failed mothers', nineteenth-century fathers were left with little direct advice as to how they were supposed to create an alternative role, especially in terms of achieving the right balance between emotional sensitivity and moral leadership – a balance that was assumed to come naturally to mothers. This was part-and-parcel of the culture's uncertainty about what we might call middle-class 'male values'. 'Even at their toughest and most conservative', argues Matthew Sweet, 'Victorian theorists and polemicists failed to offer a uniform, coherent blueprint for proper masculine behaviour'.[13]

Although motherhood was widely considered to be 'natural', endless quantities of advice were published to help new mothers produce healthy children and manage their homes. Pye Henry Chavasse's *Advice to Mothers* (1839) ran to countless editions; other popular titles included Henry Frank E. Harrison's *Advice to Mothers How to Rear Their Infants Healthily* (1882), Dr Alfred Fennings's *Every Mother's Book* (1858) and William Buchan's rather quaintly titled *Advice to Mothers on the Subject of Their Own Health; and on the Means of Promoting the Health, Strength, and Beauty of Their Offspring* (1803). According to Sally Shuttleworth, such were concerns about the physically poor condition of women and the risks of inherited disease, that 'the functions of maternity were the object of fierce scrutiny and control'.[14] With fathers, bodily separateness from the child meant there were no such acute health issues to discuss. Though there was a *British Mothers' Magazine* (1845–55), which became *The British Mothers' Journal* (1856–63), edited by Mrs J. Bakewell; a *Mother's Magazine* (1842–62); *Mother's Friend* (1848–59); and *Mother's Companion* (1887–96), there was apparently no niche market for fathers' supportive literature, any more than there is today. The British Library catalogue lists no Victorian periodicals beginning with 'Father's' (*Father's Companion*, or the like), though advice to fathers was sometimes hidden away in 'home' or 'family' magazines, especially for the lower classes. Poole's *Index to Periodical Literature* (1882), covering the first three quarters of the nineteenth century, lists only a handful of articles concerned with fathers and fathering, and most of these refer to the Church Fathers, or to serialised fiction about fathers and children.

Under 'Mothers', though the list is still surprisingly short, there are articles on the duty, influence and education of mothers, as well as 'middle-class' mothers and 'mothers of great men'.[15] If the term 'fathers of great men' lacks the same resonance, so do the notions of the duty, influence or education of fathers. Sarah Ellis, who instructed the Women, Mothers, Wives and Daughters of England, felt no call to advise the fathers, except parenthetically, through her advice to their wives.[16] Natalie McKnight even suggests that Mrs Ellis sees a mother's duties as 'being nothing short of maintaining and developing the child's complete physical, mental, and spiritual health, pretty much without the help of father'.[17] Ellis also makes the point that there is 'no escape' from the duties of being a mother, whereas (though she does not say so explicitly), being a father has always been a more casual responsibility, to be accepted or not, largely at the father's own will. The frontispiece to her *Women of England* shows a triangular-shaped family group on a sofa, consisting of a mother being embraced by two daughters, with a boy sheltering by her side, while in the doorway stand two men in dark coats, either coming in or going out, and pointing their fingers towards this tableau of domestic bliss. The men's liminality in the domestic scene is perfectly symbolised by their position in the doorway, looking slightly bemused by what they see. Dressed in dark colours as a further contrast to the whiteness of the women and children (the only boy is already darkly dressed like his father), the men look as if they would be happier out of the house and at their club or office. Ellis's unshakeable belief in the subordination of women to men within the home, though by no means founded on any conviction of male moral superiority, must have made her reluctant to engage directly with the reformation of male behaviour.

Fathers' absence from the domestic scene was not always the norm, however. In his work on the history of the family in colonial America, Steven Mintz has shown that in the seventeenth and early eighteenth centuries, the father was the dominant parent, and domestic advice books were directed towards men rather than women.[18] In England, at a similar period and beyond, fathers were themselves regarded as a source of wisdom, as shown in the titles of books such as the widowed Dr John Gregory's *A Father's Legacy to his Daughters* (1773), or the early-Victorian Samuel Thompson's *A Father's Advice to His Daughters on Entering into the Marriage State* (1844). The frontispiece to *The Family Friend* (Vol. 11, 1849–50) is dominated by an illustration of a father with a book on his lap, reading to his surrounding family. As my chapter on Kingsley shows, fathers also featured in lesson books for children, giving advice about science, history and religion, but they came to be eclipsed by mothers whose natural qualification for the teaching role was more readily recognised.

Within Victorian working-class culture, the father's role tended to be seen as more central and natural than it was in some middle-class homes. William Cobbett argued in his *Advice to Young Men* (1829–30) that the presence of servants in the middle-to-upper classes impeded good relations between fathers and children, whereas working men had more 'hands-on' experience of looking after their growing families. Moreover, he equated active fatherhood with good citizenship and moral worth, strenuously denied that it made a man effeminate, and reminded his readers that 'the honourable title and the boundless power of father' came with lifelong responsibilities.[19] Richard Oastler's *The Home* (1851), a conservative paper which took as its motto: 'The Altar, the Throne, and the Cottage', similarly offered its working-class readers positive images of home life to offset the heartless atmosphere of the mills. Several issues were prefaced with poems celebrating the domestic happiness of the working man in the pre-industrial golden age, such as 'The Cottage Fire' by historian Agnes Strickland, which climaxes in the father's return home at the end of the working day:

> His rosy prattlers round him press,
> With smiles of infant glee;
> The youngest nestles to his breast,
> The elder climb his knee.[20]

Nevertheless, fatherhood in all classes was recognised as problematic by the Victorians, and was widely discussed in the public domain, albeit not in the same places as motherhood. Instead, it emerged largely in spaces dominated by male hegemonic discourse: parliamentary debates, newspaper journalism and in the law courts, where an entirely male assembly continued for much of the century to defend the father's privileges, while slowly giving ground to a growing recognition that society was changing and the old traditions would no longer answer. Mostly, in nineteenth-century Britain, fathers were written *about*, rather than directly advised. Though their behaviour was more often criticised than applauded, the underlying reluctance to tackle fathers head-on with their shortcomings produced a vague malaise in the culture, rather than the passionate activism generated by concern for women's rights. Pulled three ways between biological, social and legal definitions, blamed (by implication) for not embodying the gentler, more nurturing characteristics of motherhood, Victorian fatherhood was in all aspects of its performance a seemingly stable idea under persistent attack by a combination of neglect, complacency, shifting public opinion and legal reform.

'BOUNDLESS POWER': FATHERHOOD AND THE LAW

The sixty-four years of Victoria's reign saw a gradual erosion of the father's 'sacred' and 'natural' rights to what amounted to exclusive ownership of his offspring. The catalyst for this decline in respect for fathers was largely the legal and cultural focus on the breakdown of middle-class marriage, which inevitably exposed disturbing examples of how husbands and fathers behaved in the home. As separated and divorced mothers began to claim an equal or morally superior right to custody of their children, judges, church leaders and Members of Parliament found themselves locked in argument as to what exactly a father's rights and duties entailed. Despite almost continuous discussion of the mother's claims around issues such as child custody, the Poor Laws, marriage, divorce, and marriage with one's deceased wife's sister, there remained an underlying conviction in favour of the father's custody rights, which took the whole century to undermine. 'Nothing can be clearer than that, according to English law, the parental power is vested in the father alone', *The Times* reported in 1864. 'It is he who while he lives is permanent guardian of the children, and entitled to the control of their persons during the age of minority.' While conceding that younger children and girls belonged more rightly to the mother, this editorial nevertheless insisted that 'we must here, as ever, adapt human laws to the natural inequality of the sexes, and give the superiority of right to that which cannot but have the superiority of power'. Twenty years later, in 1884, there was still a basic legal and common understanding that 'The children belong to the father.'[21]

While concern existed about the working-class father, this centred largely on his role as a good provider. As Sonya Rose argues, parliamentary debate about the Factory Acts in the 1840s 'reinforced the idea that men were responsible for the economic well-being of their families, whereas wives were responsible for motherhood'.[22] A good working-class father, therefore, was a man who could keep his family out of the workhouse and put wholesome food on the table; he also avoided the alehouse, and helped his sons into apprenticeships. Although there were ongoing arguments about the bastardy clauses in the Poor Law Amendment Act, working-class fatherhood perhaps seemed easier to regulate than the middle-class version where there were subtler nuances of education, religion and personal morality at stake.[23] Victorian anxiety about fatherhood came to rest essentially on the plight of the middle-class man whose marriage had somehow foundered, making the welfare of his children a new cultural responsibility.

In the nineteenth century, the father's role – at least as discussed in the public domain – was primarily legal, and his 'ownership' of any children of his marriage was a point of principle widely accepted for most of the period. Caroline Norton's campaign to have the mother's rights acknowledged on an equal basis is too well known to need reiterating here; it was the first serious legal challenge to the supremacy of the father, which opened the doors to further assays, not least from Norton herself, through the remainder of the century.[24] Though the Infant Custody Act of 1839 permitted a separated mother of unblemished reputation to retain custody of any children under the age of seven, the law was clearly at odds with the burgeoning feminist subculture in declaring the father the only parent with legal rights over the children; it was another thirty-four years before the 1873 Act extended the mother's custody rights to older children, up to the age of sixteen. As a *Times* commentary of 1865 indicates, however, the court had the power to infringe a father's rights, 'and when the common home has been broken up by the conduct of the father it frequently exercises its power in favour of the injured mother'.[25] The point was that the father had a prior claim unless he forfeited it by his own misconduct. Only proven cases of domestic violence or blatant adultery were likely to cost him his paternal rights.

Not that the father's position was by any means clear-cut, given the language in which it was defined. As stated in *Blackstone's Commentaries on the Laws of England* (1765–9), which remained the primary source of law and morality at the start of the Victorian period, his responsibilities sound obvious enough, but closer observation of the wording exposes immediate ambiguities. The father is first and foremost a provider 'for those descended from his loins', but Blackstone then refers to 'this natural obligation of the father to provide for his children'. The contradictory phrase, a 'natural obligation', implies that this responsibility is both instinctual and yet somehow enforced. In begetting children, Blackstone elaborates, parents have 'entered into a voluntary obligation' to support and preserve their offspring.[26] Equally complex is the grey area between 'rights' and 'duties'. Whereas a father is legally expected to provide for children under the age of twenty-one, he is not necessarily obliged to 'maintain his idle and lazy children in ease and indolence' (p. 437). As later sections of this book will show, maintaining idle sons was indeed a real problem for many Victorian fathers as an epidemic of lethargy seemed to drain the energies of middle-class sons in the closing decades of the century.

On the other hand, the law was ever mindful of children's rights. It would not 'suffer a parent at his death totally to disinherit his child, without expressly giving his reason for so doing' (pp. 435–6). In his attempts to construct a fair balance between the needs of fathers and children, Blackstone creates a scenario of negotiated responsibilities predicated on mutual reasonableness. He is aware that the balance can go awry, but assumes that in rational households it will not. As for the mother, she has no legal power over her children anyway, so her role in the family triangle is for Blackstone's purposes irrelevant to the discussion. When Thomas Talfourd began campaigning in Parliament for the mother's custody rights in the late 1830s, he initially asked for *access*, presumably because the award of full custody seemed at that stage unrealistic.[27]

Fatherhood is therefore initially mooted in terms of 'voluntary' and 'natural' 'obligation': terms referring back to the mixed biological and legal compulsions of the relationship. In fact, as Allen Horstman notes, many couples petitioning for divorce were childless, or had already made arrangements for their children, but this was not enough to halt the steadily mounting challenge to the father's authority in the social structure, caused by legislation in favour of women's guardianship of children.[28] While it was recognised that women were bound to have closer physical ties to babies and small children, the responsibility of a father for his older children, especially in relation to their education and religious guidance, remained a contentious issue. Certain high-profile court cases, such as the custody battle between Annie Besant and her husband Frank (1873/1878–9), or the fight for religious authority between Leopold Agar Ellis (a Protestant) and his Catholic wife Harriet (1878), gave judges and journalists alike the opportunity to revisit the old arguments about paternal ownership of children. As Leonore Davidoff *et al.* argue in their discussion of the Agar Ellis case, 'What all the judges involved in this dispute agreed about was the absolute authority of fathers over their children, an authority which was derived from nature, and confirmed by religious and civil practices.'[29] During the court hearings *The Times* reported many pronouncements by the judges that pitted the notion of the father's 'natural' authority as guardian and 'trustee' of his children's welfare against the mother's essentially emotional claims, which remained unrecognised by the law. The language used in such cases is particularly strong in challenging alternative interpretations: phrases such as 'absolute control' and 'absolute authority' are used of the father's position. Even so, *The Times* acknowledged that some of what it was asserting might sound extreme for the age: 'even in these days', the newspaper admits, 'it is a mere recognition of fact to admit the father's title to govern his family'.[30] As for a case like the Besants', where the father was a clergyman and the mother a self-proclaimed agnostic, *The Times* wondered what would have happened had their religious positions been reversed: 'Would the authority of the father survive in such a case to keep the children under his educational influence despite the resistance of the mother? We cannot profess to answer this question.'[31]

This rather strange throwaway remark acknowledges that the father's authority in such cases would not be infinitely elastic, and would therefore not be infallible in all situations relating to his children. Joint parental rights might have seemed the obvious solution to increasingly acrimonious custody cases but, as Ben Griffin has shown, opposition to joint parental guardianship of children remained deeply ingrained, with Clause 2 of the 1886 Guardian of Infants Act – a clause proposing such joint guardianship – disappearing in the course of parliamentary debate.[32] Although the second reading of the debate on 26 March 1884, as recorded in Hansard, began with a strong sense of mothers' inequality in the eyes of the law, MPs quickly raised the alarm about what they called 'duality of control', 'two authorities in the household', 'this double authority' and 'a dual jurisdiction' if mothers were to be given equal power with fathers, especially over issues of education and religious upbringing. The MP Thomas Collins declared: 'It was a monstrous thing to enable a wife to say that her husband's wishes with respect to the education of his son should not be fulfilled.'[33] It was not until 1925 that the Guardianship of Infants Act recognised the equal rights and responsibilities of both parents in awarding custody of their children.

Once the welfare of the child became the main concern, as it did towards the end of the century, the father, in effect, had to compete with the mother for custody, especially of sons. As even destitution and cruelty were sometimes overlooked in such cases, it seems fitting to ask why a father's rights were considered quite so sacred, to the point where he had to be exceptionally immoral or lawless to forfeit his custody claims. As we have seen, this reluctance to concede ground to mothers comes partly from a religious conviction that the father is the supreme source of authority (in effect God's representative in the family), and partly from a fear of creating disputed authority and dissension in the home. Equally important, though, was the underlying distrust of mothers' ability to take command of the household beyond its purely domestic functions. For all decisions relating to schooling, religious direction, financial support and careers, there remained a deeply rooted conviction that only fathers would have the worldly experience to provide reliable guidance, especially in relation to the upbringing of boys.

The nineteenth century, therefore, witnessed a lengthy and painful struggle to admit wives into a more equal legal partnership with their husbands so far as the management of their children was concerned. In the long, tortured parliamentary debates about the guardianship of infants, especially, MPs wrestled with a sense that young children needed a mother's love and tenderness, which a father's relationship with his children could not replicate in exactly that form. At the same time, few were willing to accept the mother as sole guardian of her children, except in extreme circumstances. The discussion of fatherhood that follows in subsequent chapters needs to be viewed in the light of the cultural mixed messages of the period. Neither parent was sufficient alone: mothers failed because they could not provide materially for their children, and fathers failed because they lacked the emotional tenderness of mothers. The difference was that while mothers had everything to gain, fathers were steadily losing what had been indisputably theirs for as long as anyone cared to remember.

VISUALISING FATHERHOOD

If all the moral fervour of the age seemed concentrated on the mother as emblem of nurturing love, as against the father's inevitable outward-facing involvement with the material world, attempts to visualise the father-figure in art reflected a similar cultural anxiety. Much of the art and literature of the period both represented and created a sense of paternal inadequacy or redundancy compared with the centrality of the mother by hearth or cradle. Where the father does occupy the place of honour, he often seems inactive, a family figurehead, while his wife and children bustle about in the background. In the major oil paintings of Victorian domestic realism, fathers tend to be shown in drawing-room armchairs, commanding the scene, most famously in William Powell Frith's *Many Happy Returns of the Day* (1856). As the father of nineteen children – twelve with his wife and seven with his mistress – Frith was well qualified to present an image of paternal satisfaction tinged with mild detachment.[34] Working-class fathers, by contrast, are more likely to be shown as victims of a harsh economic environment, as in Thomas Wade's *Carting Turf from the Moss* (c. 1867), in which an exhausted father-figure pulls an equally exhausted horse and overburdened cart, his wife and daughters ineffectually trying to help. George Hicks's *The Sinews of Old England* (1857) offers a more positive image of the working man with the father-figure balancing a pickaxe on his shoulder and supporting his adoring wife and child.[35] A favourite topic among Victorian artists was, however, the domestic scene *without* the father – for example Charles West Cope's *A Life Well Spent* (1862), which shows four young children circling a mother equipped with book and knitting. Though they look comfortably off and untroubled, there is no sign of a husband or a father to support them or, conversely, to disturb their peaceful harmony. Jane Maria Bowkett's *Preparing Tea* presents a young mother buttering toast while looking out of the window at the distant train bringing her husband home, while two little girls make toast and bring in slippers. These pictures make the viewer focus on someone who is not there, and share the sense of his absence. The women and children are clearly one half of the domestic equation, and function as a group, while the father is separate and (literally) an outsider.[36]

More negative pictorial images of the father stress the damage he has done to the family by his recklessness with money. Robert Braithwaite Martineau's *The Last Day in the Old Home* (1861) is the best known of these narrative paintings, whose detailed domestic interiors tell a story – in this case of cheerful and feckless gambling by a father who still seems unaware of the misery and ruin he has brought upon his old mother, wife and children – but there are others that repeat the tale.[37] Like Hogarth, Frith painted a kind of rake's progress called *The Road to Ruin* (1878), which features a family man in an elaborate smoking jacket failing to protect his wife and children from the bailiffs. In the final scene, he is alone in a garret, locking the door and apparently preparing to shoot himself with a pistol, which lies ready on the table. The only traces of his wife and children by this stage are a cradle and some toys: either they have left him, or they are out trying to sell the wife's paintings to buy food.[38] The point of this and other narrative paintings of a similar kind is to stress the father's crucial but precarious role at the heart of the family's prosperity. Where the mother is presented as a victim, doing her best to make ends meet, the full weight of moral responsibility is borne by the father. As Davidoff and Hall argue, fatherhood was 'part of a moral destiny', and it is this view of the role that Victorian artists and writers repeatedly addressed.[39]

Artists, like novelists of the period, enter the debate about fatherhood by offering disturbing images of families adrift in a world where fathers were abdicating their responsibilities, or mothers proving they could provide an emotionally secure retreat without a husband. Though mothers are far from sinless in Victorian artists' impressions of family life, they seem less pivotal to a family's fortunes than the father because they are rarely the main breadwinners. Since, in Joseph Kestner's words, the majority of representations of men and masculinity in Victorian painting 'are overwhelmingly by male artists', the fissures and failures they expose derive from within a masculine culture.[40] Where the artist was also a father, different angles emerge, as the 2007–8 Tate Britain Millais exhibition demonstrated. Millais's 'fancy pictures' of children may not show them interacting with father-figures, but many of them were modelled by his own eight sons and daughters, and expressed his increasing sense of mortality, as well as his pleasure in children. Following the death of his second son George in 1878, Millais embodied his feelings as a bereaved father in the bleak landscape of *The Tower of Strength* (1878–9); the following year he painted his daughter Sophie as *Princess Elizabeth in the Tower* (1879), the doomed daughter of Charles I.[41] Luke Fildes's *The Doctor* (1891), which shows the anxious waiting of a medical man by a child's bed, was also inspired by a son's death.[42] Artists' impressions, too varied to cover adequately here, joined the other cultural forces interrogating what exactly 'fatherhood' entailed, and what wider resonances, such as reminders of mortality, the appearance of beautiful and vulnerable young children suggested.

An alternative to paintings of fathers and children might have been daguerreotypes and photographs, but few exist of the fathers featured in this study. Darwin was daguerreotyped with his first son William in 1842, but not with his other children; there are several well-known photographs of Gladstone and Huxley with their grandchildren, but not with their own young sons and daughters, or of Dickens and Matthew Arnold with theirs. Even Prince Albert was usually photographed either with Victoria, or with a group of children, rather than just one. Though fathers feature often in large family group photographs, there is little evidence that intimate portraiture of a father and child was popular among the middle-class intelligentsia with which this book is concerned. Whatever else this might suggest (including the slow and expensive nature of photography), it does not imply a sentimentalising of fatherhood in the visual imagery of the period on the scale applied to motherhood, though as later chapters show, fathers faced with the imminent or recent death of unphoto-graphed children, belatedly had memorial pictures taken.[43]

FATHERING AND FATHERHOOD

'Fathering' is not the same as being a father in that a childless man can assume paternal responsibilities for children who are not his own, while a biological father remains a father even if he ignores his offspring and plays no part in raising them. In its reference to looking after a child, 'fathering' perhaps differs from 'mothering', in the suggestion of mentoring, eco-nomic support or social protection, while 'mothering' hints at a cosseting emotional defence from the dangers of the outside world. Alternatively, 'fathering' possibly implies a more intermittent kind of relationship with the child, whereas being a mother was understood to be full-time and permanent. There is, however, a vagueness about all these terms, which makes their precise application problematic for a study of this kind. Worse still is the modern version, 'parenting', which tends to flatten gendered difference in a way that would have been alien to the Victorians, committed as they were to an accepted definition of motherhood, if not of the standard responsibilities of fathers.

There are many examples of non-biological fathering in Victorian culture and literature, much of it stemming from the male professions, especially teaching and the church. A 'paternalist' manufacturer might accept fatherly responsibility for hundreds of employees, mostly adults, and try to regulate their habits and leisure time by promoting rational pursuits and comfortable living conditions in factory villages. Chancery judges had a paternal responsibility for wards of court, as Gilbert and Sullivan comically recognised in *Iolanthe* (1882); church leaders were fathers of their flock; and headmasters, such as Dr Arnold, who were biological fathers, were also *in loco parentis* for scores of boys, who retained a lifelong emotional attachment to them. Godfathering is another variant on the paternal role, which even the agnostic scientists Darwin, Huxley and Hooker performed for one another's sons, replacing spiritual mentorship with a broader kind of masculine comradeship. Most of the fathers discussed in the next chapters combined the roles of biological father with some kind of fatherly responsibility for other people's children or the wider community. The differences between these roles are not always easily discriminated, with some father-figures appearing more emotionally involved than real fathers. The subtleties of this are perhaps best traced in Victorian novels through imaginative exploration of what it feels like to be a father or to be denied biological paternity. Some of the most striking examples include Dickens's Joe Gargery in *Great Expectations*, unknowingly partnered with the convict Magwitch (perhaps an echo of *Oliver Twist*'s good father-figure Mr Brownlow, doubled with the criminal Fagin, both providers of food and shelter), and George Eliot's Silas Marner, an isolated miser who finds a child (Eppie) on his threshold and raises her as his own daughter, while she in turn rejects her biological father, Godfrey Cass. Whereas Eppie is given a choice between two father-figures, Dickens's Pip initially has no choice. Joe, who is actually his brother-in-law, gives him a home and an apprenticeship, but is more of a brother and fellow-sufferer than a patriarch, while Magwitch, who describes himself as Pip's 'second father', is essentially a caricature of the father-as-provider, telling his 'dear boy': 'You're my son – more to me nor any son. I've put away money, only for you to spend.'[44] Magwitch's concept of fathering crudely embodies the theory that a father compensates for his own disadvantages by spoiling his son, but expects unconditional gratitude in return. He is part of Dickens's lifelong engagement with the meaning of fatherhood, more specifically the *earning* of it by men who have mixed motives. Few of Dickens's father-figures actually deserve the respect that people grudgingly show them, though many insist on their dignity, which seems to be their chief characteristic. George Eliot's surrogate fathers tend to be more sincere, and take their responsibilities more seriously, even if they are not always successful. These include *Middlemarch*'s kindly but bumbling Mr Brooke, Dorothea and Celia's childless bachelor uncle, and, in *Daniel Deronda*, Sir Hugo Mallinger, Daniel's guardian who, when asked to raise him, 'declared that he would pay money to have such a boy'.[45] Another classic case is Hardy's Michael Henchard, the Mayor of Casterbridge, who is tricked into thinking the second Elizabeth-Jane is the biological daughter he 'sold' as a job lot with her mother twenty years earlier. When he discovers that she is his wife's daughter by her second 'husband' Richard Newson, he feels entirely differently about her. Ironically, however, Elizabeth-Jane thinks that Henchard has behaved exactly like a real father, unlike Newson, whom she still supposes to be her stepfather:

'It is so plain to me now. Indeed, father, it is. For, of course, you would not have done half the things you have done for me, and let me have my own way so entirely, and bought me presents, if I had only been your stepdaughter! He – Mr Newson . . . was very kind – O so kind!' (she spoke with tears in her eyes); 'but that is not the same thing as being one's real father after all'.[46]

Although fictional comparisons between real fathers and father-figures help identify the essentials of each function, Elizabeth-Jane's confused delight shows how difficult it can be to separate the two, especially as Victorian literature is more notorious for its wicked stepfathers (and mothers) than its kindly ones. So far as she is concerned, real fathers are more indulgent; in reality, much the same could be said of surrogates. As for Henchard, he never experiences true biological fatherhood as he sells his only daughter, and spends the rest of the novel seeking and rejecting alternative means of fathering. His strongest paternal feelings are probably for his son-like rival Donald Farfrae who eventually becomes his (posthumous) son-in-law.

Where the father-figures have accepted their responsibilities voluntarily – both in fiction and in 'real life' – they usually display their commitment more intensively than real fathers, being doubly conscious of the privilege. John Stuart Mill, for example, in his *Autobiography* (1873) pays fulsome tribute to his stepdaughter Helen Taylor, whose intellectual companionship he valued almost as much as her mother's. 'Surely no one ever before was so fortunate, as, after such a loss as mine, to draw another such prize in the lottery of life', he declared, '– another companion, stimulator, adviser, and instructor of the rarest quality'.[47] Different again was the situation of men such as Lewis Carroll or J. M. Barrie, who became infatuated with the children of other men. Barrie eventually adopted the Llewelyn Davies boys when both their parents died, but Carroll became estranged from Alice Liddell, possibly on the advice of her mother, possibly because he had indicated he wanted to marry her.[48] 'Fathering', which seems to encompass positive notions of mentorship, protection, care and playfulness, has always, when not biologically justified, alarmed the suspicious. Nevertheless, to all the father-figures listed in this section, whatever their actual relationship to the child, being a father was seen as an enviable privilege. In this respect, the abstract or theoretical notion of 'fathering' conflicts with the more problematic and demanding image of 'the father' conveyed by Victorian culture through its art and literature.

ROLE MODELS AND CASE HISTORIES: TAKING RESPONSIBILITY

It was always harder for theorists and writers to idealize the image of the father than it was for them to create an air of sanctity around the mother. Although fatherhood was glorified in the Fatherhood of God, with which it was often compared and confused, the language of patriarchy, as indicated by the legal cases cited above, tended towards the authoritarian rather than the loving, and there seem to have been no prominent and positive role models for fatherhood in Victorian society. Prince Albert is perhaps the nearest we come to a Victorian paternal role model, but as the next chapter shows, there were many flaws in his make-up as a father, and his German nationality initially made him unpopular with the public. More recent social studies of role model development have suggested that men traditionally reject the previous generational model and take their fathers as negative, rather than positive examples. Kerry J. Daly, in a small study of late-twentieth-century American fathers, concludes that their paternal role models, 'when there were any at all, were fragmented and disjointed', drawn as much from the exemplary behaviour of their mothers and wives as from their fathers.[49] While social conditions in modern America are very different from those of Victorian Britain, Daly's social learning theory can be applied surprisingly easily to the fathers in my case history chapters, who largely lacked positive role models in their own upbringing.

The methodology used for the following chapters relies strongly on the case history as a means of providing a framework and structure. It provides space for a fuller analysis of the fatherhood experience than we find in most biographies, and allows for parallels and comparisons in a range of responses to the anxieties and tragedies of family life. Novelists, poets, churchmen and scientists predominate because they were best able to articulate the implications of their experiences, and they have left some of the most frank and intimate records. Clearly there are many other equally important examples who could have been chosen, such as Tennyson and Browning, both fathers of promising sons with little sense of direction; Mr Barrett, thundering Victorian patriarch *par excellence*; or Patrick Brontë, father of one of the most extraordinary families of the nineteenth century. Other interesting cases would have been Robert Southey and William Makepeace Thackeray, in effect made single fathers by their wives' psychological instability. My aim, however, was to move beyond the over-familiar and purely literary, to include fathers who represented other areas of the Victorian intelligentsia and establishment. These examples cannot be said to be 'representative' of attitudes to Victorian fatherhood, any more than a Manchester tradesman or a Hampshire farmer might be, nor were most of them directly in conflict with the legal issues outlined earlier in this introduction; but they were all affected in one way or another by the contemporary cultural uncertainty about masculinity in general, and fatherhood in particular. Moreover, they were all in a position to influence social attitudes, if only by example. 'Influence' is of course notoriously hard to measure, but curiosity about the personal lives of famous men drove a modernising agenda in life-writing, especially in commemorative newspaper articles and obituaries. Huxley's son Leonard was repeatedly asked to describe his father's character, and responded with a set of anecdotes about his drawings and absences, as did the Darwin and Dickens children with descriptions of their fathers' domestic habits. John Guille Millais, son of the artist, included in his father's *Life and Letters* (1902) a chapter on 'The Man and His Home Life', while Herbert Gladstone felt more should have been said in the Morley biography about his father's private character.[50] In some cases, what was memorable about these men is specifically bound up with their experiences as fathers: Dean (later Archbishop) Tait is today probably best remembered for the tragic loss of his five daughters to scarlet fever in 1856, an event recently rediscovered and scrutinised by critics such as Pat Jalland and Laurence Lerner, among others.[51] Similarly, Charles Kingsley's *Water-Babies*, a children's book, has stood the test of time more successfully than most of his writing for adults, while Darwin's despair at his daughter Annie's death, the subject of Randal Keynes's reappraisal of his life in *Annie's Box* (2001), revived interest in the personal tragedy underlying his discovery of evolutionary theory.[52] In selecting these particular examples, my intention has been to restore the experience of fatherhood to a more central position in the lives of high-achieving Victorian men, and to evaluate its effect on their writing, their decisions and their developing responses to the world around them.

Biography analyses the different influences on an individual's life, but it usually does so chronologically, taking each event as it comes. My approach differs from 'straight' biography in a number of ways. First, most of my case histories are paired or grouped with others, to highlight shared relationships and experiences. They are designed to emphasise both parallels and differences, as well as the ways in which Victorian men communicated with each other about matters that were essentially private and personal. Most of this correspondence is about their own feelings and only tangentially about their wives', whose experience of loss or anxiety we largely infer from incidental asides. In these private spaces, the fathers displace the mothers by positioning themselves at the emotional centre of their family life: a situation that was intensified by pressure to appear publicly in control of their feelings. Second, each chapter deals with only a few aspects of each subject's life. It makes no claim to be an exhaustive narrative of all that happened to them as fathers, which readers can discover from the many traditional biographies already in existence. Instead, each case history considers their cultural reception of fatherhood: the turning points in their lives when the experience of being a father impacted on their work, their construction of responsibilities and duties, and their emotional response to family tragedy. In some cases, discussion is geared around one or two major issues, such as Huxley's loss of his temperamental artist daughter Marian, or Kingsley's development of a scientific catechism style of teaching his son Grenville. Because of his public profile – as Prime Minister, Archbishop of Canterbury, Head-master of Rugby or popular novelist – each father had the opportunity to

clarify or develop the conditions in which fathering was performed. He
could, for example, try to educate his own children, as Prince Albert,
Charles Kingsley and Gladstone did, or, like Darwin, Tait and Benson,
he could agonise about the connection between his own physical or
spiritual health and the inherited guilt of his children. All these case
histories are to greater or lesser extent discussions conducted between
men among themselves and with the wider public who read their books
and followed their achievements. Given the contested nature of fatherhood at the time, their experiences both demonstrate the wide range of
fathering styles available to men in the nineteenth century, and expose the
uncertainties that even confident and successful public figures encountered in their attempts to raise their children according to their own
religious or moral standards.

Masculinity studies, now rapidly proliferating, provide a theoretical
underpinning to the case history approach. Victor Seidler's experience,
though separated from the Victorians' by religious differences as well as
a hundred years in time, nevertheless meshes with that of men like
Dr Arnold and Charles Kingsley, whose sense of their own masculinity
was both strengthened and tempered when they became fathers. Seidler's
observations on the history of fathering may apply mainly to post-1960s
versions of masculinity, but they provide a useful starting point for a
study of Victorian men's self-doubt and uncertainty in the absence of
positive paternal role models. Employing what he calls 'an Enlightenment vision of modernity', Seidler emphasises men's need to find a way
of expressing and valuing their emotions without appearing to be
'feminine'. He argues that 'Emotional needs were a sign of weakness and
therefore were often suppressed as a threat to male identities.' The point
of his book title – *Man Enough* – is that post-Enlightenment men have
always had to keep proving themselves, to show that they are 'man
enough' to justify their commanding position in the home and in society
at large. Being present at his son's birth and immediately bonding with
him became, for Seidler, an alternative way of achieving complete masculinity. 'I never thought I would become a father myself', he recalls.
'Somehow it felt strangely connected to becoming a man in my own
right.' Nevertheless, he still found time spent with babies and small
children 'challenging' because 'so little seems to happen': for a man
geared to the notion of constant, measurable activity, letting time slip by
in play can be disconcerting and unsatisfying. 'You literally achieve
nothing', Damon Syson confirms in a recent *Observer* magazine article on
stay-at-home-fathers.[53] Whether or not the paternal instinct came

'naturally' to men is an issue highly important to the Victorian fathers chosen for this discussion, as is the distribution of their time between masculine work and unproductive domestic play.

Michael Lamb's work with American fathers returned to the issue of changing paternal responsibilities. Whereas in 1975 he described fathers as the 'forgotten contributors to child development', among today's perceived duties of the father he lists breadwinning, providing emotional support to the children's mother as well as the children themselves, and 'direct interaction' with children. According to his research, fathers tend to be more interested in and involved with their sons than with their daughters; however, 'mothers' interactions with their children are dominated by caretaking, whereas fathers are behaviourally defined as playmates.[54] Evaluating Victorian fathers without a consciousness of what we expect from today's fathers is difficult; likewise, using transcultural or anachronistic models of fatherhood is self-evidently full of risks. The reality is that research on family practices has always been beset by uncertainty as to how representative the behaviour of any one father or individual household can be, and what the means of gauging his success. There have always been 'hands-on' models of fatherhood in the past that sound remarkably like the popular modern concept of the 'new' father today; conversely plenty of 'Victorian heavy fathers' still exist in the twenty-first century, though probably less so now in the middle classes. The area of greatest uncertainty, which the succeeding chapters try to explore, is that identified by Michael Lamb as contributions to child-development through 'direct interaction': in other words, play, education, emotional support and involvement, care in illness, one-on-one dialogue, and other activities apart from those shared with the mother.

For many nineteenth-century men, becoming a father opened up the possibility of a new kind of communication, which could be playful, irrational and purely entertaining, as much for their own amusement as for their child's. It released a vein of humour in them, if not for the first time, at least in a new way. Even a serious-minded father like Southey, who was often dismayed by his brother-in-law Coleridge's offhand attitude to his children's education, was not beyond addressing his eldest daughter Edith (at nineteen) as 'Very magnificent and most dissipated Daughter', or inventing a particularly extravagant style of language to tell his seven-year-old Isabel about a royal levée he had attended: 'O Isabel, if you had seen how grand I was that day, when I went to visit the King! I had no powder in my hair, that being no longer required at a levée, but I had a bag, and lace at my shirt, and lace ruffles, and gold buckles on my shoes, and at my knees, and a cocked hat in my hand. Think, Isabel, how grand I must have been.'[55] This is a kind of nonsense writing that forms a special language between father and child. Far from upholding any notion of patriarchal dignity, it becomes a place where fathers can enjoy their children's company, away from the more rational and disapproving eye of their mother. It therefore inverts the usual binaries separating paternal linear language from the unregulated, playful, passionate expression traditionally associated with mothers, complying more with Victor Seidler's proposition that men should discover new forms of communication to express their more intimate emotions.

For fathers such as Darwin and Thomas Hood, the nonsense language of children was something to be encouraged. Apart from being creative and entertaining, it allowed them as fathers to explore aspects of themselves that normally had to be repressed, especially their delight in absurdities. Though the two most famous nonsense writers of the age, Lewis Carroll and Edward Lear, were childless (albeit from large families), a kind of informal nonsense writing, found in Victorian fathers' private correspondence, emerges as intimately connected with the experience of fatherhood – which even Carroll and Lear enjoyed by proxy in their relations with other men's children. John James Ruskin's correspondence with his only son John shows the father compromising his dignity as a 'papa' to collude with his son in playing verbal games outside both their relationships with the wife and mother, Margaret. Margaret's unease about John's poetic effusions has been discussed by David C. Hanson, who suggests that her concerns were both Evangelical and sexual: 'excessive excitation' was something to be avoided on both counts.[56] John James, however, positively relishes his son's verbal precocity, and the two vie with each other in narrating their adventures. Margaret, for her part, sensed that the father's relationship with his son was different from her own, producing outbursts of 'exuberant mirth so common with him when you are at home'.[57] Certainly greetings of 'Hollo hollo papa' seemed presumptuous to John himself (Vol. 1, p. 175), but John James's response is mostly one of amused indulgence. If John could begin a letter 'Ha ha ha, he he he, ho ho ho' (Vol. 1, p. 177), or confess 'Oh Papa we do miss you so much so very much so excessively much so super-excessively much so inexpressibly much' (Vol. 1, p. 220), John James could catch the mood, albeit more purposefully, and 'commence this Letter exclaiming wonderful, wonderful wonderful – Do you ask what is so very wonderful – your Latin Lesson sent to me' (Vol. 1, p. 209).

Ultimately the relationship between father and children outlined in this study is tragi-comic. While birth announcements are made in a state of relieved elation, and christenings arranged to reinforce professional bonds with other men, all were aware of the precariousness of a child's life, and all except Kingsley suffered the death of at least one child. It was the reliving and retelling of short lives and painful deaths, even more than the trauma of birth, that forced many Victorian fathers to confront for the first time the real meaning of fatherhood. These auto/biographical memorials of children's lives that many of them felt compelled to create reveal more of their developing relationship with their children than anything else they wrote. In their exclusion of all but passing references to their wife's grief as their co-mourner, these unpublished diary-narratives seem to have been the one place where bereaved fathers could write freely and privately examine the mixture of guilt, pride, incomprehension and shame that characterised their state of mind. They are now uncomfortable to read: a painful retracing of the child's precocious development, the protracted deathbed scenes with the fluctuations of hope and despair, the desperate prayers, and then the struggle to come to terms with the child's loss. The recent revival of critical interest in sentimentality has scrutinised the suspect pleasure the Victorians seemed to gain from reading accounts of all types of death, not just those of children, and has defended its moral purpose. Sentimental reading is traditionally a female taste, even though the most archetypical sentimental deathbed scene (Little Nell's) was created by a male novelist. In arguing that the 'sentimental fiction of the early and mid-Victorian period also served to enshrine the cherished totems of middle-class respectability – the pure woman, the sanctified hearth, the innocent child, and the charitable benefactor', Miriam Bailin endorses the connection between sentimentality and the feminine, the 'charitable benefactor', though gender-neutral, being the only possibly male factor in her list.[58] This immediately raises the question of where Victorian fathers situate themselves in relation to the sentimental, especially the deathbed narratives of their own children. Julie-Marie Strange, who has made a study of bereaved working-class fathers, reminds us that 'the historiography of grief is a history of love and longing, emotions that have tended to be associated with femininity and domesticity', while Bailin specifically links the sentimental with a protest against disturbing cultural and social transformations of the nineteenth century, and a reaffirmation of ideal values.[59] As my discussion of the Taits, Bensons and Gladstone shows, Victorian fathers had to find a way of appropriating the sentimental, while acknowledging that it expressed feelings in conflict with their publicly avowed masculine Christianity. What aesthetic pleasure (if any) fathers gained for themselves in writing these narratives, and how much (if any) religious solace will be explored in the following chapters.

'So common an affliction ought not to so weigh me down', Southey wrote, upset by the sight of his niece, Sara Coleridge, soon after the death of his first daughter Margaret at the age of one. 'Yet she was not a common child', he defended himself.[60] Southey and Coleridge are of course separated by half a century from Darwin, Gladstone and the other grief-stricken fathers discussed in the following chapters, but they are mentioned here because their close identification with their children, and quest for a way of articulating their experience of fatherhood, make them fit inaugurators of a dialogue engaged in by many of their Victorian successors. Not all of these fathers' comments are addressed to other men, but many of their more self-reflexive ones were, forcing them to invent a language to describe events normally associated with a female subculture: their response to childbirth, their engagement with babies and small children, their management of relationships with older children, and their judgement of themselves as fathers. It was by comparing experiences, such as their grief at the death of one child, or their pride in the uniqueness of another, that nineteenth-century fathers developed their own alternative subculture which was essentially private and unreported: a view of fatherhood largely at odds with the public image vented in the news-papers and parliamentary debates, or in the visual images of fathers that portrayed them as living outside domestic constraints. For many, fatherhood was an unmapped adventure, ending a time of actual adventure, such as travel for scientific discovery. It might extend – given the size of their families, and difficulty in placing adult sons in work – from their twenties until the end of their lives. In constructing a private language for their interaction with children, interrogating their religion when it seemed to fail them and comparing their offspring, the fathers discussed in the following chapters were embarking on a moral journey of domestic accountability. If fraught with tragedy and disappointment, it enabled many scientists, poets and clergymen to find their own voice and a place for the father in the unceasing debate about the function and purpose of the family in Victorian social culture.

CHAPTER I

The failure of fatherhood at mid-century: four case histories

'Papa is an oracle and what he decides must be right.'[1] This is doubtless what the typical authoritarian Victorian father would have liked his children to think of him, as the Princess Royal did of Prince Albert; but such adulation was extreme, even for adoring daughters, and the culture produced no universally acknowledged ideal father-figure, who can be used to calibrate a series of well-meaning failures. Gladstone's children proudly defended him throughout their lives, but there is much in his diaries and letters to disqualify him for the title of perfect role model. Many other fathers (Kingsley and Darwin, for instance) were admired by their children, but it is hard to find anywhere in fiction or history an ideal typology of fatherhood, or a helpful body of theory, save in legal documents, comparable with that directed towards mothers.

All the following chapters are concerned at least partly with failed fathering, but this initial collection of case histories establishes the cultural expectations and pitfalls of Victorian fatherhood through four examples where failure was both acute and conspicuous. Two of them – Prince Albert, the most prominent father of the nation in the early Victorian period, and Dean Tait of Carlisle, who subsequently became Archbishop of Canterbury – were both high-profile exemplifications of the ways in which fathering became a public issue, prompting open discussion. For the most part popular opinion was critical of Albert – at least until towards the end of his life – while sympathy for Tait's losses was instinctive and universal. The cases of Thomas Hood and G. H. Lewes were chosen because they illustrate the complications of juggling responsible fatherhood with, in Hood's case, an unpredictable professional career, and in Lewes's, a scandalous private life. What most unites these disparate examples, however, is that they all faced additional pressures from the conflict between their private family concerns and their public visibility. Discussion of their cases will consider the management of failure in Victorian fathering, and the response, both public and private, each catastrophe occasioned. It will also explore the extent to which social and cultural expectations of the time contributed to the misdirection of each family, and how far each of these fathers was, in effect, experimentally mapping out his role in a domestic context over which he himself lacked confident control.

ALBERT, ALBERT EDWARD AND VICKY

'*None* of you can *ever* be proud enough of being the *child* of SUCH a Father who has not his *equal* in this world – so great, so good, so faultless', Queen Victoria rebuked her heir, the teenage Prince of Wales, in 1857.[2] As the most prominent father-figure of the nation, Prince Albert makes an ideal starting point for a study of Victorian patriarchy. Victoria could never praise him enough, either dead or alive, nor sufficiently exhort her children to regard him as their oracle. So far as she was concerned, he was the perfect father, and she hoped all her sons and daughters would emulate his virtues and spread them through Europe, via carefully planned dynastic marriages designed by Albert himself. In the event, he died before more than one child could be married, and even this ambitious marriage – of his eldest daughter Vicky to the future Emperor of Germany – failed to transform the politics of northern Europe as he had intended. This trajectory of hope, disappointed ambition and loss not only typifies the experience of many of Albert's Victorian contemporaries, but also brings us closer to understanding what the Victorians expected of an exemplary father.

So far as the Royal Family were concerned, the Prince had stepped into an empty breach. Victoria's own father, the Duke of Kent, had died when she was less than a year old, and his brothers, George IV and William IV, while fathering large illegitimate families, had failed to establish themselves as respectable royal patriarchs like their own father, George III. Albert's father, Duke Ernest of Saxe-Coburg-Gotha – a well-known womaniser – was no role model either, and his mother had died when he was twelve. Though George IV had provided a much-loved heir in the form of Princess Charlotte, her death in childbirth in 1817 plunged the Royal Family into a succession crisis. The post of virtuous royal father had therefore been vacant for several decades when the birth of the Princess Royal on 21 November 1840 confirmed Albert's credentials as a properly masculine family man. He had at least fulfilled the prime duty, which was the provision of heirs.

From the start, however, Albert's whole position as royal father was fraught with irreconcilable contradictions. It was essential for the Queen to marry and produce an heir, but Albert was soon accused of fathering too many. Alarmed lithographs on the theme of 'Annuals' (children springing up like hardy plants) greeted the arrival of the first few children, with 'John Bull' wondering how much they would cost him in maintenance, education and eventually dowries;[3] while in 1844, 'A Royal Nursery Rhyme for 1860', drawn by John Leech, was captioned 'There was a Royal Lady that lived in a shoe, / She had so many children she didn't know what to do.'[4] A friendlier lithograph of 1843, titled 'The royal family at home', shows Albert on all fours giving baby Alice a ride on his back, while his two older children pull him about like a horse; likewise a loyal illustration to *A Book of British Song* (1842) makes him the apex to a family pyramid of nestling wife and children, the embodiment of a perfect family man with his arms round as many of them as he can reach. When photography became more common in the 1850s, Albert is shown towering above a sprawl of small people in bonnets and kilts, gazing with a preoccupied air towards one side of the group.[5] Either way, while the Royal Family, for the first time since the early days of George III, began to look like the exemplary bourgeois family it was meant to be, it prompted alarmed debate over how such a household was to be financed by the nation. Unlike the typical bourgeois father, Albert was not exactly the family breadwinner.

Moreover, if Albert's initial function as progenitor of heirs was obvious enough, the extent to which he was meant to be actively involved in raising them was less certain. The birth of his daughter, however, gave him not only full adult male status for the first time, but more significantly real use as a working consort. Having supported his wife through the birth, he later that day chaired a meeting of the Privy Council: a pattern repeated each time another child was added to the family. In effect, the Queen's disabilities as a woman, evident with every confinement, gave him an active purpose, which he had lacked as mere husband: sheer biology had helped him where protocol and tradition remained immovable. Albert was also determined to be fully involved in running the nursery; he arranged the christening ceremonies and, according to *The Times*, 'with the natural pride of paternity', often took visitors to see the infant Prince of Wales.[6] His alarm over one-year-old Vicky's weight-loss and feeding problems occasioned one of his fiercest marital arguments with the Queen, when he accused her of starving the child.[7] Although the episode was bitter at the time, Victoria later quoted with approval Albert's sayings about being a fully involved father. 'Papa', she told the married Vicky in 1859, 'says that the men who leave all home affairs – and the education of their children to their wives – forget their first duties'.[8] His next daughter Alice who, like her older siblings, 'went to Papa' for an hour's lesson every evening, later recalled learning the details of house design and décor from him informally: 'If I have any taste, I owe it to dear Papa, and I learned so much by seeing him arrange pictures, rooms, etc.'[9] In turn, Queen Victoria took him for *her* father as well, and even her mother. Still regretting her solitary childhood, she confided in Vicky: 'He was my father, my protector, my guide and adviser in all and everything, my mother (I might almost say) as well as my husband.'[10] Being everyone's father, as well as his wife's mother, was clearly a lot to ask of this twenty-one-year-old, who, in the Queen's eyes, at least, straddled traditional gender boundaries in terms of his general all-round usefulness.

However, it was the children's more formal education that was Albert's chief concern, assisted by his faithful adviser Baron Stockmar. Perhaps because the Queen never made any great claims to intellect, it fell naturally to her more earnest husband to map the children's course of study. Vicky had even looked forward to his teaching her own children, if she died prematurely, or even if she did not.[11] Indeed, Albert's role as his children's instructor was something noted by many obituary writers after his death. The *Saturday Review*, for example, remarked that he had performed 'in a most exemplary manner' his duties towards his children's education: 'This he did, it may be truly said, with the solicitude of a father added to the solicitude of a prince. Nor have his anxious labours proved vain; for, so far as his children have come before the public, they have won golden opinions in all quarters.'[12] *Fraser's Magazine* agreed that 'No children have been more assiduously cultivated', not realising how irksome this teaching was to the Prince of Wales.[13] Although he tried, according to Philip Magnus, to treat his children as peers, and enjoyed their company more than the Queen did, Albert made the mistake of assuming that what had suited one child would equally suit another. This was despite his scientific study of his children as they were growing up, and his acute awareness of their different personality traits.

Albert was in some ways a Darwinian father, years before Darwin published either his *Origin of Species* (1859) or his 'Biographical Sketch of an Infant' (1877). Darwin's children were roughly the same age as Albert's, with the eldest being born in 1839, a year ahead of Vicky, and the two families increasing over roughly the same period of time. 'There is certainly a great charm, as well as deep interest in watching the development of feelings and faculties in a little child', Albert observed in 1843, 'and nothing is more instructive for the knowledge of our own nature, than to observe in a little creature the stages of development, which, when we were ourselves passing through them, seemed scarcely to have an existence for us.'[14] Albert's comments suggest more than just a transient interest in his children's progress. He related what he saw back to himself, and outwards again to the differences of personality, his interests being both psychological and physical. Later references to his children in his letters remain highly conscious of 'steps' and 'stages' in their development, supported by his active tutoring. Like Albert, Darwin observed his children's moral as well as physical development, and was amused by his eldest son William's habit of referring to his actions in the third person.[15] Writing to Vicky, now married and living in Berlin, Albert was similarly fascinated by the behaviour of his youngest daughter, two-year-old Beatrice, who had come into breakfast, 'moaning "Baby has been so naughty, poor baby so naughty," as one might complain of being ill, or having slept badly, &c.' Albert noticed how 'the child felt she was not responsible for her naughtiness, and regarded it rightly as a misfortune for the "I", which appears to her still as a third person, that is, as something outside herself (*als Object*).'[16]

His comments on Vicky as she grew up show how pleased he was with her combination of childlike simplicity and increasingly adult awareness, both of her political surroundings, and of human relationships. Albert urged her to impart 'the progress of her inner life' in return for his, and 'to take a constantly active part in fostering it'.[17] After her marriage he wrote to her every Wednesday, and seemed to be equally at home discussing the advantages of constitutional government, and the best way of recovering from a difficult childbirth – as hers had been with her first son, the future Kaiser Wilhelm II. For him and the Queen there was always a conflict between their wish to see their children make dynastically useful marriages while they were still young, and – for their daughters especially – parental concern at the physical strain early marriage would place on them. Albert's anxieties as a father were just as intense when his eldest child was married as when she was still at home being systematically prepared for her putative future as Empress of Germany. As a father, therefore, Albert saw his role as one of lifelong commitment to enhancing all his children's physical and psychological wellbeing.

With Victoria as dependent on him as their children, he appeared to be the stronger parent of the two, missed when he died at the end of 1861, primarily for his advice and support, which as Vicky carelessly indicated were more satisfying than her mother's. For example, there was no one to discuss religious controversies with: 'What a pleasure it was to write to dear Papa and tell him all one thought –', she sighed to her mother, who pretended not to mind the affront to 'old Mama's wits'.[18] Everything he had believed in or had pronounced to be good was adopted uncritically by mother and daughter. 'Whatever I hear or see I always think what would Papa say what would he think [*sic*]', Vicky told her mother when she was separated from him only by marriage and not yet by death.[19] Moreover, Albert never revealed any jealousy of his daughter's position, unlike Victoria who, as she watched her two eldest girls marry and have children, needed to maintain that *her* husband (even after his death) was better than theirs; even, when Alice's first baby was born, that she herself would have liked a tenth – a strange comment in the light of all her earlier complaints about men (even Prince Albert) not fully realising the suffering they inflicted on their wives in pregnancy and childbirth.[20]

In evaluating Albert's contribution to the Victorian debate on fatherhood, we are faced with the challenge of appraising a saint: someone whose perfections as a father were reiterated both by his wife and his eldest child in the most extravagant language of worship. The Queen's habitual phrase for him, in her letters to Vicky, was 'adored Papa', a view her daughter fully reciprocated. 'He was too great, too perfect for Earth that adored Father whom I ever worshipped with more than a daughter's affection', Vicky insisted after his death.[21] The feelings of the other children are harder to gauge. The youngest hardly knew him, and Vicky was the only one to be fully prepared for marriage and remain in regular dialogue with him afterwards. The country at large, judging by the obituaries, treated him with the profound respect they had begrudged during the first ten years of his marriage, making the excuse that it had not been possible previously to 'know' Albert as a human being. Black-edged newspapers and periodicals acknowledged his worth as a family man, while recognising that few outside court circles could appreciate just how zealously he had worked for his children's moral development. By contrast, Charles Dickens, whose children's ages, like Darwin's, roughly corresponded with Albert's, scoffed at the fuss about him: 'Prince Albert's death was a very sad thing for his family. He was neither a phaenomonon [*sic*], nor the Saviour of England; and England will do exactly without him as it did with him. He was a good example of the best sort of perfectly commonplace man, with a considerable desire to make money . . .'[22]

For Dickens, Albert had little importance beyond his own family circle, where he was a typical bourgeois intent on his own advancement. Though this view undervalues his major contributions to the cultural life of the country, especially the Great Exhibition of 1851, it reminds us of Albert's middle-class ordinariness in the eyes of a cool outsider, and one father's sense of the limitations of another, faced with the Royal Family's eagerness to idealise him. If the perfection of the father was not widely theorised in the mid-century period of Albert's predominance, the two Victorias, mother and daughter, evolved a way of verbalising it for themselves in their exchange of letters, in effect establishing a blueprint for flawless fatherhood. Albert is seen as unceasing in his efforts for all the children: a tower of strength at the very heart of the family who, despite his growing tiredness and despondency, was still negotiating terms with Bertie and urging Vicky to safeguard her own health. His wisdom on all matters, it went without saying, was wholly dependable.

Obituary writers of the time were concerned for the fatherless children the Prince had left behind, especially the twenty-year-old Prince of Wales whose future now hung in the balance. *Fraser's Magazine*, characterising Albert as 'the prudent father of our future King', maintained that 'we have long looked on him as an example to every one of us in our families ... If character were inherited, we shall have no anxiety.' On the other hand, the reviewer conceded that the 'mother's influence is often the most effective...', and much would depend on the Queen's ability to pull through her bereavement.[23] Arthur Helps, reviewing the Theodore Martin biography of Prince Albert in 1875, which revived another round of Albert-reappraisals, specifically recommends him as a role model: 'Throughout the narrative it is clearly to be seen that the Prince Consort was a good husband, and a kind master; such a man, in short, as may be adopted by fathers for their own model, and set as an example before their sons.'[24] Both *Blackwood's* and *Fraser's* also pressed the role-model idea: *Fraser's* (1862) claiming that the Royal Family had 'set a pattern which every household in England according to their degree may do well to imitate' (p. 126); while *Blackwood's* (1876) refers to 'that faultless pattern of a pure and happy domestic life, set forth to all classes in the Palace itself'.[25] Praise for Albert as a husband and father even found its way into Mary Elizabeth Braddon's 'bigamy' novel, *Aurora Floyd* (1862), which recalls the sad day when the poor wept 'for a widowed Queen and orphaned children in a desolate palace', mourning the 'spotless character of him who was lost; the tender husband, the watchful father, the kindly master, the liberal patron, the temperate adviser, the stainless gentleman'.[26]

In fact it was not until the serial publication of Martin's monumental biography between 1875 and 1880 that many of the more human anecdotes about Albert and his private relationships became widely disseminated, at a point in the century when the fashion for unsympathetic fictional fathers was burgeoning. 'The public failed to appreciate him, because he was too good for it', *Blackwood's* concluded bluntly in 1875. Indeed, the public was unsure 'in what manner it ought to conduct its dealings with the almost perfect man thus unexpectedly thrown upon its hands'.[27] Both Queen and country now competed to do justice to a man who appeared superior to them all. This made his impact as a role model even harder to evaluate, given that his private virtues were slow to emerge, and that he seemed too exceptional to be easily imitated.

Moreover, much of what he had set out to achieve with his own family, especially his eldest children, has now been cancelled out or critiqued by historical events. Dying in December 1861, Albert never knew that Vicky and her husband Fritz would rule Germany for a mere three months of 1888, and that she would be as unpopular in her adopted country as he had been in his. 'Sitting at [Albert's] feet', argues Hannah Pakula, 'Vicky imbibed a rigidity in political outlook that would prove less than helpful to a girl embarking on life in a foreign culture' (p. 75); while Princess Alice caught diphtheria from nursing her children, and died prematurely in 1878. By contrast, Bertie, about whom his parents worried so fruitlessly, succeeded his mother in 1901, enjoying a nine-year reign of easy-going popularity.

As a father-figure and a role model to the early and mid Victorians, therefore, Albert occupies a crucial but ambiguous position. He certainly demonstrated all the virtues of what we would now call 'hands-on' fathering, being eagerly interventionist and directly involved in the educating of both daughters and sons. He was ambitious for them all, but not at the cost of their happiness, and he thought he understood the differences in their needs and personalities. Initially caricatured for being irresponsibly fertile, he was then idealised as the perfect husband, father and consort, whose guidance of his children was cut off at the point when they most needed it. In every aspect of his life, an easy relationship with the public evaded him. As a model father to the nation, he sends out contradictory messages: not least because those responsible for mediating them took too long to make up their minds about him. Perhaps this in itself is a symptom of contemporary cultural confusion about what it was exactly that a model father was supposed to do. In the event he was mourned largely as a husband, because it was his wife, the Queen, whose sense of bereavement was extreme, while the children's grief was more circumspect. Their loss, though acknowledged, was seen as less acute than Victoria's and, unlike her, they found a way of moving forward in their fatherless lives.

In June 1840, Thomas Hood's two children – Fanny aged nine, and Tom aged five – were detained without their parents in Ostend as hostages against a debt of £150 owed by their father. In desperation, Hood turned to his publisher, Richard Bentley, for an advance on articles not yet ready for *Bentley's Miscellany*, pleading 'you will feel as a man & especially if you be a father the nature of the demand upon me'. This was indeed the ultimate disgrace for Hood, who had been all his adult life both a dedicated father and a hopeless manager of money. 'It was never thought possible that a boy & girl of 5 & 9 years old could be detained – it is not perhaps legal – but they are in the people's power & I am doomed just now to feel how might overcomes right.'[28] In order to release them, there seemed no alternative but to sell Bentley the copyright of his novel *Tylney Hall* (1834). What was already a complex relationship between his writing, his earnings and his family thus became formally for him a public embarrassment, further enmeshing him in long-standing arguments about copyright and fair deals for professional authors.

The situation had arisen because the family had been living, for five years, first in Coblenz and then Ostend, as an alternative to declaring bankruptcy. While he was in Germany, he struggled with the language and the way of life; his drinking became a problem, and he briefly joined a battalion of Polish soldiers on the march as far as Berlin. On one occasion he told a 'Frau' that he had 'come 50,000 miles, was married at 14, and had 17 children'; as he really, in his words, 'looked a Grand Turk, she believed me like Gospel.'[29] When Hood's health, never strong, collapsed in April 1840, he returned home to England for medical treatment, his wife Jane joining him in May and leaving the children with friends. To add to Hood's troubles, he had thus to choose between his own needs and his children's, obliging his wife to do the same. The children languished in Ostend for another few weeks, before in July they could be released and brought home.

Much of Hood's short life (1799–1845) illustrates the tensions between his responsibilities as a father, his precarious career as a largely comic writer and his poor health, sparked by a childhood bout of scarlet fever, and later by the lingering effects of rheumatic fever. His children's needs intensified his compulsion to succeed as a professional writer, but he often suggested the two situations, of father and author, were incompatible in the conditions prevailing at that time. Because copyright laws failed to protect them, Hood felt that British authors were stateless nobodies, little better than street-sellers, 'quack doctors' or 'Punch and Judies'.[30] When the father-author was also in continual ill health, another burden was added to the already intractable situation. Nevertheless, he was amused when he overheard a conversation between his two small children, which revealed their sense of his difficulties as a writer: 'I one day overheard a dispute between Tom and Fanny as to what I was. "Pa's a literary man," said Fanny. "He's not!" said Tom; 'I know what he is." "What is he, then?" "Why," says Tom, "he's not a literary man – he's an invalid." '[31] Tom's innocent comment implies that his father cannot be both a literary man and an invalid: the two states are incompatible, as being an invalid is a full-time occupation.

In writing to and about his children, Hood oscillates between a type of fantasy-prose akin to the Romantic prose writing of Lamb, his close friend; pure sentimentality (as in 'To My Daughter on Her Birthday'); and a comic depiction of himself as a father burdened with responsibility, prefiguring the way Dickens complained about his experience of fatherhood. Both of Hood's children, Frances (known as Fanny, b. 1830), and Tom (b. 1835), followed their father into the profession of writing, and both devoted themselves to editing their father's works and letters, keeping his reputation alive during the mid-Victorian period. One of his biographers, John Clubbe, summarises their efforts as worthy, but limited in scope and effect: 'Brother and sister kept close, revered almost to the point of worship their deceased parents, and led lives seemingly untroubled by their society's problems.'[32] Hood's own description of himself towards the end of his life, in 1844, was as 'strictly a domestic man myself, finding my comfort for many evils in the bosom of my family'.[33] His attempts to juggle these various uneasy states provide a commentary on how he defined the role of a father in the 1830s and 1840s, in the context of contemporary expectations, especially among his coterie of male literary friends, who included Charles Lamb, Charles Wentworth Dilke and John Hamilton Reynolds, brother of Hood's wife Jane. As a magazine writer and poet who made occasional forays into longer prose narratives, Hood benefited from the early-nineteenth-century rise of the periodical and newspaper market, especially that aimed at middle-class readers with a taste for lighter literature. After working on the *London*

Magazine, *Athenaeum*, *Punch* and the *New Monthly Magazine*, among others, he started new ventures of his own, including his *Comic Annuals* (1830–9) and *Hood's Magazine* (1844–5), but by the time of the latter, he was already too ill to maintain it for long. His biographer, J. C. Reid, sums up the tragi-comedy of his contradictory life:

A jester who was always ill, a public comedian loaded with debts and anxieties, a man of poetic talent living in an age that scarcely valued poetry, a writer almost evenly divided between melancholy, pathos, farce and fun, and who was both true poet and versifying journalist, a practical-joking, pensive, laughing, worrying man, filled with Jacques's 'most humorous sadness', at the heart of his personality lies duality.[34]

Reid rightly stresses Hood's fondness for puns and wordplay, which he started using in jokes about fatherhood before his daughter Fanny was born. 'Every day I am a step-father to being a parent', he told Dilke; whereas the birth announcement itself played on the double meanings of 'sun' and 'son': 'Jane was taken ill on Friday evening, & on Saturday Morning at 6 presented me with a little daughter – tho it was *sun*rise.'[35] In describing his children to others, he highlights whatever is bizarre or entertaining about them, whether their appearance, behaviour or what they say. To Maria Dilke (Charles's wife), for example, he describes Tom, not quite one, in the following terms, finally comparing him with a bumper edition of a periodical:

Tom, Junior, who came to Cologne a little 'shabby, flabby, dabby, babby', has grown a young Kentuck, who can lick his father – as hard as nails, and as brown as rusty ones. – For his temper, only fancy mine 'with sugar'. So unlike Jane's 'warm without'. Then he is already so good on his legs. I wonder he ever required D[ilke]. 'to stand for him' [i.e. as godfather], and as to talking he can say papa when he likes. I have no doubt he only don't cut his teeth because he don't *choose*. In bulk, he is really a double number, but a good deal more amusing. (*Letters*, p. 192)

This account of Tom gives Hood every opportunity to indulge his love of playful language, which includes a quotation from one of his own poems, 'Domestic Asides; or, Truth in Parenthesis', an appropriately double-edged title for a comic piece about social hypocrisy. The poem, from the *Comic Annual* of 1831, refers to an absent 'Little Clara': 'I should have loved to kiss her so – / (A flabby, dabby, babby!)'. The phrase evidently pleased him so much that he recycled it in another long letter to Maria Dilke in January 1836, to describe calves killed at nine or ten days old: 'poor things mere flabby dabby babbies' (p. 216). The rest of his description of Tom revolves round puns on standing, nails and alcoholic drinks, for Maria to decode as best she might.

In writing to Fanny, he invented a more fantastic style, which he knew the child was too young to read for herself, but assumed someone would read to her. One from Ramsgate, written when Fanny was not yet three, describes children sea-bathing out of machines, and liking 'the fun of paddle daddleing – but some of them are afraid & squall & squeak like the pigs when Moot [a servant?] is killing them. – & while they are squalling the sea goes dab into their gaping wide mouths, & the water is so salt it makes them spit & splutter like frogs in a gutter' (*Letters*, p. 150). As the letter develops, Hood increasingly relies on mini-rhymes and sounds for comic effect: children on donkeys 'niddle noddle' their heads, one is 'kicked off splash dash into a wave', and he signs off as 'your own dear Parby-barby'. The overall effect is of a kind of pre-Lear nonsense writing, dependent not only on word-sounds but fantastic images, such as his expecting to see the nodding children's eyes dropping out 'like green gooseberries'. When one child fell into the water, all the others 'laughed at him & grinned till I thought their wide mouths would swallow their ears'. It was perhaps hardly surprising that Fanny eventually became a children's author in her own right.

Hood wrote in a similar vein to other children besides his own. Those of 1844 to Jeanie, May and Dunstanville ('Dunnie'), children of his doctor, William Elliot, again about seaside life, also describe for the children's amusement a surreal world heightened by punning and word play, which turn ordinary features of the beach into a grotesque fantasy. His letter to May repeats, with variations, the self-consuming image of the children swallowing their ears: 'I think I see *you* being dipped in the sea, screwing your eyes up, and putting your nose, like a button, into your mouth, like a buttonhole, for fear of getting another smell and taste!' (*Letters*, p. 628). Almost every aspect of the sea becomes for Hood in these letters the occasion for a pun or some other kind of word play. He suggests to Dunnie that he must have become 'instead of a land-boy, a regular sea-urchin' (p. 625), while his sister Jeanie is urged to dip her doll in the water among the mermaids, to see if she grows a tail and becomes a 'doll-fin' (p. 626). Carroll-like, there are jokes about oysters and lobsters, and one in which he imagines himself transformed into all three Elliots:

Childhood is such a joyous merry time I often wish I was two or three children! But I suppose I can't be else I would be Jeanie & Dunnie & May Elliot. And wouldn't I pull off my three pairs of shoes & socks & go paddling in the sea up to my six knees. And Oh how I would climb up the down & then roll down the ups on my three backs & stomachs. (*Letters*, p. 627)

Hood's comic style is at its best and its most inventive in letters like this, where there is no need for the formal narrative that proved his undoing in longer prose writings. He seems totally at liberty to invent a new way of expressing himself by recalling the sensations of childhood and exploring the interchangeable identities of adult and child. In the poem 'Youth and Age' he imagines a father and son wanting to swap lives with one another, each believing that the other has the better deal (Anstey's later novel, *Vice Versa* (1882), plays with this at length). It is impossible to tell whether the father has the last word purely by accident or design, but it certainly matches the spirit of Hood's letters to the Elliots and Fanny:

> Impatient of his childhood
> 'Ah me!' exclaims young Arthur
> Whilst roving in the wild wood,
> 'I wish I were my father!'
> Meanwhile, to see his Arthur
> So skip, and play, and run,
> 'Ah me!' exclaims the father,
> 'I wish I were my son!'[36]

Children – his own and others – were not, of course, his only inspiration in developing his comic style, but they, and his experience of married and domestic life generally, liberated in Hood a playful talent for nonsense writing at a period shortly before first Lear and then Carroll began to publish. Though he often sees life from a child's perspective, Hood writes more regularly from a father's point of view. He can sometimes be emotional, as in his poem 'Lines on Seeing My Wife and Two Children Sleeping in the Same Chamber' (written in Coblenz in November 1833), which, John Donne-like, describes his family as his whole earth and heaven, his 'universe of love' lying together in the one room, but Hood's fatherly writing about children is more often briskly comic. In 'A Serenade', for example, he empathises with an increasingly desperate father trying to make his son fall asleep:

> 'Lullaby, oh, lullaby!'
> Thus I heard a father cry,
> 'Lullaby, oh, lullaby!
> The brat will never shut an eye;
> Hither come, some power divine!
> Curse his lids or open mine.' (lines 1–4)[37]

Similar to this is his 'Parental Ode to my Son, Aged Three Years and Five Months', which begins as a Romantic address, but quickly begins to undercut itself with the reality of the child's behaviour:

> Thou happy, happy elf!
> (But stop, – first let me kiss away that tear) –
> Thou tiny image of myself!
> (My love, he's poking peas into his ear!) (lines 1–4)[38]

One more perspective for Hood, in his family writing, is the son's. As with much else in Hood's make-up, the cynical satire spoken by his father persona in many of his poems contrasts with the affectionate parent–child relationship in his unfinished novel, *Our Family*, serialised in *Hood's Magazine* between May 1844 and February 1845. Although this is a comic serial, which includes much ironic humour at the expense of the rich and pretentious, at the heart of it lies enormous respect for their doctor father from his twin sons, one of whom – Rumbold – narrates the story. *Tristram Shandy*-like, the novel begins with the narrator expatiating on the situation of his birth: not the birth itself, but the perspective of those waiting and discussing the event downstairs, and the whole tale (albeit unfinished at Hood's death) never progresses beyond the twins' christening and vaccination. *Our Family* recounts a succession of disasters that seem to follow upon each other naturally enough, but which are also aggravated by the doctor's bad luck. Underlying everything he does is the consciousness that he must provide for his twin sons. When adverse circumstantial evidence makes him resign from his duties in looking after the workhouse, he sees before him 'very distinctly, a Wife, two dear Twins, and a household to support, but no clear prospect of that indispensable requisite, a livelihood'.[39]

As his own life neared its end, Hood's vacillations over whether it was right to accept a state pension became the final twist in his attempts to balance his duties to his family with his self-respect and independence as an author. Hood prided himself on being essentially a 'clean' writer, whose blameless work his own children would be able to read 'without a burning blush on their young cheeks to reflect that the author was their father'.[40] Nevertheless, he felt he had not been appreciated by the state in any way that would benefit his family, either before or after his death, prompting him finally in July 1844 to permit a pension application to be made on his behalf to Sir Robert Peel, 'as it might enable me to make some slight provision for my children – whom I am but too sure to leave, like the children of literary men in general, to a double lament, – for the author of their being, & for his being an Author' (*Letters*, pp. 630–1). Even in this depressing situation Hood could not resist the temptation of a pun; but Peel's eventual offer of a £100 pension, to be settled on a close female relative or on himself (it was assumed he was near death) was disappointing. He told his doctor that he was 'exceedingly tempted to decline it' (*Letters*, p. 663), but wrote thanking Peel as 'a Man, a husband and a father', as well as an author (*Letters*, p. 665). To the end of his life, which came six months later, in May 1845, Hood both pressed his claims as a family man, and appealed to the domestic sympathies of anyone whose help he needed.

Hood's experiences as author and father were inextricably entwined. Frustrated by his limited earning powers, angry about the low standing of authors, whom he described in his copyright letters as 'immortals without a living' (*Works*, Vol. VI, p. 396), and always anxious about his children's long-term welfare, he was deeply conscious of the contradictions inherent in being a father, an invalid and a 'literary man'. He was never able to provide securely for his children, and was often both embarrassed and angry about his financial position and precarious state of health. In exploiting his mature writing to act out the various positions of the beleaguered father, he achieves his most inventive comedy in the private nonsense letters he wrote for, and about, his own and his friends' children. Here, liberated from financial care and public reputation, in a seaside world full of mermaids and polka-dancing crabs, he could escape into a comic fantasy of word play and endless punning, making something positive of the double meanings that otherwise distressed him as author/father. Perhaps it is no coincidence that the two greatest nonsense-writers of the period – Lear and Carroll – were both childless bachelors who could indulge their love of fantasy without any pressure to provide for others.

THE CARLISLE TRAGEDY: DEAN TAIT'S GIRLS. 1856

'Oh good archbishop you are better than I', Margaret Oliphant confessed in her *Autobiography*, as she compared Archibald Tait's tragedy as a bereaved parent with her own.[41] Whereas all of Oliphant's children predeceased her over a period of forty years, Tait had lost five young daughters to a virulent form of scarlet fever in the space of as many weeks in the spring of 1856. Oliphant found some comfort and fellowship in reading Tait's memorial volume on his wife and son, *Catharine and Craufurd Tait* (1879), his response to two further bereavements that happened twenty-two years later, but while she recognised the parallels between them ('Tait must have been exactly my age when his Craufurd died, sixty-six and a half'), she knew there was a world of difference between their ways of handling family tragedy.[42] Tait was a believer, while Oliphant's faith had been badly shaken by the loss of her sons Cyril and Cecco: 'We are none of us pious like him and his wife, not praying together or talking as they do – too little, I know too little' (p. 84). Moreover, she winced at the public display of private emotion that Tait, in his grief, had exposed to the world. 'I did not like his book', Oliphant complained. 'I thought it too personal, too sacred for publication . . .' (p. 84).

Oliphant's comments go right to the heart of the problem we have in reading bereavement narratives like Tait's. Not only has our culture largely lost a shared belief in the Christian afterlife, and the comfort of praying together as a family; the glorification of suffering and saintly children 'minimizes the ugliness of death', as Laurence Lerner puts it, 'in order to make sadness pleasing' – in itself a suspect pleasure.[43] More recently, David Hughes's *The Lent Jewels* (2003) confronts these 'suspect pleasures' in his discovery of the Taits' story as he tries to make sense of his own situation in the light of their unshakable faith. He admits to finding both the Taits sexually charismatic – to the extent that he pairs Archibald with the mysterious 'Walter', author of *My Secret Life* (*c.* 1888–94), a pornographic history of sexual adventuring around the time of Tait's translation to the Bishopric of London in 1856. The Taits fascinate Hughes for several reasons, not least because of the intensity of the couple's emotions as they weather their daughters' deaths. Like Oliphant, he feels a grudging jealousy of their religious life together, which seems so out of reach in contemporary times, but from initial scepticism about their passivity in the face of so much misery, he comes to respect them as friends and guides through the meaninglessness of modern experience. 'I was asking Tait as a man, and Catharine as a woman, and the girls as a family, to indicate to me gifts I was not using, as well as teach me services I could give', he presently admits.[44]

The Taits' tragedy was truly shocking. Between 6 March and 8 April 1856, their five daughters, one after the other, sickened with the symptoms of scarlet fever, and, though the course of the illness varied (the eldest was ten, the youngest nineteen months), the outcome was the same for all. Victorian medicine could do little to help, other than offer palliatives, leeches, hot baths and port wine. The longest-surviving daughter, eight-year-old May, held out for a fortnight, and her parents were hopeful that

Figure 1   Archibald Campbell Tait. From a photograph by John Jabez Edwin Mayall, engraved by D. J. Pound.

one daughter at least might be saved, but she too eventually succumbed. The sole survivors were the new baby, Lucy, who was only a month old when the first child fell ill, and the only boy – Craufurd, aged six – who saw each of his sisters taken away to die. Neither of the parents caught the disease, though Catharine was barely recovered from childbirth.

This was more, however, than a family tragedy, severe though it was. The ramifications of the Taits' experience raised many questions concerning the nature of religious faith, especially in relation to parenthood. What was the appropriate response of a mother and father whose family was decimated by an apparently God-sent epidemic? Were the Taits being punished for failings of their own, or was their faith being tested by the worst of all trials for devoted parents? And where did the experience leave Tait as a religious professional whose first loyalty was to God? He was not like the controversial and charismatic preacher, Edward Irving (1792–1834), who, when his young children fell ill, believed it was going against God to call in medical help.[45] Doctors were in and out of Tait's Deanery throughout the five weeks of illness, and additional doctors sent for after the first two children had died. Arguably Tait's fatal error of judgement was to keep the children in Carlisle when scarlet fever was known to be in the town, but his own miraculous deliverance, on Easter Sunday of 1848 from rheumatic fever while he was Headmaster of Rugby, gave him a stubborn faith that all would be well.

Tait's life was chequered by ill health. He was born with club feet, which were straightened by a rough technique involving tin boots, and throughout his adult life he was susceptible to serious illness. In 1843, a year after succeeding Dr Arnold as Headmaster of Rugby, Tait married the earnestly religious Catharine Spooner. By all accounts he was an undistinguished headmaster, and his appointment to the Deanship of Carlisle in 1850 took him permanently out of schoolmastering and into a successful career in the church. His reputation as a family man positively aided his advancement to Bishop of London in 1856 and then Archbishop of Canterbury in 1868. Canon Fremantle confirmed in a *Good Words* obituary of 1883 that Tait 'would never have had so great a hold on the convictions and the affections of his fellow-countrymen and fellow-Christians but for his pure and beautiful family life'; while 'men of all kinds and degrees, far and near, found themselves drawn within the alluring shade of his sorrow . . .'[46] Queen Victoria herself, believing that few archbishops had been 'more respected and beloved', wished that she had seen his 'holy deathbed' and received his blessing.[47]

'[A]lluring shade of his sorrow' is a telling phrase, which sums up Tait's cultural appeal as a tragic Christian father-figure. Both he and his wife kept journals of their daughters' final illnesses, but whereas Catharine's was published in *Catharine and Craufurd Tait* (1879) under the Archbishop's supervision, his own journal remains in manuscript in

Lambeth Palace library. Pat Jalland, who has analysed both journals, thinks they were written for different purposes: whereas Catharine's is 'exemplary and consolatory, as well as therapeutic', her husband's 'seems to have been written for his eyes alone, as part of the private daily diary in which he normally accounted to God, in Evangelical manner, for his life'.[48] Catharine's evidently circulated in manuscript before it was published: Gladstone's daughter Mary described it as a 'beautiful account' when she was lent it in 1864, which suggests she regarded it as consolation literature.[49] Tait's diary, on the other hand, reads more problematically as a father's quarrel with himself and God in the hope of understanding what had happened to his family. There were good reasons why its publication would be withheld.

Tait's position in the home during his daughters' illness was very different from his wife's. His was essentially a liminal presence, recalled in his memory of 'the bright forms that used to welcome me at the Railway Station or on the threshold of our home'.[50] His presentation of himself arriving home from travel is significant here: throughout the journals of both parents, he is reported as coming in and out of rooms; his real work lies elsewhere, and he remains essentially a visitor in this world of ailing girls with 'bright' souls. Even when the eldest child Catty was first ill, Catharine says that her 'Father still only came to the door, but lived in prayer for his first-born'.[51] On the first night of illness, when he knew that five-year-old Charlotte ('Chatty') was unwell, he had actually been out to dinner; back at home, he 'sat some time in [his] study and was very dreary' (p. 3). David Hughes, visiting this study for his *Lent Jewels*, imagines it as the place where Tait escaped 'the small crises that were the daily currency of family life beyond the door, but not the large ones' (p. 141). Catharine, however, recalls that the children liked to prepare their lessons in this study: 'they would lie down without disturbing him, and dearly did he love the little hum which, like a sweet song, soothed him in his own work'.[52]

What exactly was Tait's role as the Christian father of a sick family? Laurence Lerner, who ignores Tait's diary, argues that 'the central figure of any child death must surely be the mother' (p. 211); other memoirs of the time, however, suggest that it was not unusual for fathers to help nurse their children through illness, and Dickens, Macready, Darwin and Gladstone certainly performed these offices. Though he was constantly in and out of the sickroom, Tait's memoir is full of self-recrimination, mainly for not realising how bad things were. It is hard to agree with Pat Jalland's view that his 'account of his children's deaths was more prosaic and less emotional than his wife's' (p. 135): there are moments of extraordinary passion in his memoir, not least because he clung to his children's physical presence. Both parents comment on their daughters' beauty – enhanced, ironically, by the flushed cheeks and bright eyes of their illness – but Tait finds it particularly hard to give up the feel of their bodies. His journal includes additional memoirs, afterthoughts or extra notes, scribbled on the blank pages opposite each of the formal diary pages. One of these recalls the moment when he held the newly dead Chatty in a passionate embrace:

Shall I ever forget the anguish of that moment as I folded my darling little child in my arms – and felt her heart still warm though life was fled – I threw myself upon the bed – and soon putting all the others out of the room I took her in my arms and kissed her lifeless form – my darling bright little [illegible] girl – who loved me so very dearly – who for months past had never met me anywhere without gently kissing my hand – How shall I express the shock – that one brief day shd have taken her from us – and I felt that I had not prayed for her as I ought to have done the night before having no fear that she was in any danger. (pp. 25–6)

In this passage, Tait reveals his need to have Chatty to himself one last time, and to rekindle the exclusive relationship he had with her, without the intrusive presence of the others. Elisabeth Bronfen's argument, in *Over Her Dead Body* (1992), that the conjunction of death, art and femininity forms a disturbing undercurrent to Western literature, helps to explain some of the conflicting implications of this scene, which would not be out of place in a gothic novel. According to Bronfen, the 'feminine corpse inspires the surviving man to write, to deny or to acknowledge death, while at the same time the corpse is the site at which he can articulate this knowledge'.[53] This corpse can just as easily be a child's as a woman's: the deaths of Little Nell and Harriet Beecher Stowe's little Eva from *Uncle Tom's Cabin* are cited later in the argument. Bronfen's emphasis on the male observer of the beautiful female corpse supports the interpretation of Tait's response as partly self-reflexive. 'Any articulation of another's death, it seems, inevitably returns to the surviving speaker', Bronfen argues, not least because 'it is coupled with a realisation of one's own mortality' (pp. 15–16).

As a religious professional, Tait's role was primarily to intercede with God for his children's lives, but his faith in prayer was to be severely tested over the next few weeks, as was his confidence in his own purpose as father of a family. He quickly arrogates to himself moral leadership of the household, but there is still little he can do other than manage the developing crisis. 'In the morning of the 6th', he recalls in his journal, 'I was up soon after six having given orders that no one but myself shd break the sad tidings [of Chatty's death] to my other darling children' (p. 27). Fearing the worst, he had all their pictures taken, and a daguerreotype of Chatty lying dead on the sofa. At this stage Tait was already planning a memorial window in the Cathedral, just for her (as Gladstone would do in thanksgiving for his daughter Agnes's survival), though ultimately it was dedicated to all five daughters. Tait, in other words, was busy memorialising his daughters in a variety of different ways, even as they were gradually slipping from him, nor was it enough for him just to remember his daughters, or to trust that God had them in his safekeeping: he had to *see* them, in every possible configuration, mental, spiritual and material.

The greatest trial for both parents, but especially the father, was the news that their eldest daughter Catty had been taken ill. Again, his pleasure in her appearance, as he looks at her through the window, is as much aesthetic as spiritual: 'I never thought her really beautiful before but that night she did seem really beautiful', he admits. 'Alas the heightened colour was the beginning of the awful fever.'[54] May too 'looked beautiful when she was brought into the day nursery in her blankets' (p. 75) and 'Francy [Frances] especially with her clear complexion and white hair looked lovely in her black clothes' (p. 50). Tait takes leave of each daughter in this way, and is shocked when his wife cuts off Catty's 'beautiful hair' (p. 70). Seeing her partly as a replica of himself – 'Without her hair she looked very like the little bust of me in Park Place' (p. 71) – he hoped that like himself she would experience the 'joyful change' of recovery on Easter morning as he had done eight years earlier at Rugby.

This was the ultimate test for Tait. He was so convinced Catty would recover – a holy child and her father's favourite – on Easter morning, that he refused to abandon hope. Unlike Chatty's case, which he had seriously underestimated, with Catty he prayed fervently himself and, as Catharine recalls in her journal, 'sent to all the churches to ask that prayer might be made for her and for us' (p. 348); but when Catty pointed towards heaven, as if ready to depart and join her sisters, Tait burst into tears. Both he and his wife describe this episode in their diaries, remembering that Catty wiped away his tears, but whereas Catharine fled from the scene, unable to bear any more, Tait stayed, before venting his grief privately in an unorthodox, non-Christian way. 'The grey light was beginning. I thought of rushing into the Abbey ground & shrieking aloud. I lay down on the floor in the dining room of Mr Gipp's house below where she lay dead' (p. 87).

Catty's loss agonised both parents for a long time afterwards, but for her father, her death was especially poignant. As he pushes the vocabulary of religious sentimentality to the extreme, his grief-stricken gestures have a gothic extravagance, and his memories lurch from the conventionally pious to the sensuous and secular. 'She and sweet May who was about a year old', he remembered that summer, 'used to chase each other naked about the drawing room before they went to bed May crawling and Catty running' (opposite p. 127). On another occasion, in the Lake District, Tait thought he saw Catty leading her 'beautiful band' of sisters hiding themselves in the woods.[55] He remembered her wiping away his tears, not just on her own deathbed, but when he recalled early losses of his own (Vol. XL, p. 12). The cult of the beautiful, sensitive child was something he knew and understood, even if it was unnamed by him and unrecognised; likewise his innocent, [pre-]Freudian tribute to Catty as loved more intensely than her sisters. 'I seem to mourn for her – as a husband almost wd mourn for a wife, (p. 28) he admits in one of those naked moments of self-analysis that occasionally shock modern readers of Victorian family discourse. The visions of his children were so intense that he worried 'lest the desire of seeing my sweet children departed take the place of the desire of seeing the Lord Jesus Himself' (p. 27). Tait says little about his wife's handling of this aftermath of their grief, though he admits she has more 'genuine piety' (p. 9). Her comments on their tragedy were more publishable, perhaps because she had always intended them to be so. Whereas Tait argues with himself and God, lamenting: 'Oh God thou hast dealt very mysteriously with us –', her diary ends on a less raw note, as she tries to summarise the meaning of what they have experienced: 'Thus were we called upon to part with these five most blessed little daughters, each of whom had been received in prayer, borne in prayer, educated with prayer, and now given up, though with bitter anguish, yet with prayer and thanksgiving.'[56]

Catherine Robson argues that for the Victorians perfect childhood is 'always exemplified by a little girl'.[57] This is all the more so when the girl has lived a saintly life and died dispensing wisdom and comfort to those around her, as Catty and the others did. Tait's daughters seem to join Dickens's Little Nell, Wordsworth's Lucy and daughter Catharine, and De Quincey's sister Elizabeth in that constellation of idealised girls whom nineteenth-century men lament as permanently beyond their reach. Robson notes that the narrative of *The Old Curiosity Shop* repeatedly focuses on Nell's body – both her living body and her corpse – as if to emphasise its precious materiality. For all his Christian piety, Tait too could not get his daughters' physical presence out of his mind: it was not enough for him to think of being reunited with them subsequently in heaven – he wanted to hear their voices and see their beautiful faces in this life. Robson further argues that for the Victorian gentleman, the little girl represents 'an adult male's best opportunity of reconnecting with his own lost self' (p. 3). In other words she represents an innocence and unsullied purity that he can no longer recapture in his adult life. Tait clearly identified himself with Catty, as his quoted comments show: she was both an aspect of himself, and a saintly 'Other', interacting with all that had so far happened to him and permanently changing who he was. His delight in his daughters' collective beauty as young children had to be sacrificed to his faith that they would be waiting for him in heaven. Freud's dismissal of any meaning in his daughter Sophie's death sixty years later in 1920 provides a sharp contrast with Tait's struggle to thank God for, in effect, lending him his five daughters. So far as Freud was concerned, Sophie's death, at the age of twenty-six, from influenzal pneumonia, was a 'meaningless, brutal act of fate . . . a joke played on helpless, poor humans by higher forces'.[58] Language of this kind was simply not an option for Tait, who has to cast his grief in terms of biblical reverence, addressed to a personal God: 'But tho' thou slay us yet will we trust in thee' (Vol. XL, p. 2). In the journal entries written in the later spring and early summer of 1856 at Hallsteads, a house on Ullswater, Tait's gothic grief gives way to Christian resignation.

If Tait's life as a father was in conflict with his dedication to God, his career in the church was awkwardly aided by his tragedy. This is not to suggest that Tait's advancement happened through some kind of 'sympathy vote', but commentators could hardly avoid noting his terrible experiences as a father and their effect on his spirituality. Henry Wace, writing in the *Quarterly Review* at the start of 1883, argues that if Tait's rapid progression up the church hierarchy had been in any danger of compromising his simplicity of character, 'it was effectually averted by the heavy blow which desolated his household at Carlisle'. After praising Tait's 'manly resignation', he claims:

it cast over his whole future life the solemnizing light of another world. Perhaps, especially when thus borne, it conciliated towards him a degree of sympathy which is often denied to those who rise rapidly to great place in the Church of the State. He was felt to be united with those over whom he presided in the experiences which most closely touch their hearts; and the intense interest aroused by the Memoir of his wife and son bore striking witness to the depth of this sympathetic feeling.[59]

The evidence suggests that Queen Victoria herself was behind his preferment, first to London and then to Canterbury. According to P. T. Marsh, 'The Queen, in common with the higher levels of English society was moved by Tait's recent tragedy and may out of sympathy have pressed Palmerston to nominate him'; while Elizabeth Longford, describing Tait in her biography of Victoria as 'the first Primate to become her friend', suggests that when he was promoted to Canterbury, seven years after Prince Albert's death, 'perhaps it was partly because Mrs Tait, though not of course a widow, had lost five children from fever in one month'.[60] Though essentially it was his broad-church principles that attracted her, there is little doubt that the Queen, like everyone else, was touched by what had happened to Tait, marked out as he was in a way that protected him from hostile criticism.

As a comment on the cultural reception of fatherhood, Tait's tragedy of 1856 seems archetypically Victorian. It was not only in keeping with the taste for deathbed narratives of saintly children written by sorrowing parents; their narratives yield a strange kind of forbidden satisfaction and morbid enjoyment, even for modern readers like David Hughes, who not only reads and then reconstructs their story, but also needs to share the intimacy of the Taits' virtuous lives. If today's readers are mostly aghast at the mind-set of parents who could resign five daughters to God, however unwillingly, there is another aspect of Tait's story that concerns his own experience of fatherhood in more earthbound ways. His narrative lets slip the unsayable about his daughters' beauty in illness and death as well as life. It celebrates the appeal of their bodies as well as their souls, and it voices his helplessness as a religious professional who could not make God listen in his hour of need, but who accepted promotion to high office partly, at least, on the strength of what he had endured on their account.

G. H. LEWES: 'THE VERY BITTER PLEASURE OF CHILDREN'. 1859 AND 1869

My last example is a very different case history from the previous three: a fatherhood 'scandal' in the sense of children being caught up in their father's public disgrace, of which they were initially unaware, and which did not directly concern them. The three surviving sons of George Henry Lewes and his wife Agnes Jervis – Charles Lee (1842–91), Thornton Arnott (1844–69) and Herbert Arthur (1846–75) – were not introduced to their father's new partner – Marian Evans, or 'George Eliot' – until 1860, six years after he had originally eloped with her to Germany. Throughout the early years of this relationship, Lewes had to keep leaving his home with Eliot, itself of unfixed tenure, to visit his sons, and after 1856 escort them to and from their boarding school at Hofwyl, near Berne in Switzerland. Although his wife Agnes had begun bearing Thornton Hunt's children in 1850, Lewes paid his wife regular maintenance, and never divorced her. In registering Agnes's first two children with Hunt as his own, Lewes in effect condoned her adultery. The strangeness of the Lewes story begins with this fact alone. Why would any father, at a time when family law was so inflexible, acknowledge another man's children as his own, thereby disqualifying himself for divorce and remarriage? Eliot's biographer Kathryn Hughes suggests it may have had something to do with the death, just two weeks before a new son's birth, of the fourth son of Lewes and Agnes, St Vincent Arthy, at the age of two: 'In the midst of despair it may have been that the joy of a new child, even another man's, went some way towards filling the void.' For her, however, the real explanation is that, 'despite the façade of moral flippancy which offended so many, Lewes was a man of integrity'. He had agreed with Agnes that monogamy was difficult to sustain, and if either of them wanted a relationship with someone else, this should be accepted.[61]

Perhaps the story starts even earlier, with Lewes's own absconding father, John Lee, who left his partner and three sons when George Henry (1817–78), the youngest, was only two, and went to join his customs officer brother in Bermuda. Lewes, whose parents never married, was told that his real father had died, not that he had gone away: his mother then married Captain John Gurens Willim in 1823, a stepfather Lewes never much liked. Rosemary Ashton has suggested that he was probably unaware of his own illegitimate status, and that he had a set of half-siblings.[62] Unsurprisingly, being a father remained problematic for Lewes for the rest of his life. He mostly lived apart from his own three boys, and failed to incorporate any of them except Charles into his household with George Eliot. Like Dickens's sons, they proved difficult to place in professions, and the recourse of sending two of them to South Africa ended in tragedy. 'Thornie' contracted tuberculosis of the spine while he was out in Natal, trying to establish himself as a farmer, and came home to die at Lewes's home with Eliot a few years later, while Herbert, also farming in Natal, died six years later of bronchitis in Durban. Though the remaining son, Charles, settled down to a steady job in the Post Office, Lewes's well-meaning efforts as a father were largely a failure, with two sons predeceasing him. In 1859 he told them, at Hofwyl, of his relationship with George Eliot; 1869 was the year Thornie came home to die.

The account of this revelation is given in Lewes's journal for 13–16 July 1859. He had made arrangements to spend a few days with the boys, so that they would have plenty of opportunity to discuss the situation with their father, and he took them out on country walks to make the talking easier. They were lying on the moss in a wood when he actually broke the double news that his relationship with their mother had collapsed, and that he was now living with George Eliot. 'They were less distressed than I had anticipated', Lewes noted, 'and were delighted to hear about Marian. This of course furnished the main topic for the whole day.'[63] It seemed as if the secret that had been withheld for five years had been safely communicated, and that his relationship with his sons had survived intact. Nevertheless, subsequent letters swarm with a surplus of mother names (Agnes, Lewes's own elderly mother, and now Marian), while he holds sway as the only meaningful father.

In his letters to the boys, first at their school at Bayswater, and then at Hofwyl, Lewes called himself both 'Pater' and 'Papsy', and addressed them as 'My dear Pups', until Charles married in 1865, whereupon he and his wife Gertrude became 'My dear Children'. The tone is friendly, affectionate and informative, but only about the side of his life that involved work and travel. Initially, he continues writing as if he is a single man: even in 1854, the elopement year ('Here I am in the capital of the Grand duchy of Weimar'), talking mainly of his own work and literary social life, such as Thackeray's invitation to write for his new journal, *The Cornhill Magazine*, and George Smith's personal visit by carriage to make him a tempting offer (*Letters*, Vol. III, p. 195). Once the George Eliot secret was out, he was able to be more open about the kind of life they were leading, and the nature of their welcome as 'quite European celebrities', even if they were still *personae non grata* at home.[64]

All three sons were less academic than he had hoped, but while Charles was biddable and anxious to please, the younger two gave cause for concern. Lewes intended Thornie for the Civil Service, but when he failed his final examination and talked of going to Poland to fight the Russians, Lewes thought farming in Natal might be a more appropriate kind of adventure. As Kathryn Hughes observes, the possibility of Thornie's permanently living with the Leweses in London was never considered a serious option.[65] As for Bertie, his writing was so poor that competitive exams would have been humiliating for him, and farming was thought to offer the best chance of an independent livelihood, supported by his older brother. The pattern of energetic, vigorous fathers trying to place lethargic sons in professions for life will feature many times in this study. It was clearly a problem for men who had themselves worked hard to overcome adverse family circumstances, but whose sons, protected by their fathers' success, either felt discouraged by the comparison with themselves, or unmotivated to make similar efforts. Read alongside his theatre reviews as 'Vivian' in *The Leader* during the 1850s, his letters to his sons construct a narrative of self-conscious denial as a father managing a long-distance relationship with his children.

'Vivian' was a persona Lewes created for himself in the weekly radical newspaper to which both he and George Eliot contributed articles. *The Leader* was founded in 1850, ironically enough in a joint venture with Thornton Hunt, Lewes's successor with Agnes, and provided commentary on current affairs, literature of the day, and other matters of general interest. Lewes wrote long literature reviews under his own name, but for his roundup of theatrical news, he invented a louche bachelor, 'Vivian', who lets slip little personal details in between advising his readers on the best shows playing in London's theatres. A running theme in the reviews is women's perverse attraction to married men, to the neglect of bachelors like himself, while he dismisses as noisy and tasteless the disorder of married households full of 'obstreperous children, who dislocate my watch-chain and press their jam-stained fingers on my lavender trousers'.[66]

Whenever he writes about families and fatherhood in *The Leader*, Lewes as 'Vivian' distances himself as an outsider to marriage. His contempt for married couples may disguise a certain envy, but he often sneers at their domestic complacency. 'One is always the son of somebody; but, happily, one is not always the father of somebody', he declares in a review of a comedy by Joseph Stirling Coyne, *The Hope of the Family*. This review is particularly scathing about sons ('if one has a boy there is always the hope that he may run away');[67] even closer to the bone was 'How to Make Home Happy', a *Leader* review of a farce by William Brough in November 1853. 'As I have *no* home', Vivian announces, 'and that home is not happy, I really stand in need of his secret'. Before seeing the play, Vivian claims his idea of how to make home happy would be to 'keep late hours, – be sarcastic on shopping – admire the way Mrs Jones dresses, – think Mrs Brown's children are "perfectly managed", – bring a friend home suddenly to dinner on Saturdays, discover that "other people" manage to get whatever cannot be got at home, and you will infallibly make home happy'.[68] There is a cynical contradictoriness in this and many of the other 'Vivian' passages, which portray a man at odds with the majority view of family life, or else subversively say what others privately feel but cannot speak aloud. Only when a children's entertainment needs reviewing, such as *Anderson the Wizard* at St James's Theatre in April 1851, does he wish he had a child to share the experience: 'This is an announcement to make me "wish I were a boy again"', he says of the *Wizard* show, '– or at any rate, that I were the father of a family, – that I might take my noisy children to see this wondrous man. Decidedly one *ought* to be the father of a family! I shall make arrangements to become such.'[69]

Already the father of a family, Lewes enjoys pretending to be a proud bachelor wondering what it must be like to be a father, experiencing what he calls, citing Tertullian, 'the very bitter pleasure of children'.[70] If this had been his lot in life, he muses, he imagines himself spending his evenings 'enlightening their young minds and setting them copies in round text! If! Ah if!' The children he imagines here are very different from another bachelor's – 'Elia', alias Charles Lamb – whose essay 'Dream Children' (1823) can otherwise be seen as a similar exercise in imagining himself the father of a son and daughter, telling them stories of their great-grandmother, only to find that these are 'dream children' of his imagination: 'and immediately awaking, I found myself quietly seated in my bachelor armchair, where I had fallen asleep ...'[71] The difference is clearly that Elia romanticises his 'dream children', whereas Vivian sees them as a 'bitter pleasure': nevertheless, both experiment with a bachelor fantasy of fatherhood, which is the fireside companionship of children with the father as the dominant figure, ordering the evening's entertainment.

It is easy to take the 'Vivian' reviews as an acid counterpoint to the reality of Lewes's actual life (at this stage he was not living with Marian Evans, but he knew of Agnes's affair with Hunt, and he was responsible for the upkeep of a growing family of children). More interestingly, they allow Lewes the freedom to offer a general running commentary on the options open to Victorian middle-class men, and the hypocrisies of a family-orientated society. 'Vivian' looks ahead to the world of Oscar Wilde (curiously enough, Wilde used the same name, spelt differently, both for one of his own sons, and for his dialogue 'The Decay of Lying'), where bachelors, conceivably in 'lavender trousers', long for dinner-parties and the theatre to lift their boredom, only to be just as bored there, while envying the married men who have real homes to go to. Vivian's London society of the fifties sounds as discontented and frivolous as Wilde's of the nineties, yet underlying the façade of elegant boredom combined with jealousy and contempt for domestic men is a feeling of exclusion. Lewes seems to be using his Vivian persona to disappear underground, away from his paternal responsibilities, and to reassess the attractions of being alone. When he was invited to revive Vivian in the 1860s, he declined, feeling he had outgrown the role: 'My objection to Vivian is first that V. was a personality which I can no longer maintain being too airy & foppish for a grave signior about to be a grandfather.'[72]

In making a permanent home with George Eliot, Lewes resumed the role of father, albeit largely at a distance, and provided a new mother for his adult sons. Eliot's letters look forward to their own ageing as a 'comfortable old couple', but in fact there was little comfort in this final phase of Lewes's experience of fatherhood.[73] He spent a painful five months nursing Thornie, an episode famously commemorated by Henry James, who turned up at 'Mrs Lewes's guarded portal' soon after the invalid's return in May 1869. With Lewes out trying to buy painkillers, James focused on Eliot: 'It infinitely moved me to see so great a celebrity quite humanly and familiarly agitated', he recalled; he himself took a cab to leave a message with the doctor, as the invalid's 'father's return still failed'.[74] As recounted by James, the father and son are the background figures in the drama, his own quiveringly new 'relation' with George Eliot the focal interest; and as both the Leweses described the tragedy of Thornie's death, Lewes attributes to Eliot the greater sense of loss: 'She had lavished almost a mother's love on my dear boy, and felt almost a mother's grief. I was better prepared, having never from the first had much hope of his recovery . . .'[75] In responding to condolence letters after Bertie's death six years later, Eliot often spoke philosophically for both of them: 'What can we do more than try to arrive at the best conclusion from the conditions as they are known to us?' she said to John Cross, as she inevitably wondered whether sending Bertie to Natal had shortened his life; while to Sara Hennell she confided that 'the boys seem all to have inherited an untrustworthy physique'.[76]

Of all the fathers discussed in this chapter, Lewes seems to have had the least pleasure in his children's companionship. He stopped living as a father with his children in the early 1850s, when the eldest was barely ten; after that they always lived somewhere else, until two of the three left Europe altogether in the 1860s. Eliot's presence impacted on the relationship, initially as someone to be talked about; then as the 'little Mutter' whose activities are reported in letters, until the narrator and subject change places, and she tells the boys about their 'little Pater'. Lewes assured the boys that Marian's arrival would not damage his own relationship with them; nevertheless, beginning with the 'Vivian' articles, and then through his letters about his own and Eliot's careers, Lewes's writing disowns or displaces his fatherhood as much as it acknowledges it, until the moment when he hears of Thornie's illness, and admits: 'The vision of him haunts me incessantly'.[77] As Lewes is frightened into the simplest, most direct use of language ('Dreadfully shocked . . . A dreadful day . . .'), Eliot increasingly speaks for both of them, engulfing the father's voice in the adoptive mother's: 'This death seems to me the beginning of our own.'[78] Nothing Lewes said about his own fatherhood seems to have retained the richly intoned resonance of this comment by the parent who was not even the son's biological mother.

CONCLUSION

Each of these fathers can be said to have 'failed' for different reasons. Prince Albert was too ambitious for his eldest children, Hood failed as a man of letters to provide adequately for his family, Tait's Christian faith could not save his daughters or console him for their loss, and Lewes's ambivalence about fatherhood seems to have been answered by the poor health and low achievements of his three sons. More than anything, they were powerless against the ravages of contingency, whether in the form of disease, poverty or just low achievement. If their role was above all to protect their children, none of these four succeeded; moreover, their different experiences show that this basic assumption was well nigh impossible to guarantee. Fatherhood had failure built into its very purpose and fabric, even more than motherhood, which – for all its perfections – was subordinated to fatherhood in the eyes of the law.

On the other hand, measured by different standards, their failure was not necessarily absolute. None of Prince Albert's children died during his lifetime, and he was perhaps guilty of nothing worse than unrealistic hopes; Hood's children had a predominantly happy childhood, despite his financial shortcomings, as did Tait's, whose beauty and piety were universally admired; while Lewes constantly concerned himself with his sons' futures even as he was enjoying his escape with George Eliot. Despite the very obvious differences of circumstance, all identify a role for themselves that was distinct from the children's mother's. Loosely speaking, this encompassed a wider sense of possibility for their children. The mother is relegated to a more humdrum role of domestic carer while the father sees his children in a broader landscape, whether a reformed and united Germany, a comic seaside, a South African farm or guiding their father from the vantage-point of the next world.

The cases that follow explore less acute examples of failure, but build on themes initiated by this chapter: the father's inability to protect his children from illness, death or inherited weakness; his desperation to place sons on promising career paths; his underlying fear of responsibility for the lives of others, and his attempts to seek out identities other than those of the traditional Victorian patriarch and breadwinner. These are not self-satisfied trajectories, despite each father's success in public life. In fact it could be said that each man's private domestic career as a father developed against the grain of his external profile, and became known to the public only towards the end of his life, or via his obituaries. Over the course of the century the nature of a man's relationship with his children became a matter of increasing public curiosity. As they ploughed their way through piles of *Lives and Letters*, Victorian readers looked for clues to a man's personality in the way he managed his work at home against the noise of children playing outside the private masculine sanctum of the study.

CHAPTER 2

Theatrical fatherhood: Dickens and Macready

On 4 July 1857, Charles Dickens staged a production of his and Wilkie Collins's collaborative venture, *The Frozen Deep*, before a private audience of Queen Victoria, Prince Albert and other members of the Royal Family. The Queen had especially requested the performance, but Dickens refused to give it at Buckingham Palace, as he did not 'feel easy as to the social position' of his daughters appearing there in the guise of actresses.[1] What was indeed remarkable about the play was that Dickens himself, his brother Alfred, his two daughters Mary and Kate, and eldest son Charley, as well as his two sisters-in-law Georgina and Helen Hogarth, all acted in it, as if it were still the private dramatic production at home in the schoolroom that it had originally been. In fact its first performance had occurred on 6 January 1857, to celebrate the twentieth birthday of Charley Dickens, which coincided with Twelfth Night. *The Times* marked the anomaly of its public/private circumstances by heading its review 'Tavistock-House Theatre', and observing: 'It would be absurd to apply the term "private" to the theatrical performances that take place at Tavistock-house, the residence of Mr Dickens's family.'[2] To reinforce the point that his daughters were not professional actresses, but members of the family, their names were given in the 'Tavistock House Theatre' playbill as 'Miss Kate' and 'Miss Mary'. When the play went public in Manchester later that year, to raise money for the widow and daughter of his old friend Douglas Jerrold (adding another dimension to its family associations), Dickens decided to pull his daughters (but not his son) out of the production, and replace them with professional actresses. One of these was Ellen Ternan, with whom he then embarked on an illicit romantic relationship. The curious thing is that for the Ternans, too, *The Frozen Deep* was a family affair, as Ellen's mother and sister were both involved in the production; while for Dickens, his intense absorption in the play marked the last stage of his marriage, as he separated from his wife Catherine the following year.

The Frozen Deep is therefore a major symbolic milestone in the life of Dickens as a family man, encapsulating the complex and problematic nature of his domestic politics and the relationship between his home life and public reputation. The theatre had long been a home-based activity for him: he had been interested in amateur theatrical performances since childhood, and as a married man regularly assembled a cast of friends to act plays in his house. Once his children were old enough to participate, they too were included, and their schoolroom commandeered to provide both stage and audience seating area. Comments in his letters indicate how enthusiastic he was about transforming his domestic living space into a theatre. Unlike Sir Thomas Bertram in Jane Austen's *Mansfield Park* (1814), where the returning father is shocked to find an amateur actor 'almost hallooing' on a makeshift stage in his billiard-room, Dickens rechristened his home 'The smallest theatre in the world', appropriating for himself as actor-manager the name of his own Mr Crummles from *Nicholas Nickleby* (1838–9).[3] Charley Dickens recalls how his father was fascinated by his son's toy theatre, 'a perfect Drury Lane among its brethren'. Before long, Dickens had taken it over, and employing Clarkson Stansfield, the landscape painter, to provide the backdrops, staged a 'spectacle called the "Elephant of Siam"'.[4] There followed increasingly ambitious productions of children's plays, such as Planché's *Fortunio*, in which one of his younger sons, Henry Fielding Dickens, played the lead role. 'My children have a little story-book play under paternal direction once a year on a birthday occasion', Dickens told Planché, encouraging him to come and see for himself.[5] His first 'grown-up' play, as he called it, involving his amateur theatrical company of friends and family, was an earlier Collins melodrama, *The Lighthouse* (performed in 1855), which he described as 'our domestic freak.'[6] For a man notorious among his children for neatness, he seems to have relished every aspect of the chaotic preparations. 'The house is full of spangles, gas, Jew theatrical tailors and Pantomime Carpenters', he reported, while in the run-up to *The Frozen Deep*, there were 'four stage-carpenters, entirely boarding on the premises, a carpenter's shop erected in the back-garden, size always boiling over on all the lower-fires . . . and a legion of prowling nondescripts ever slinking in and out'.[7] Certainly, if the engraving *in The Illustrated London News* review is anything to go by, the results were spectacular. In the melodramatic final scene, Dickens, playing the explorer Richard Wardour, lies on the ground in rags before all the people whose lives have become entangled with his, framed by a realistic cavern structure, with a ship on the sea visible through archways.[8]

The upheaval of the house, the sending out of invitations and general sense of bustling anticipation brought a respite from Dickens's mundane domestic life, which by the mid 1850s was under considerable strain. His wife Catherine rarely figures in his excited letters about the theatricals and never acted in them herself: whereas the amateur acting group gave him, in effect, an alternative family, composed of male friends and young adult children. When the time came for the 'depressed agonies of smashing the theatre' and the resumption of normal household routines, Dickens's emotional flatness is palpable. 'The Theatre has disappeared', he tells his actor-friend William Charles Macready, Prospero-like, at the end of January: 'the house is restored to its usual condition of order, the family are tranquil and domestic, dove-eyed Peace is enthroned in this Study, fire-eyed Radicalism in its master's breast'.[9] This last phrase about himself, implying ominous domestic frustrations, stands incongruous and unexplained at the end of his account of a house otherwise restored to quiet normality.

Luckily for Dickens, there was an excuse to revive the play in the summer as a means of raising funds for the Jerrolds, but this meant a move out of the domestic space into a small theatre, the Gallery of Illustration in Regent Street, where a decade later W. S. Gilbert would be staging his earliest operas. Although the domestic performances had attracted many prominent public figures, including, on one night, four judges sitting in a row, as if trying a case, they had been invited guests in Dickens's own house; now they were paying money to see a play in a public place, which inevitably altered the status of his daughters and sisters-in-law.[10] The reviewers handled their task as delicately as possible, almost universally praising the 'ladies' for their 'natural' performances – the *Saturday Review*, for example, appreciating the realism of the drawing-room dialogues: 'Everyone accustomed to professional theatricals must, on this occasion, have felt how novel a charm it was to hear the ladies of the play talk like ladies.'[11] In other words, they talked like ladies because they *were* ladies, and not professional actresses. As it was, Dickens's responsibility for his daughters as father-actor-manager became more complicated at this point, not least because Mary, by then nineteen, had to play a woman torn between two lovers: one acted by her father, and the other by Wilkie Collins, who would a year later set up the first of his two ménages with a mistress. When Maria Ternan (Ellen's sister) took over this role a few weeks later, she was so moved by Dickens's death scene as Wardour that 'the tears streamed out of her eyes into his mouth, down his beard, all over his rags – down his arms as he held her by the hair'.[12] The watery intimacy of this response in a complete stranger shows how emotionally volatile the whole production must have been. As it was, most of Dickens's women were playing characters waiting for a lover, brother, husband or father absent on an Arctic expedition. *The Frozen Deep* was essentially a play about four women on tenterhooks about four men; its families are fragmented, seeking support from friends in the light of household collapse, while the men set up an alternative community of huts in the Arctic. While the women's emotions were all loyal and worthy, the casting of parts did not reflect the actual family configurations of the Dickenses; the roles were more compromising for the women, especially when they had to say lines such as 'Can a girl like Clara be fonder of her Lover than I am of my Husband?'[13] The only one who seemed to be speaking in character was Katey, playing Rose Ebsworth, the rather spoilt daughter of an absent father, who complains in the play: 'I must have my father near me, or I can never enjoy myself as I ought.'[14] Dickens, as the misogynist, obsessive Wardour, plays not a father, but a man who feels betrayed by women as lovers.

When the play took a further step into the public arena – in being performed at the Free Trade Hall in Manchester – Dickens claimed the space was too big for his daughters' untrained voices, and removed them from the cast. 'The place is out of the question for my girls', he insisted. 'Their action could not be seen, and their voices could not be heard.'[15] Perhaps the problem was more that they *might* be heard, and would therefore appear on the stage as professional actresses. Though Maria and Ellen Ternan were more or less the same age as Mary and Kate Dickens, all being born between 1837 and 1839, Dickens invariably refers in his letters to his daughters as 'girls' and the imported actresses (including some older ones) as 'the professional ladies'. The implications are clear enough; and when Kate Dickens, thirteen years later, asked her father to help her become a real actress, he was adamant that she was 'clever enough to do something else'.[16] Nevertheless, Dickens insisted that the experience of being in a production like *The Frozen Deep* had been an excellent discipline for his 'young people', who by then were beginning to worry him. To correspondent after correspondent he explained that the play had taught his children a 'remarkable lesson' in 'patience, perseverance, punctuality, and order: and, best of all, in that kind of humility which is got from the earned knowledge that whatever the right hand finds to do, must be done with the heart in it, and in a desperate earnest'.[17]

The Frozen Deep represents a high point in Dickens's life, before his domestic world began to collapse around him. In bringing his family on to a public stage, it also marks one of several occasions (the most famous being the *Household Words* announcement of his impending separation from his wife) when Dickens dissolved the boundaries between the private domestic sphere and its public exposure.[18] In turning his young daughters into actresses (Katey was only fifteen when she appeared in the farce *Mr Nightingale's Diary* after *The Lighthouse* in 1855), Dickens not only risked their reputations, but also appeared to compromise his own responsibilities as a protective father. On the other hand, directing his children in a play – a highly artificial situation – gave him complete control over them in confined conditions, unlike the more difficult challenge of establishing them as independent adults in the real world. In this respect he was at his happiest as a father when the role (a word used advisedly) came closest to being a performance or a linguistic game. His children's births and christenings easily fitted this requirement, as did his descriptions of their antics as small children. It was when they became awkward adults – unmotivated sons, daughters who married the wrong men – that his ability to perform the role of actor-manager-father was severely tested. Even then, in his frequent descriptions of himself as prematurely old and grey-haired, or as despairing over sons who meant well but were unemployable, he exaggerates and dramatises. Wherever he can, he makes a drama of his children, merging them with the identities of his fictional characters, and orchestrating their performances like a Vincent Crummles displaying his 'Infant Phenomenon'.[19] In his early years as a father, it is indeed to *Nicholas Nickleby* – that mixture of melodrama and theatrical comedy – that Dickens turns most often for comic analogies; but faulty, un-self-critical fathers, who stand on pomp and ceremony, appear in most of his novels. Mr Micawber; *Bleak House*'s Mr Turveydrop, 'a model of Deportment'; Mr Dorrit, 'Father of the Marshalsea'; and Flora Finching's father, Mr Casby, known as 'The Last of the Patriarchs', are all poseurs of a similar kind. The showmanship of fathers, as the outward, deceptive face of a shambolic family, is a distinctively Dickensian hallmark, connected to his lifelong sense of the father's role as essentially performative and theatrical. It remains problematic in his literary texts: at worst pompous, self-regarding and false; but at best, exuberant and life-affirming. In Mr Sleary's circus, in *Hard Times* (1854), 'all the fathers could dance upon rolling casks, stand upon bottles, catch knives and balls, twirl hand-basins, ride upon anything, jump over everything, and stick at nothing'.[20] One senses that Dickens himself would like to have been as versatile.

This chapter is not a study of Dickens's fictitious fathers, a subject that has been already extensively discussed by critics such as Hilary Schor and Dianne Sadoff.[21] Rather, it is an examination of the way Dickens responded to the cultural challenges of becoming a father: partly through his heightened awareness of the difficulties of the role, but more generally through his handling of the dividing line between his fictitious children and his real ones. Sadoff suggests that Dickens's father-figures embody an 'image of improvidence and profligacy' (p. 4), and that he 'continually imagines the father–son relationship as an economic one' (p. 26), while Schor is interested in the daughter's role as a transmitter of values. My concern is more with Dickens as a self-conscious orchestrator of special effects – tears, laughter, even mesmerism – through control of his children as players and characters of his own devising. His inability to make them successful, beyond the euphoric stage performances exemplified by *The Frozen Deep*, drives him into increasingly inventive ways of reconfiguring their identities for the entertainment of other people. By contrast, his close friend Macready, who regularly performed father-roles on the London stages, repudiated all hints of connection between his children and his theatrical roles, though it was finally impossible for him to escape the tragic parallels.

Appropriately enough, *Nickleby* was dedicated 'as a slight token of admiration and regard' to his new theatrical friend, the actor-manager William Charles Macready (1793–1873), whom Dickens met in 1837, the year Charley's birth made him a father. Macready and his wife Catherine (née Atkins, 1806–52), a former actress, had a large family of sickly children, whose number Dickens, in an unusually ribald joke, was afraid Macready might expand from 'eight' to 'eighteen' before he was done. Even 'twenty-eight' are mentioned, Dickens himself having only six children in 1846 when this letter was sent.[22] In due course Dickens became godfather to the Macreadys' son Henry, and Macready reciprocated for Dickens's second daughter, Kate Macready. When the Dickens parents travelled to America in 1842, the Macreadys agreed to watch over their young children, and when Dickens read him *The Chimes* in 1844, Macready responded by 'undisguisedly sobbing, and crying on the sofa'.[23] The two men initially shared a taste for the free flowing of tears and laughter, and then a growing disillusionment with the experience of fatherhood. If Macready's children were ailing and tubercular, Dickens's were lethargic, without the excuse of weak constitutions. As a great tragedian, Macready, who shrank from letting his children see him act, often internalises his paternal drama in tragic terms, whereas Dickens, initially at least, objectifies his experience of fatherhood as a lively domestic comedy. Even his declarations of hopelessness have a melodramatic tinge, as if Crummles himself might have spoken them: 'Why was I ever a father! Why was *my* father ever a father!' he asks himself towards the end of his life, despairing over his sons' futures.[24]

Both men found several ways of exploring and addressing their anxieties about fatherhood: Macready in his regular diary entries, and in the patriarchal roles (King Lear; Prospero; and Virginius, in Sheridan Knowles's play of the same name) that he acted on stage alongside women who were *not* his daughters (though one became his wife); and Dickens in his letters, but most obviously in his fiction, where a long line of patriarchs, from Mr Dombey to R. Wilfer, exhibit the full range of fatherly vices and virtues. As Trev Broughton and Helen Rogers have argued, 'No writer contributed more to the stereotype of the stern, unbending, Victorian paterfamilias than Charles Dickens, whose misguided and unfeeling fathers – Pecksniff, Dombey, Gradgrind – had to learn (largely from women) the cost of paternal neglect, the joys of intimate parenting and their paternalist obligations to workers and the poor.'[25] If anything, his harsh, selfish or unloving fathers are more memorable than the gentle and heroic, who are few enough (though more numerous than his good mothers). His most affectionate father-figures are often those who have no actual children of their own, but take an adoptive interest in the fatherless children of others: Mr Brownlow in *Oliver Twist*, Sol Gills in *Dombey and Son*, Mr Jarndyce in *Bleak House* and Joe Gargery in *Great Expectations*. The implication is perhaps that these men have the time, the spare emotional capacity or the money to be fond of children; all but Joe significantly lack even a wife.

Over a period of thirty years, Dickens and Macready met regularly at each other's houses, socialised with each other's families and took a keen mutual interest in each other's professions. Both had suffered from their fathers' inability to manage money; indeed both their fathers had been imprisoned for debt at a point that impacted on their sons' education, and the teenage Macready had had to abandon his ambition of becoming a lawyer to go on the stage. Unlike Dickens, who turned his home into a theatre, for Macready the split between home and his profession was marked by the journeys to and fro between the West End of London and Elstree, where his wife and children lived until 1840. 'Left my dear, my blessed home, its quiet, and its joys, to enter on a task for which nature and taste have disqualified me', is a typical diary entry for 1837, the year he met Dickens.[26] Moreover, he was very different from Dickens in despising the means by which he was forced to earn a living. His diary entries show him often deeply resenting his profession, hating his work – not least because it left him at the mercy of fickle audiences – belittling his own performances and falling out with actor-managers. He worried constantly about whether his career would provide him with enough money to support his ever-increasing family, and several times embarked on gruelling American tours to boost his funds; but no alternative profession seemed open to him. Far from encouraging his children to follow him into the theatre, and form an acting dynasty like the Kembles, Macready panicked if they showed any signs of wanting to follow in their father's footsteps. When they put on an after-dinner performance of Milton's *Comus* in the drawing-room, he observed: 'they recited the poetry very well indeed, and only gave me a fear lest they should imbibe a liking for the wretched art which I have been wasting my life upon'. When a friend suggested his daughter Katie might become an actress, he declared in his journal that he would 'rather she were taken early to God's own rest than exposed to such a fate', the tragic irony of which became apparent when Katie died at thirty-three, a published poet.[27]

The gap between Macready's working life and his domestic escapes to Elstree creates a rhythm and structure to his diaries. Whenever he is at home, he finds time in between learning his lines to hear his children say their lessons. He punishes them (with deep reluctance) when they seem deliberately uncooperative, and often blames himself for anything that appears amiss with his household. Worries about sick children left at home pursue him on his return to the West End, where they unsettle his on-stage performances; on other occasions, he reminds himself of them as an incentive to work harder. A more conventionally religious man than Dickens, he resorts to pious formulae by way of urging himself to improve: 'I recalled two or three times to-night in the play the claims of my children on my exertions as a stimulant to me; I should also think of them as a check to my intemperance of disposition and great imprudence.'[28]

In fact the gap between stage and home is less marked than Macready implies. Many diary entries show how closely his two worlds converged, even though to him they were antipathetic. Because he often prepared at home for forthcoming productions, he alternated tasks: 'Began the day with packing up things for the theatre; looked over my children's sums, and read in *Hamlet*', he records in a typical entry of 1838.[29] Sometimes, indeed, he failed to balance the two sides of his life appropriately, and his concern for his children caused him to fail on stage. 'Returned home and assisted Willie in his exercise', he mentions in January 1840, referring to his eldest son, '– *instead of attending to my own business*, and *reading my part*. I did it most reluctantly, but could not bear to leave him to his own apprehensions.' That night he forgot his lines in *Mary Stuart*, which he had known six weeks earlier, and came off stage in 'a state of desperate fury'.[30] For Macready it was never entirely clear whether his children were a hindrance or a consolation as he doggedly pursued a career to which he felt bound because of them.

One of Macready's most important contributions to stage history is his 1838 restoration of Shakespeare's original *King Lear*, which had been dropped for the previous 150 years in favour of Nahum Tate's 'happy ending' version, in which Cordelia marries Edgar. As Dickens himself noted in an approving review, Macready shone in the role of agonised father, whether raging at Goneril or despairing over the inert body of Cordelia. 'Mr Macready's representation of the father at the end', wrote Dickens in the *Examiner*, 'broken down to his last despairing struggle, his heart swelling gradually upwards till it bursts in its closing sigh, completed the only perfect picture that we have had of *Lear* since the age of Betterton'.[31] Dickens was by no means the only observer to note the passion of Macready's stage performances as a father. A *Times* reviewer of 1845 affirmed that 'Mr Macready's Lear is one of his most impressive delineations'; a view reiterated in 1849 when his 'agony of bereavement' over Cordelia's death was singled out for praise.[32] After his death, when reviewers of the *Reminiscences … Diaries and Letters*, edited by Sir Frederick Pollock (1875), recalled the roles for which he was best remembered, Lear, Virginius and the father in Knowles's *William Tell* (1825) were often cited, though an 1837 entry in his diary admits that he 'detested' the latter because of the part's 'unmanliness'.[33] Where there was scope to improve a part and make it more convincingly domestic, Macready adapted it accordingly. W. B. Donne, writing for the *Edinburgh Review*, claims that '[T]he grave look of love which Virginius fixed upon his daughter, his demeanour in sacrificing his darling, are remembered by many even unto this day.' Not only had Macready put some real human emotions into the stiff Roman soldier, including private 'home-joys', but in the part of William Tell, 'he displayed similar powers for delineating intense pathos and paternal love'.[34] Much of Macready's professional life was therefore spent simultaneously being a father and acting fatherhood on stage: transforming Roman soldiers and other heroic figures into middle-class domestic Victorians. He had originally become an actor to help his bankrupt father; subsequently his acting

Figure 2 'Was occasionally pretty good, but I was not what I wished to have been' (Macready, *Reminiscences*, Vol. II, p. 99): W. C. Macready as King Lear (1838) with Helen Faucit as the dead Cordelia.

career had to sustain his growing family of children. Though the stage was hardly a place for children, in Macready's case it was always unavoidably connected with issues of family responsibility and harrowing emotion, which often came close to his own personal experiences. Acting Virginius and Lear, who both go mad with grief over the deaths of their daughters, provided him with an outlet for articulating his experiences as a tragically bereaved father.

For Dickens, the language of fatherhood was a parody of the grand style – playful, experimental and self-consciously extravagant – for example in announcing the birth of each of his ten children to his (mostly) male friends. Their arrivals are staged performances, as with Charley's in 1837 when, after suspenseful scene setting, the baby is revealed with a flourish: 'After a day and night of watching and anxiety', he explains to his publisher Richard Bentley, 'I was yesterday made – not a Member of the Garrick Club; but a father'.[35] In fact Dickens was made a member of the Garrick that same month, soon after being appointed editor of *Bentley's Miscellany*, which meant that his public recognition as part of the literary and theatrical elite coincided with his becoming a father. Although the connection between these two events was entirely fortuitous, it seemed symbolically to link Dickens as a father with the theatrical world that the Garrick represented. The auspicious nature of Charley's birth was sealed by another announcement – in a totally different style – to the illustrator George Cruikshank: 'According to all established forms and ceremonies, I ought to have written on Friday Evening last, to duly acquaint and inform Mrs. Cruikshank that Mrs. Dickens had at a quarter past six oClock P.M. presented me with a son and heir –.'[36]

By the following December, Dickens has further adapted the mock-formal style to advertise the baptism of the 'living wonder': 'We christen an infant phaenomonon [*sic*] on Saturday', he tells Samuel Lover; while William Jerdan is informed: 'We are going to bring within the pale of Christianity on Saturday next, an infant "whose name is velocity, and nature, genius" and in honor of him and his faith assemble a few friends in the evening to music and a rubber.'[37] Although Dickens remained a believing Christian to the end of his life, he was not beyond building his children's christenings into a personal extravaganza. 'A babby is to be christened and a fatted calf killed on these premises on Tuesday the 25th, Instant', he tells another male friend in 1840. 'It (the calf; not the babby) is to be taken off the spit at 6.'[38] Not surprisingly perhaps, Macready (as godfather) felt the tone on this occasion was all wrong: 'Rather a noisy and uproarious day – not so much *comme il faut* as I could have wished.'[39]

As the births went on relentlessly, Dickens's language became increasingly exotic, if not grotesque. Henry Fielding Dickens, born in 1849, was announced in a letter to Macready as 'what the Persian Princes might have called a "moon-faced" monster'; while his youngest child,

Edward Bulwer-Lytton, born in 1852, was a 'golden baby . . . a perfect Californian little Duncan – his silver skin laced (internally) with his golden blood' – an oddly applied adaptation of Macbeth's description of his murdered King. Of all his children, 'Plorn', as the youngest was known, attracted the most elaborate childhood nicknames coupled with the highest praise, albeit always tinged with irony: 'The Plornishghenter is evidently the greatest, noblest, finest, cleverest, brightest, and most brilliant of boys.'[40] Unfortunately, he turned out to be nothing of the kind, but Dickens was always prepared to hope for the best in small children and believe in their potential. By this time he was in fact rather tired of boys, and would have preferred another daughter: 'but never mind me', he complained when his fourth son Alfred was born in 1845.[41] Even Edward's arrival was dismissed disparagingly to some correspondents. If he was a golden Scottish King at the moment of birth, Dickens told Angela Burdett Coutts particularly ungraciously that 'on the whole [he] could have dispensed with him'.[42] There were to be other awkwardly judged associations between his children and literary characters who meet a violent or premature end.

Dickens's sons were nearly all named after living writers who were also invited to be their godfathers: hence Walter Landor (1841–63), Francis Jeffrey (1844–86), Alfred D'Orsay Tennyson (1845–1912), Sydney Smith Haldimand (1847–72) and Edward Bulwer Lytton (1852–1902). Only the eldest, Charles Culliford Boz (1837–96), was named after an uncle and his own father (twice), and the sixth after one of his favourite novelists, Henry Fielding (1849–1933). Dickens hoped their godfathers would both inspire and help his sons as they made their way through the world, and in naming them after a bevy of journalists, novelists and poets, he was bringing his children into a literary circle of his and their own. Their nicknames, which he often changed, seemed to reflect what was happening in his own writing career, borrowing the names of his early fictional characters such as Sampson Brass from *The Curiosity Shop* (Alfred) and Chickenstalker from *The Chimes* (Francis). 'Plorn' seems to pre-date the Mr Plornish of *Little Dorrit* (1857), introduced in Chapter 12 as 'Long in the legs, yielding at the knees, foolish in the face, flannel-jacketed, lime-whitened'.[43] Rarely did the nicknames sound flattering, or compliment either child or godfather. Walter was sometimes known as 'Young Skull', Sydney as 'Ocean Spectre' and Alfred as 'Skittles' ('I call him so, from something skittle-playing and public-housey in his countenance').[44] When he strung them all together in letters, he created an instantly comic chorus, sometimes coining exceptionally preposterous names for the occasion: 'With best love to Charley, Mamey, Katey, Frankey, Right-follarollidedee- rightfollarollorà, and the Jolly Post Boy', he ended a letter to his wife in 1852; while some of the earlier nicknames surface in a greeting of 1846 to John Forster: 'Kate, Georgy, Mamey, Katey, Charley, Walley, Chickenstalker, and Sampson Brass commend themselves unto your Honour's loving remembrance.'[45] Significantly, the older children quickly acquired affectionate shortened versions of their real names (Mamie's 'Mild Glo'ster' and Katey's contrasting 'Lucifer-Box' soon disappeared), while the numerous boys, from Walter onwards, were made into comic turns to enliven Dickens's letters. As his biographer, Peter Ackroyd, has observed, 'in giving them all nicknames he was in a sense turning them into fiction, too'.[46]

Sometimes the children's fortunes seemed to follow their fictional counterparts' all too closely. While his most successful son, Henry Fielding, was nearly called Oliver, but saved by his father's fear that he would 'constantly be chaffed about "Oliver asking for more" ', his daughter Dora's short life of less than a year seemed to mimic the decline of David Copperfield's Dora and reach the same fatal conclusion.[47] Dora died of convulsions in April 1851 – bizarrely enough while Dickens was out making a speech at a meeting of the General Theatrical Fund – but her birth the previous August had already seemed to bode badly. As with his joke about not taking the baby, but the fatted calf, off the spit, Dickens discriminates awkwardly between the two Doras as he tells his wife, writing from Broadstairs where he was working on *Copperfield*, that he is unsure when he will be returning to town: 'It depends upon Dora – I mean *my* Dora.' Arguably, both Doras were his, but to John Forster he explained more brutally: 'I have been very hard at work these three days, and have still Dora to kill.' A further joke the next day repeats the distinction: 'I have still Dora to kill – I mean the Copperfield Dora – and cannot make certain how long it will take to do.'[48] As Peter Ackroyd comments, 'As if he could mean anything else. But how strange it is for him to call his infant child after a character whom he intended to "kill".' His daughter Mary insists, by contrast, that Dickens found it hard to write the death of Paul Dombey, 'and how it would have been impossible for him to have gone through with it had he not kept constantly before his eyes the picture of his own Plorn alive and strong and well'.[49] Nonetheless, the frisson of fictional children dying while real ones survived was an effect that Dickens repeatedly courted, juxtaposing the writing of novel episodes with letter narratives in a way that brings the two into unsettling conjunction. Other family names were recycled as characters, with results almost as bad: his second son Walter (who died in India) shares his name with Walter Gay of *Dombey*, who is exiled to the West Indies, and mistakenly thought to have been lost at sea, while his second daughter Kate was born in the same month as the first publication of *Nicholas Nickleby* in volume form after serialisation. Though Kate Nickleby ends happily married, the plot dices edgily with her virtue at the hands of her uncle Ralph and his network of lascivious business contacts.

For Macready, it was impossible to joke about the death or suffering of a child, even though the nature of his work repeatedly involved him in staging agonising scenes of paternal loss. Apart from Lear, one of the parts with which he was most associated was the title role of Knowles's *Virginius*, which climaxes with the 'honour' killing of his daughter Virginia by her father. Like Lear, Virginius eventually goes insane with grief, which for Macready was painfully close to the bone. Acting it in 1850, the year before he retired from the stage, he noted in his journal that he was 'quite overcome in the betrothal of Virginia; for my own dear girls were in my mind; was not this to "gore my own thoughts, make cheap what is most dear?" '[50] Although Macready is never entirely specific about what he dislikes so much about the stage (partly he was intemperate and had ferocious rows with managers, partly he felt degraded by it), he evidently felt it was inimical to family life. For as long as possible, he prevented his children from seeing him act, but when they watched his farewell performances in January and February 1851, he eagerly recorded their doubts as well as his own. Though he regretted that his eldest daughter Christina, known as Nina, had died in 1850 before she was able to see him on stage, he noted her reluctance: 'latterly she had begun to doubt whether she should like to "disturb her idea of *Pearse* [her nickname for her father] himself, by associating him with any assumed character" '. His second daughter Katie felt much the same, tearfully explaining after a performance of *Othello* that she 'did not like to see me associated with such minds as those about me'. Clearly his children shared his worry that the demarcation between his theatrical and his home lives was insufficiently distinct. Far from being offended, Macready felt pleased they had been properly prepared for any risk of moral contamination. Nor did it discourage him from 'trying to produce a powerful effect' on them a few evenings later as Macbeth.[51]

If the protection of Macready's children preoccupied him throughout their short lives, their presence haunted him still more after their deaths. The death he took hardest was that of his three-year-old daughter Harriet

Joanna, known as Joan, in 1840. It is clear from his diaries, which faithfully record the anniversaries of Joan's birth and death, year after year, that he saw himself as somehow morally responsible for her death because of his own supposed condition of guilt. His redundancy as she lay dying was, like Archibald Tait's, a further source of torment. 'Catherine waved me back with her hand', he wrote on the day Joan died,

and begged me not to come – that I could do no good. I felt – I do not know what I felt – a strange agony, a weight at my heart and head, that made me irresolute and tortured what to do. I had nowhere to go, no one to go to. All were around this blessed precious infant making despairing efforts. I threw myself on my bed and, wrapping the coverlid over my head, lay in a state of misery such as I never felt before, till dearest Letty [his sister] came down to me in tears, wrung my hand, and spoke a few words to me.[52]

When Nina died ten years later in 1850, the situation was very different. Returning to Hastings from a theatrical tour of Ireland, Macready nursed her himself through her final few days, as his wife Catherine was in London eight months pregnant, and in no condition to watch her eldest daughter die. This time he was able to say prayers and read aloud at her request; he also kept a private record of his 'Thoughts and Feelings' about his daughter, which might serve for his own or his other children's future reference. Viewing the record objectively, he admitted that though she was 'a most pure and upright spirit', there were 'indications of the prospect of an after life not so happy as her happy childhood and youth'.[53] Like Dickens, he found small children far less problematic than older ones, whose eventual function in the outside world had to be negotiated. Joan therefore is remembered as a beautiful angel, contrasted with his own dismal state as a perpetually suffering and sinful father. She seemed more important to him even than his living children: 'I think of her with a sorrow and a love that seems to me stronger than my feelings are to any of those dear ones whom God has spared me', he admitted to his diary on the second uncelebrated birthday after her death.[54]

It was therefore particularly painful to him that Dickens was disposing of Little Nell from *The Old Curiosity Shop* a mere two months after Joan's death. 'Asked Dickens to spare the life of Nell in his story', he recorded, '. . . and observed that he was cruel. He blushed . . .'[55] When Dickens ignored him and killed off Nell as planned, Macready felt a 'dead chill', and dreaded reading the full description; when he did, however, it seemed both painful and truthful: 'Sensation, sufferings have returned to me, that are terrible to awaken; it is real to me; I cannot criticize it.'[56] What he perhaps did not sufficiently appreciate was

Dickens's own emotional involvement in Nell's decline. Numerous letters testify to his 'heartbreak' (a term used in several) over her death and his inability to let go of the story. 'I am, for the time being, nearly dead with work – and of grief for the loss of my child', he told George Cattermole in January 1841, once more confounding a fictional child with one of his own.[57] If anything, his grief over his fictional children sounds more heartfelt. He had, after all, complete control over them, and did not have to defer to a wife and mother with an equal share in their welfare.

Most of the fathers discussed in this book at some point in their lives had to deal with the death of at least one child, and felt compelled to describe and discuss the event in diaries and letters. With Macready, Dickens and, later, Darwin, it was necessary for the father to break the news of the death to the mother, who was for some reason temporarily separated from the sick child; but it remains the case that the father often internalises the grief uniquely to himself, dwelling on his own feelings rather than his wife's. Macready presents himself as engaged in a lifelong and intense relationship with the dead Joan, who seems to represent for him his need to be connected to an image of sinless virtue emanating from himself as father. In his diary references to Joan he writes of his own loss, rather than his and Catherine's jointly as parents. As with Archibald Tait, reference to Catherine Robson's theory of the perfect nostalgic reconstruction of childhood appearing to Victorian men as embodied in a little girl helps explain the nature of Macready's obsession with Joan, who is often mentioned in conjunction with a consciousness of male guilt. Robson specifically refers to Little Nell as the figure who embodies a Victorian masculine longing for three places of safety: 'respectively the perfect childhood, the rural past, and the protected and stable home'.[58] In standing for the peaceful haven of Elstree and the happy home he left behind whenever he returned to London's West End, Joan, as Macready's most perfect child, retained precious resonances as his own unsullied Little Nell.

The interactions with Dickens's texts continued for both fathers. Following Nina's death in 1850, Macready was comforted by reading Dickens's sentimental story, 'A Child's Dream of a Star', which appeared in *Household Words* (6 April 1850).[59] In this story, a bereaved brother is consoled by the thought that his sister is an angel belonging to a clear shining star, which they have both befriended. As the child's baby brother, mother and daughter subsequently die and he imagines them all united in the star, the brother is sustained throughout his life by the thought of his family supporting one another and waiting to welcome him at the end of his long life. Dickens, in fact, in confronting his feelings first about Dora's death, and then that of his adult son Walter, sounds more philosophical than Macready, even if he did admit a 'foolish dislike to leaving the little child shut up in a vault': both an implied disavowal of his own sentimental 'Star' story, and a repulsion he had in common with Gladstone over the death of his daughter Jessy.[60] Though he often consoled bereaved friends with the thought that their children had been spared the distresses of a longer life, Dickens's views on child death are hardly those of an unquestioning, conforming Christian. Far from imagining his daughter translated into an angel or a star, he was but too well aware of her as a vulnerable little body left alone in the ground, a decaying reminder of his own failure to save her.

It was undoubtedly easier for both Dickens and Macready to idealise the death of a little girl than the loss of an incompetent young male. Dickens's long account of Walter's death in 1863, in a letter to Angela Burdett Coutts, harps on the boy's financial mismanagement as a soldier serving in India, and his own quarrels with him as a frustrated father. 'He had always been in debt, poor boy, and I never could make out how', Dickens confessed; moreover, he had also discouraged him from applying for home service. In the end, his sudden death from an aortic aneurism while he was in Calcutta, heading home on sick leave, prompted further self-reflection from Dickens on the relationship between his dissolving family and his own writing and literary imagination. Responding to Miss Burdett Coutts's recommendation that Walter's death might encourage him to look more kindly on his estranged wife, Dickens claims that 'a page in my life which once had writing on it, has become absolutely blank', and that 'it is not in my power to pretend that it has a solitary word upon it'. Later he recalls being disturbed by a funereal-looking prop he had carried as the Goddess of Discord at his family's New Year's Eve charades; though he altered the shape of it, its shadow, projected on the wall, still made him think of death and funerals. 'All this would have been exactly the same if poor Walter had not died that night', he rationalised, but added: 'See how easily a marvellous story may be made.'[61] Even in tragic circumstances such as these, Dickens fictionalises his children and sees them as inextricably connected with the intense functioning of his own imagination. Although he predeceased another unsuccessful son, Sydney, who died in 1872, Dickens was not beyond prefiguring a further death as the most convenient solution to the hapless young man's financial difficulties. 'I fear that Sydney is much too far gone for recovery', he wrote a few days before his own death in 1870, 'and I begin to wish that he were honestly dead'.[62]

The story enacted by most of his sons, however, was of languor and failure, caused both by hopelessness with money, and a lack of passionate commitment to a career. This is a remarkably recurrent feature of Victorian literature, which finds its way into numerous novels, including Dickens's own, most notably in *Bleak House*'s Richard Carstone, though many of his young adult heroes find it hard to settle into meaningful work. Time and again, both in the experience of actual Victorian families and in fiction, promising young men reach adulthood only to become mysteriously inept in a way that rarely happens with daughters (though they of course have no career expectations). Real life examples include Margaret Oliphant's two sons Cyril and Cecco, who both died in their early thirties, having failed to make anything of themselves in the world of adult male work. Even Archbishop Edward White Benson's sons, though all successful writers, spent much of their adult lives feeling depressed and apathetic in the face of their father's dynamic energy. Indeed, the unmotivated son in Victorian culture is often the child of a hyper-energetic parent. In the Royal Family, this was evident in the Prince of Wales, who seemed indolent and dissolute in comparison with Prince Albert. As Chapter 1 indicates, G. H. Lewes's three sons all lacked the versatile energy he had shown in writing anything and everything from theatrical journalism to serious studies of scientific theory. It is notable that all these vigorous fathers, embarrassed by under-achieving sons, sent them away to the colonies, as if exporting them from the homeland, and certainly the home, to test their mettle in a youthful civilisation. The work all these sons were expected to undertake was largely practical and physical, marking a further contrast with their father's artistic – possibly more effeminate – activity, as if in over-compensation for their own domesticity. Martin Danahay suggests that as Victorian ideology saw masculine work as physical and muscular, the work of intellectuals and writers 'could be viewed as feminine because it was often carried out in the domestic space and certainly did not involve muscles'. Indeed, because mental labour 'was not obviously a form of exertion in the same way as physical toil, it could thus be seen as idleness'.[63]

The Frozen Deep gave Dickens yet another opportunity to voice his frustrations as a father of sons lacking muscular energy. Although his character Richard Wardour is not a father, he has already acquired Dickens's own ethic of hard physical work as the source of all worthwhile human fulfilment. A vigorous speech in Act II seems to explain why Dickens sent so many of his sons to engage in muscular labour in challenging climates:

Let's do something. Is there no work in hand? No game to shoot, nothing to cut, nothing to carry? Hard work, Crayford, that's the true Elixer [*sic*] of *our* life! Hard work that stretches the muscles and sets the blood a-glowing, that tires the body and rests the mind! *(Enter Bateson with an axe.)* Here's a man with an axe. I'll do his work for him, whatever it is. (p. 135)

It seems significant that Wardour is a misogynist who blames women for men's emotional suffering. In the year before his separation from Catherine, Dickens was developing strongly held prejudices against the enervating effects of women on men, and asserting the masculinity of his own activities, however desk-bound. For Dickens, masculinity was synonymous with energy, as he endeavoured to explain to sons and friends alike, attributing the boys' constitutional apathy to their mother's influence. 'With all the tenderer and better qualities which he inherits from his mother', he complained of Charley, his eldest, 'he inherits an indescribable lassitude of character – a very serious thing in a man – which seems to me to express the want of a strong, compelling hand always beside him'.[64] When the same want of energy surfaced in one son after another, culminating in the inertia of his favourite 'Plorn', Dickens was convinced the problem was genetic, though nothing to do with him as their father. It was, however, his responsibility, rather than Catherine's, to find him a niche in the adult male world. 'If he cannot, or will not find one, I must try again, and die trying', he declared ominously, just three weeks before his own death.[65]

At the same time, he acknowledged that the Dickens name was a burden. Far from helping his sons, it might embarrass employers afraid of seeming to curry favour with the author, or it might create unrealistic expectations. 'I fear his name is too notorious to help him, unless he can very strongly help himself', he worried about his one successful son, Henry Fielding.[66] His daughter Kate remembered the issue of the Dickens name quite differently, especially at the time of her parents' separation, as she recalls in her memoirs. The situation was difficult, Kate's editor, Gladys Storey, explains, 'since Dickens had sternly impressed upon them that "their father's name was their best possession" – which they knew to be true – and he expected them to act accordingly'.[67] Her brother Henry was inclined to agree. 'It led people to expect more of me than of an ordinary young man', he recalls in his own memoirs.[68]

Though few of his own sons survived beyond young manhood, Macready worried about his eldest, William (1832–71), whose wavering sense of purpose his father noted in 1847. Like Dickens, he saw himself as being responsible for directing his sons towards the right kind of education, which would fit them for a specific career. His diaries show that he often heard their lessons, and set them 'homework' in the form of English or Greek verses to read, learn or translate. When Willie declared that he was no longer interested in becoming a clergyman, Macready tried to conceal his frustration and disappointment. 'I have *no wish* that he should adopt this course of life, but I fear that he has not energy for a lawyer', he admitted to his journal. 'I am willing to assist him to my utmost in anything he may choose, but it is time he chose.'[69] Again, it was the indifference and lack of energy in his son that disconcerted this most 'driven' of fathers, and seemed to reflect back on himself as a male role-model not engaged in a truly masculine profession. Neither father complains of his daughters' lethargy as a troubling concern. If anything, the daughters were too energetic, wanting to act, write poetry or go to art school. As they grew older, both men looked to their daughters as more reliable companions, and indeed wife-substitutes, Macready's first wife having died in 1852, and Dickens having separated from his in 1858.

Dickens's relations with his children took a new turn after the separation, when all but Charley stayed with him rather than their mother. As he battled with rumours that the break-up of the marriage was caused by his relationship with Ellen Ternan, or with his sister-in-law Georgina Hogarth, he defiantly asserted that his children supported his stance and never doubted his integrity. 'All is open and plain among us, as though we were brothers and sisters', he insisted, devising yet another role for his children. Family crisis was a great leveller, and as so often happens with voluminous correspondence, once he had devised a good phrase to encapsulate a new state of affairs, Dickens endlessly recycled it. 'Between them and myself', he wrote about his children to Catherine Gore, the 'silver fork' novelist, 'there is a confidence as absolute and perfect as if we were of one age'.[70] As Helena Michie has argued, Dickens's fictional portrayal of families often confronts the shifting definition and ethics of relationships: for example, John Jarndyce's gradual transition from Esther's guardian to intended husband to father-figure, Smike's from Kate Nickleby's adoring admirer to her 'brother' (actually cousin), or Walter Gay's from Florence Dombey's pseudo-brother to future husband. There is an embarrassment about the emotions generated by these relationships, both for the characters themselves and for the squeamish reader, which Michie argues is partly attributable, not just to Dickens's well-known sexual coyness in his novels, but also to his (and the reader's) awareness of contemporary debates about the female age of consent (it remained at twelve in Dickens's lifetime), and the Deceased Wife's Sister legislation, which made a sister-in-law the same as a blood sister, at least in the eyes of the courts. In other words, there was a genuine awkwardness about the nature of sexual relationships in Victorian families, especially when the law intervened or they were artificially constructed by the courts, as in Chancery cases like Esther Summerson's.[71] Whether or not one accepts this particular explanation, Dickens's fiction demonstrates a fascination with interchangeable or loosely defined relationships within households and family groupings. Most of his novels end with a reformulation of the family, with its favoured members editing out the antipathetic: Ralph Nickleby, Mr Bounderby, the Murdstones, Monks, Mrs Joe, Mrs Clennam, Fanny Dorrit. The happiest families are those where the members choose each other on the basis of congeniality rather than consanguinity, or the faulty father is reprogrammed to love his children differently, as in the cases of Mr Dombey, Mr Gradgrind and Mr Jarndyce. Such reconfiguring of relationships was something he found appealing within his own family in the final years of their cohabitation as father, sister-in-law and adult children.

The appeal of being a father contemporary with, or even younger than, his children – an impossible fantasy – is celebrated in *Our Mutual Friend* (1864–5), when Bella Wilfer takes her downtrodden father Reginald (her 'cherubic Pa') on a secret jaunt to Greenwich without her mother. Bella becomes the 'lovely woman' to her enamoured father, who recalls: 'But Lor, what a child you were! What a companion you were!'[72] The high point of the evening is when they look at the river and imagine

all sorts of voyages for herself and Pa. Now, Pa, in the character of owner of a lumbering square-sailed collier, was tacking away to Newcastle, to fetch black diamonds to make his fortune with; now, Pa was going to China in that handsome three-masted ship, to bring home opium, with which he would for ever cut out Chicksey Veneering and Stobbles [his employers], and to bring home silks and shawls without end for the decoration of his charming daughter. (p. 373)

This time a daughter turns her father into a fantasy figure: only Bella goes further still and sees her Pa as younger and more innocent than herself. They have always been each other's favourites, she reminds him, 'because you are not like a Pa, but more like a sort of a younger brother with a dear venerable chubbiness on him!' (p. 375). This game is intensified for Bella after her marriage, when she habitually treats him like a schoolboy released for the day: on his visits to the Rokesmith cottage at Blackheath, for instance, he endures having his face washed and hair combed by his daughter before he is allowed to sit down to supper (p. 752). Of all Dickens's numerous portrayals of fathers and daughters – and there are too many to discuss satisfactorily here – the relationship between Bella and her Pa is perhaps the most joyous, founded as it is on a shared performance of a comic partnership, acting out the roles of mother/son, sister/brother and secret lovers. The relationship is mutually both punitive and romantic. He remembers her as a bad-tempered toddler, and she likes to tease him as a 'grubby child' (p. 752); she is his 'lovely woman' to a Pa full of romantic potential – both the victims of a perpetually discontented 'Ma' whose signature-tune is the 'Dead March in Saul' (p. 371). Once she is engaged to John Rokesmith, Bella changes the game, so that Pa becomes 'the Knave of Wilfers' (p. 682), predicted by a 'fortune-teller' to be a frequent visitor to her new home. Almost everything about this forthcoming marriage is explained in metaphors and euphemisms: 'What the little fair man is expected to do, sir, is to look forward to it also, by saying to himself when he is in danger of being over-worried, "I see land at last!"' (p. 682). Having accustomed him to the prospect of her marriage, she ensures that he is the only parent present at it, and he is treated throughout the celebrations as the most important participant. Indeed, the hotel where they have their dinner is chosen because of its romantic associations as the place 'where Pa and the lovely woman had once dined together!' (p. 734). All the key episodes in the Bella Wilfer plot seem to reinforce the view that she needs only one parent and that that parent is Pa: an impression endorsed by John, after Ma's visit to their grand new home, when he observes that 'although he did not dispute her being her father's daughter, he should ever remain stedfast [*sic*] in the faith that she could not be her mother's' (p. 880).

Catherine Waters, in her study of Dickens's fictional families, argues that ultimately, the Wilfers' role-playing 'conserves the power of the institution so gleefully subverted': a view reiterated in her 'Postscript', where she suggests that Dickens's 'amazing capacity for invention is not unrelated to the facility with which [his] fictions often subvert the familial ideology upon which they are nevertheless based'.[73] Through the Wilfer subplot of *Our Mutual Friend*, Dickens creates a father–daughter fantasy relationship that excludes both mothers and sons, though not a son-in-law or a grandchild. Bella's new home, which is from the beginning hospitable, may be another alternative domestic bower, not essentially different from the one she has escaped, but it is reconfigured to make the father a welcome pet, rather than an ineffectual subordinate. Nevertheless, 'R. W.' (whose numerous names never seem to add up to anything complete or entirely dignified) remains essentially his daughter's toy, designed to serve her purposes. All his sexual needs are assumed to be satisfied by flirtation with his daughter: a reversal of the pattern established in earlier novels such as *Little Dorrit* (1857), *David Copperfield* (1850) and *Dombey and Son* (1848), where the daughter represses her own desires in order to serve a dominant father.

By the end of his life, Dickens had tried to make himself into the one and only parent who mattered to his children. Claudia Nelson suggests that Dickens even took on the female role in the household, leaving his wife with no obvious function beyond child-bearing. He is the one who nurses their sick children, makes everything orderly, and flits through the home like 'a male Esther Summerson or Florence Dombey'.[74] Overlooked in the family theatricals, never mentioned, except as a negative influence, in relation to his plans for his sons' education, Catherine Dickens is mostly ignored in her children's memoirs as well, Katey's being the main exception. Ownership of their parents' relationship and reputation passed after 1870 to all of the Dickens children who published reminiscences – Charley, Mamie, Katey, Alfred and Henry – while Henry, Charley and Alfred gave public recitals of their father's novels, and Katey illustrated *The Old Curiosity Shop*. The next generation presented him essentially as a performer, both publicly and privately, whose primary function was to entertain: to amuse them with comic songs and conjuring tricks, but in more sober mood to provide for their spiritual life with individual prayers, and a Children's New Testament or Life of Christ (written 1846). All of his children except Katey amass a collection of anecdotes demonstrating his delightful ubiquity as a father who was the life and soul of his home, the comic genius of festive parties, petting the dogs or making plum puddings in a hat. While Charley delicately suggests that when Dickens was engrossed in his writing, 'he lived, I am sure, two lives, one with us and one with his fictitious people, and I am equally certain that the children of his brain were much more real to him at times than we were', Katey more outspokenly declares that the only fault she can find with her father is 'that he had too many children'.[75] Katey's attempts to commemorate her father were repeatedly doomed to failure. According to Gladys Storey, she had always intended to paint his portrait, but 'it somehow never came off, I feared not to do him justice';

similarly, a 'life' of her father, clearing her mother of false accusations, was allegedly written and then burnt, because she was afraid she had told 'only half the truth' about him, 'and a half-truth is worse than a lie'.[76] If accurately reported by Storey, Katey's efforts to capture the essence of her father were in theory easy to plan but impossible to execute. He resisted summing up, though she thought she could do it on 'one half-sheet of note-paper' (p. 91). In the end, Storey provided the narrative, and Katey the gnomic summaries, of which perhaps the most notorious is her declaration: 'My father was a wicked man – a very wicked man.' Storey adds that this was said as she rose from her chair and walked towards the door, in a suitably dramatic gesture (p. 219). Hilary Schor cites this episode as evidence of the way Dickens weaves the story of the good daughter with that of her angry double, telling the story being the daughter's best mode of revenge.

Ultimately Dickens's experience of fatherhood permeated his entire writing life. All his novels are about families, most of them fragmented by a parent's absence, or distorted by the father's heavy-handed presence. His preference, indeed, seems to have been for alternative or makeshift pseudo-families, where members decide which relationships matter to them, as Bella Wilfer does, or Caddy Jellyby, or David Copperfield. Most of his novels end with the reconstitution of the original family along revised lines, so that, for example, Mr Dombey atones for being a bad father by becoming a doting grandfather, and Mr Jarndyce, whose chaste role as Esther's guardian was nearly compromised by his sexuality, is reinstated as honorary father to Ada's son and Esther's own children. Joe Gargery, who has proved that he deserves to be a father by his 'apprenticeship' with Pip, becomes the father of his own Pip-substitute. In each of his novels, he tends to focus on a different aspect of patriarchal experience, favouring dramatic acts of reunion and understanding, the large gestures of recognition, above the mundane management of daily decision-making. It was as if the enormity of fatherhood was too vast and complicated for him to encompass in any one character or novel, but the underlying message is that fatherhood must be deserved or earned. Within his own family, where children came unsought, too quickly and easily, he was forced to confront the differences between fantasy and reality: between his daughters as classless actresses and middle-class 'ladies', his sons as heroic imperial adventurers and lethargic squanderers of their inheritance, while they in turn made him into the caricatured theatrical father of his admirers' imagination. In noting Dickens's propensity in his writing 'to shift through the affective gears from pathos to laughter and back again', Sally Ledger is also describing the rhythms of his experience as a patriarchal showman of performing children.[77] When *The Chimes* made Macready cry, Dickens told his wife 'what a thing it is to have Power'.[78] In other words, orchestrating the emotion generated by families transformed sentimentality into control of his audience's affective response. Dickens could be powerful in a masculine way without seizing an axe or farming sheep in the colonies.

Macready's own 'afterlife' was managed more smoothly, not by his family, but by his friend Sir Frederick Pollock, who edited a careful selection from his diaries and letters, as well as the aborted 'Reminiscences', covering Macready's childhood and the start of his acting career, but ending in 1826, four years before the birth of his first child, Nina. It was left to contemporary reviewers of the Pollock volumes to have the last word on Macready's reputation as a family man, and to make the connections between the life at Elstree and his literal acting of the father's part on stage. One of the most negative was Theodore Martin, Prince Albert's biographer, whose landmark work was often reviewed in the same volumes as those dealing with Macready's reminiscences. Martin's review for the *Quarterly* regretted the actor's undignified self-exposure revealed in the diary entries, which 'tell through many years a sad tale of bad temper, of angry jealousies, of somewhat unmanly querulousness'.[79] The manliness of both men seemed questionable as their lasting image was reassessed in the light of their emotional legacy, but unlike Dickens, whose performances were his novels and letters, the exact flavour of Macready's achievement can now be recovered only by friends' and reviewers' evaluations, and by the diary entries that alternately appraise his own performances and worry about his family. The close connection between the two is perhaps best demonstrated by an entry written in 1841 after a performance of *Virginius*, which made him query 'the actual value of life' as to his own personal enjoyments. Like Dickens in the way he pitched his feelings as a father through extreme imagery, concluding 'My children are my life', he is less like him in identifying himself entirely as a father awaiting reunion with the perfect child. Ending his entry with an image of his own dead body 'stretched out in its stiff and yellow coldness', juxtaposed with a vision of 'that blessed and lovely child, my darling Joan', whose loss he felt had loosened his own attachment to life, he declares: 'I feel now, in dying, I shall have something to go to.'[80] The next world was to him a place where he could devote himself entirely to being a father to his favourite child.

CHAPTER 3

'How?' and 'Why?': Kingsley as educating father

'I should like to be a scientific man, if one can find out such really useful things by science', Grenville Kingsley tells his father in *Madam How and Lady Why* (1870). 'Child', responds his father, Charles Kingsley, 'there is no saying what you might find out, or of what use you may be to your fellow-men'.[1]

In his writings for children, Kingsley employs a conversational voice designed to encourage dialogue and intimacy with the young, which begins with his own children, and then extends outward to all child readers. He invites audience participation, so far as this is possible in a printed book, with the child's responses written in for him; but at the same time he either bewilders him with nonsense writing, as in *The Water-Babies*, or hectors him into paying attention and exerting himself, as in *Madam How*. By ventriloquising the child's side of the conversation he of course establishes a model dialogue, with only the illusion of a free exchange of ideas, and it often leads Kingsley to talk over Grenville's head. 'There – you do not understand me', he says in Chapter 2 of *Madam How*. 'I trust that you will understand me some day.'[2] One of the things Kingsley most enjoyed about tutoring the young Prince of Wales at Cambridge, where he gave him lectures and private lessons, was that (doubtless contrary to Prince Albert's expectations) the Prince paid attention well, and asked 'very intelligent questions'.[3] The asking of questions turned out to be Kingsley's favourite educational method with young and old alike, modified from a century-long tradition of teaching by model catechism. As his writing and teaching career developed, it pushed him towards an obsessive passion for questioning and being questioned, which reaches its climax in *Madam How*, a fantasy celebration of the child's two characteristic questions, 'How?' and 'Why?'.

The Kingsley brothers, Charles (1819–75) and George (1826–92), were both strangely alike and strikingly different as fathers. Both spent long periods away from their children, but whereas Charles travelled for his health, George fled largely because he found domestic life intolerable for any length of time. George indeed reads like an extreme version of Charles, sending back similar educational messages to his children. While Charles might command: 'Tell the chicks I found a real wild duck's nest on the island, full of eggs, and have brought one home to hatch it under a hen', George's version was: 'Tell the boy that I have been spearing trygons and eagle-rays. (Make him look in Yarrell's *Fishes*).'[4] The brothers' concept of fatherhood included a hearty sense of themselves as active tribesmen, who modified their hunting instincts into a passion for collecting natural-history souvenirs to bring home for their children. Mary Kingsley's memoir of George portrays him as completely anti-domestic in his tastes, 'loving to be at the wild heart of Nature, far away from the clamour and turmoil of crowded cities, listening to the lore of forests or the voices of the sea'.[5] His instincts were those of a 'natural' man, convincing him that 'the duty of a father of a family was to go out hunting and fighting while his wife kept home' (p. 202). This view is certainly borne out by his own writing: for example his ebullient account of 'Chamois Hunting', published in *Fraser's Magazine* in 1851 when he was still single and childless.[6] Mary compared him both with the explorer Sir Richard Burton, and the legendary hero Tannhäuser (p. 193), renowned for discovering the secret subterranean home of Venus, goddess of love.

Charles Kingsley, by contrast, was more a man of the seashore than the high seas. His enjoyment of nature was enhanced by opportunities to share it with his children, and reveal its deeper mysteries. He thought deeply about the role he was performing with his own children, and the relative importance of mother and father in their upbringing: issues he never entirely resolves in his turbulent educational texts for children, with their restless undercurrent of self-examination and inward debate. On his many trips away from home, Kingsley, in sending regular messages to his children, was reminding them of his presence in their lives: a point reinforced by his return, laden with outlandish gifts of nests and stones and horns. He repeatedly asserted his own role as fatherly educator, urging his wife to 'tell' the children things on his behalf, so that during his absence Fanny became his mouthpiece or surrogate educator. In his letters he was in effect employing a woman to pass on useful information, while retaining ultimate control, a model he would perfect in his children's fiction. 'Tell the darling children that I will bring them each home something pretty', he instructed his wife on a typical occasion, 'and that the woods are full of great orange slugs, and great green lizards, and great long snakes, which bite nobody, and that I will bring them home some red and blue locusts out of the vineyards'.[7] With its rhythmical lilt, bright colours and reassurances of harmless snakes, this passage sounds more suitable for children than much of his more formal published writing: not least because he was concentrating on the vivid description more than he was on any underlying moral purpose. Nevertheless, most of his messages home to his children were a reminder that he was thinking of them in relation to what he could teach them about the wider world. His writing gives the impression that he never tired of disseminating information: indeed this was something he seemed to crave, as a validation of his fatherly role. His daughter, another Mary, recalled that when she was reading at home as a child, she did so in a desultory way, not bothering to verify what she read, 'but simply asked my father questions instead of going to a dictionary or encyclopaedia.'[8]

For much of his writing life, Kingsley can be seen as trying to identify and define the father's precise role as educator, stressing the opportunities to teach and learn outside the classroom, through a more unhurried and illustrative version of the catechism style of imparting factual information, which had been the standard pedagogic method in the first half of the century. His development of different hybrid genres to embody his favourite way of teaching built on this earlier didactic style, but at the same time led him to reassess the functions of fantasy and nonsense in relation to a practical, 'hands-on' style of teaching. This use of nonsense writing was something completely alien to the sober Edgeworths. Maria and Richard Lovell Edgeworth recommend direct dialogue between parents and children as the best way to impart knowledge in a normal domestic situation where questions might arise naturally, especially in relation to mechanics and science. 'From conversation, if properly managed, children may learn with ease, expedition, and delight, a variety of knowledge', they conclude in *Practical Education* (1798), reiterating a very similar statement from their Preface; 'and a skilful preceptor can apply in conversation all the principles that we have laboriously endeavoured to make intelligible'. An Appendix of notes on actual conversations held with the numerous Edgeworth children, kept by Honora, Richard Edgeworth's second wife and Maria's stepmother, shows how some of these dialogues worked in reality. The most unintentionally amusing is their conversation on whether hot chocolate causes worse scalding than hot water or tea, where the father's barrage of questions eventually meets a baffled silence. As Mrs Edgeworth observes at one point, 'No one seemed to have any thing to say about the chocolate.'[9]

The Edgeworths' assumption is that the mother is the best person to teach the younger children, a view shared with – perhaps derived from – Jean-Jacques Rousseau in *Émile* (1762), where he also argues pointedly that the mother's position 'is more certain than that of the father': 'the right ordering of the family depends more upon her, and she is usually fonder of her children'. Rousseau believed that 'the blind affection of the mother' was likely to cause far less damage than any of the vices to which he felt fathers were particularly prone: 'Ambition, avarice, tyranny, the mistaken foresight of fathers, their neglect, their harshness...'[10] Nevertheless, even Rousseau argues that while the 'real nurse is the mother', the 'real teacher is the father' (p. 6), and fathers have a duty to educate their own children where they can. In Chapter 3, he offers some practical suggestions as to how this might work, advising the father or tutor to let his charge observe nature directly and participate in scientific experiments. In urging 'Let him not be taught science, let him discover it' (p. 131), Rousseau was laying down a system that consciously or otherwise was adopted by many early-nineteenth-century educators, the Edgeworths foremost among them, and eventually Kingsley. The key strategy, stressed by Rousseau and adopted by the Edgeworths and others, was to stimulate the child's curiosity by showing him natural phenomena, and then to 'put some brief question which will set him trying to discover the answer... It is not your business to teach him the various sciences, but to give him a taste for them and methods of learning them when his taste is more mature' (pp. 134–5). Information was to be imparted, wherever possible, by a seemingly casual conversation arising naturally from whatever teacher and pupil encountered during a normal day.

As the 'conversation' book developed, however, the dialogues became anything but casual and informal. Many were more like rigid catechisms, where the pupil was expected to give a precise definition based on a pre-learned formula. Richmal Mangnall's *Historical and Miscellaneous Questions* (1800), for example, includes a section on 'The Elements of Astronomy', beginning: 'What is meant by the Heavenly Bodies? The sun, stars, planets, and comets. What is the Solar System? The motion of the planets and comets round the sun, which is placed in the middle of them.'[11] Kingsley has fun with the dryness of these questions in the 'Isle of Tomtoddies' episode of *The Water-Babies*, where panic-stricken turnips preparing for an exam ask Tom questions such as 'What is the latitude and longitude of Snooksville, in Norman's County, Oregon, US?'[12] Moreover, in the early nineteenth century, it is usually the mother, or a mother-substitute, who directs these lessons, which by this time have largely retreated indoors.

Although 'the boy' is frequently mentioned by the Edgeworths in *Practical Education* as the child to be educated, the father is rarely addressed directly as the appropriate teacher, the sex of the educating parent mostly being unspecified. This is quite different from *Early Lessons* (1801), whose preface is an 'Address to Mothers'. Under the Edgeworth system, the father seems to come into his own in the child's adolescence – though more as a practical role model than as a teacher – when it is suggested that some active involvement in the father's affairs could be offered (Vol. III, p. 283). A set of home experiments involving levers, pulleys, wheels and axles, set out in the section on 'Mechanicks' in Volume II, seems more likely to have been aimed at the father, who, in other educational books of the period, can be found enjoying a private session of chemistry or introducing the children to simple experiments with magnets. At the end of Maria Edgeworth's own story, 'The Two Plums', for example, her seven-year-old heroine Rosamond is rewarded for making the right choice of a 'housewife' or needle-case, by being allowed to watch her father demonstrating 'several experiments with her needle and a magnet'; though the father in the Edgeworths' *Harry and Lucy* series, intended for ten- to fourteen-year-olds, delegates the lower levels of teaching to his son Harry, in accordance with Maria Edgeworth's view that children should be encouraged to educate one another. While the father turns even his daughter's damp, uncurled hair into a useful opportunity to learn about hygrometers, it is Harry who takes the practical lesson forward. Like Mr Fairchild, in Mrs Sherwood's *History of the Fairchild Family* (1818–47), who often prefers to lie on the grass at a slight remove from the rest of his family, reading a book of his own while the children read aloud from theirs, Harry and Lucy's father is a busy man with other things to do. 'They were eager to show their hygrometer to their father; but he had gone from home for a few days.'[13] The father in Jane Marcet's *Conversations for Children: On Land and Water* (1838) similarly avoids becoming involved in his wife's attempts to teach the children about volcanoes, using real sand and clay. When she brings them into his laboratory to see some chemical reactions, he refuses to put on an extended show, saying ' "No, my dears, this is chemistry, which you are much too young to understand; and I am not a conjuror to show off a number of wonderful tricks for the amusement of children. So take them away," continued he, addressing Mrs. B., "and let me return to my work".' Suitably rebuffed, Mrs B tries to console them with 'some drawing-room chemistry' involving Lucifer matches, but the message is clear: fathers were not expected to teach their children chemistry, or anything else, on a regular basis.[14]

Within twenty-five years of the new century, however, a backlash in favour of fathers as educators begins to emerge in the catechism books, with mothers being pushed into a secondary background role. While some of these dialogues were family based, and circled safely round historical questions (for example, the anonymous *Austin Hall; or, After Dinner Conversations between a Father and His Children on Subjects of Amusement and Instruction*, 1831), others seized on the parent–child discussion as an appropriate way of dealing with controversial issues that parents knew they would eventually have to tackle with their children. *Conversations of a Father with His Son, on Some Leading Points in Natural Philosophy*, for example, by the Reverend B. H. Draper (1825), consists of educational dialogues between a widowed father and his son Frank about a mixture of secular scientific subjects ('The Solar System', 'The Human Frame') and more overtly theological ones ('The Power of God'). Apart from anything else, such dialogues were a way of approaching difficult issues about the relationship of science and religion. As Alan Rauch has argued, the scientific catechism 'represented an acceptable transition from scriptural to secular material':[15] a child can be allowed to ask awkward questions about the history of creation and the age of the universe, and equally, a father can be allowed to equivocate or adapt the question to suit his own purposes. 'You have asked me a hard question, Frank', the father admits in Draper's *Conversations*. 'Perhaps what we know of creation, is as nothing compared with that which we do not know.' Addressing the problem of storms and earthquakes, which also fascinated Kingsley, the father concludes that such terrifying phenomena are to chastise man 'for his manifold rebellions'.[16] Even the more impersonal Pinnock's *Catechism of Geology* (one of a series of eighty-three 'catechism' books) confronts the 'Connexion between Geology and Natural Religion', insisting that 'Geology not only proves the existence of a Creative Power, but also of the general superintending providence of God, and of his special interference from time to time with the usual order of things on the surface of the globe.'[17] Such model dialogues would have had obvious appeal for Kingsley, who never lost his belief in God, but wanted equally to acknowledge the wonders both of Genesis and evolution in his geological teaching. As he put it succinctly in his lecture 'How to Study Natural History', 'God's earth and God's word will never contradict each other.'[18]

Even the more relaxed of these dialogues was like a mechanical
catechism, however, with Pinnock's series dividing the debate into
straightforward questions and answers (headed 'Q' and 'A') with no
pretence of a fictional situation. Though Draper's *Conversations* and the
Austin Hall dialogues used named fictional characters and provided some
kind of a social context, Kingsley, in the Edgeworth tradition, wanted
more for his educational texts – both a more convincing physical world to
act as his outdoor classroom, and a more realistic child to interact with
the knowledge-imparting father – a child who would occasionally be
bored or lazy in his responses. A different kind of model altogether was to
be found in the popular children's tale of *The Swiss Family Robinson*
(1812–13). This legendary, but highly unstable text, told by Johann David
Wyss to his children, and revised by his son, Johann Rudolf, was in fact a
prime example of two-generational cooperation, which started when the
father told his sons stories, derived from *Robinson Crusoe*, about a whole
family shipwrecked on a desert island. J. Hillis Miller sees the purpose of
The Swiss Family Robinson to be as much to teach natural history as
religion, though as the father is a Swiss pastor, who conducts family
services on the beach, the religious perspective underlies the whole venture. As Hillis Miller observes, 'God is praised for his benevolence and
wisdom in creating all these living things.'[19] The Wyss stories consist
almost entirely of the father teaching his four sons how to make useful
equipment out of what they find on the island and rescue from the ship,
interspersed with dialogues about the animals, birds and plants they
discover around them. Wyss's goal was apparently to 'awaken the curiosity of [his] sons by interesting observations, to leave time for the activity
of their imagination, and then to correct any error they might fall into'.[20]
A classic example of this kind of exchange occurs in Chapter 22, when
father and sons are working together planting bamboo canes to support
the young trees they are trying to grow. 'Whilst we were hard at work our
conversation naturally turned upon the best manner of raising trees, and
the boys overwhelmed me with questions.'[21] The whole point is that the
boys ask questions because they are excited by and engaged in what they
are doing, which is in itself a healthy outdoor activity. After his intro-
ductory exposition, his second son Ernest asks 'where all the different
fruit trees came from'; while Jack, the third son, is gently put right about
the non-European origin of cherry trees: 'They are named cherries after
Cerasus, a state of Pontus, in Asia, from which place they are said to have
been first carried to Rome by Lucullus, a Roman general, who lived about
seventy years before Christ' (p. 120). As Hillis Miller notes, the father

takes himself very seriously, and entirely lacks self-criticism: 'He is, on the contrary, rather self-congratulatory and self-approving'.[22] When the boys make some kind of useful discovery for themselves, he is quick to extend their initiative further and tell them something still more valuable, as when the examination of a turtle shell in Chapter 15 switches to discussion of some white roots found by Ernest. The father congratulates him on discovering manioc, which can be made into a bread substitute: 'But it must be carefully prepared, for it contains a dangerous poison' (p. 86). Informative footnotes on each new botanical or zoological discovery add all the information that could not naturally be incorporated into a conversation between father and sons. As for the mother, she is always present in the background, but she is essentially little more than a pro-vider of meals and home comforts. She never goes out adventuring, rarely teaches the boys and sometimes needs to be instructed herself: as when Fritz proposes to make pemmican (that preserved meat most of us now associate with Arthur Ransome's *Swallows and Amazons*), and she has to ask him what it is (Chapter 33). As the mother of sons on the brink of manhood, Elizabeth's role is to guarantee a stable home for them to return to, but otherwise to accept that they need the mental and physical space to develop their survival skills, more actively supported by their omniscient father.

The father as an omniscient guide is indeed very characteristic of children's educational literature in the first half of the nineteenth century. One of the most famous (indeed notorious) fathers of the time is Mr Fairchild in Mary Martha Sherwood's immensely successful *History of the Fairchild Family*, published in three instalments between 1818 and 1847. Sherwood's strictly Evangelical philosophy ensures that each epi-sode teaches the three Fairchild children that they are born sinners with a wicked nature – as indeed are their parents – and the only way they can combat this is by daily self-examination and vigilance over their own actions. Mr Fairchild's teachings, however, sometimes combine secular subjects with religion, as when in Volume I he teaches his children the use of a globe: 'You shall come into my study, and I will teach you a little every day; and we will talk about the various nations and people who live on this globe.'[23] In Volume II we learn that he carries a small microscope in his waistcoat pocket: 'He often used this to show the children those beauties of flowers and insects which are too small for the naked eye to perceive' (Vol. II, p. 230). On this occasion, by way of illustrating the beauties of the Bible that are not always perceived on a detached first reading, he shows the children and their neighbour a common mallow and the wing of a diamond beetle, 'works of God's own hand' (p. 232), which are much more beautiful than a piece of man-made silk. Although Mr Fairchild's notoriety comes from his taking the children to see a corpse dangling from a gibbet (a warning against sibling rivalry), and he overlooks no opportunity to remind them of their innate human depravity, he is also highly involved in their upbringing, and teaches the youngest child Henry Latin. Moreover, the Fairchild parents are just as concerned for their two daughters, Lucy and Emily, and many episodes are devoted to correcting their childish faults, as well as their brother's and other children's in the neighbourhood. Several comments in the stories remind us that the father of a family and God the Father are at times synonymous, as Mr Fairchild reminds Henry: 'I stand in the place of God to you, whilst you are a child; and as long as I do not ask you to do anything wrong, you must obey me' (Vol. 1, p. 266). While the mother is more involved in the teaching process than Elizabeth Robinson in Wyss's book, she never challenges the father's authority, and usually defers to him where more severe chastisements are necessary. Whatever Mr Fairchild does for a living, he puts it aside for days at a time to concentrate wholeheartedly on his children's moral and intellectual upbringing.

This contextual background to Kingsley's writing for children clearly indicates his roots in the educational tradition of the late eighteenth and early nineteenth centuries, even if he also felt frustrated with it. His irritation with the 'Cousin Cramchilds' of the children's book publishing world is evident enough in *The Water-Babies*, where he more than once ridicules the Peter Parley series (1827–60), authored by Samuel Goodrich of New England. Again, these books attempted to chat their way through informative material on the natural sciences, history and geography, helped along by a discursive narrator, but what presumably most annoyed Kingsley, at least in the British magazine version (1839), was their stated declaration: 'I do not mean to tell you anything but what is strictly true.'[24] *The Water-Babies*, by contrast, continually teases the child as to its truthfulness or otherwise, especially over the issue of whether water-babies actually exist. Just because nobody has ever seen one, does not mean they do not exist, is the gist of Kingsley's argument; whereas 'Cousin Cramchild' (like 'Aunt Agitate' – Mrs Marcet or Harriet Martineau perhaps? – or Dickens's M'Choakumchild in *Hard Times*) prefers everything unambiguously cut and dried: 'Some people think that there are no fairies. Cousin Cramchild tells little folks so in his Conversations . . . And Aunt Agitate, in her Arguments on political economy, says there are none.' The narrator of *The Water-Babies*, however, insists that there must be fairies because 'this is a fairy tale: and how can one have a fairy-tale if there are no fairies?' Sensing that a child reader might query this – 'You don't see the logic of that? Perhaps not?' – he dismisses it with the remark: 'Then please not to see the logic of a great many arguments exactly like it, which you will hear before your beard is grey' (pp. 34–5). What makes Kingsley's stance as father and narrator inconsistent is this habit of simultaneously educating and teasing the child reader into a state of questioning bewilderment, as the inscribed 'reader response' of many passages implies.

In the Preface to *Madam How and Lady Why*, he complains that the children's books of his own childhood were 'few and dull and the pictures in them ugly and mean'; but an honourable exception was *Evenings at Home* (1792–6) by John Aikin and his sister Anna Laetitia Barbauld, which Kingsley praises for its story 'Eyes and No Eyes', the moral of which is: 'One man walks through the world with his eyes open, another with his eyes shut; and upon this difference depends all the superiority of knowledge which one man acquires over another' (*Madam How*, p. ix).[25] Kingsley prefaces *Madam How* with the injunction to his boy readers to 'use your eyes and your intellect, your senses and your brains, and learn what God is trying to teach you continually by them' (p. xi). Digressing into a warning about the Tree of Unreason, which is even more deadly than the poisonous upas, he openly acknowledges his readers' bafflement before they have even begun the main body of the text: 'There, you do not understand me, my boys' (p. xiii). As indicated earlier, this will not be the only time he catches himself talking above his listeners' heads, and even draws attention to it. The contradiction or puzzle at the heart of so much of Kingsley's writing for children, especially *The Water-Babies*, is why he so often writes in a heavily allusive and digressive style inaccessible to children. Though a father who wrote specifically for his own family, he alternately explains and defines, insisting on exactitude of speech and comprehension, while mixing fantasy with fact, and nonsense with common sense, pursuing his own separate stream of consciousness which rhetorically excludes the child reader. This is something that contemporary reviewers were quick to identify, especially when the publication of Kingsley's *Letters and Memories* two years after his death invited a round of reappraisals. The *Edinburgh* reviewer was typical in declaring that whatever the range of opinions expressed about *The Water-Babies*, most would agree that 'it is not a child's book. A little child cannot make head or tail of it; a bigger child would consider it altogether beneath the dignity of the teens...'[26] Kingsley does, however, openly confess the problem and justify it in *Madam How*, with the comment: 'It is good for little folk that big folk should now and then "talk over their heads", as the saying is, and make them feel how ignorant they are, and how many solemn and earnest questions there are in the world on which they must make up their minds some day, though not yet' (pp. 181–2). The questions he is so keen for his child listeners and readers to ask him are thus just the first stage towards understanding the vast moral issues all adults must eventually confront for themselves. To ask difficult questions, for Kingsley, is an essential part of becoming a fully responsible adult citizen of the world, and to give teasing replies is to stimulate further curiosity.

In his books for children, Kingsley tries to establish this habit of asking questions, and begins, in 'The Wonders of the Shore', his 1854 review article, which was eventually developed into *Glaucus* (1855). Though this was meant to be a review of other scientists' work, including Philip Gosse's, Kingsley uses it mainly as a springboard to publicise his own concerns about 'the education of our children', and his faith in natural history as a purifying influence. Apart from anything else, the study of natural history provided a good way for fathers and children to spend time together in the fresh air, sharing their discoveries, as he recalls in both *Glaucus* and 'Wonders', where he recalls the happy days spent wandering among rock pools, with memories of:

the laugh of children drinking in health from every breeze, and instruction at every step, running ever and anon with proud delight to add their little treasure to their father's stock, and of happy friendly evenings spent over the microscope and the vase, in examining, arranging, presenting, noting down in the diary the wonders and the labours of the happy, busy day.[27]

This passage, repeated in the two texts, embodies Kingsley's idea of the happy family, made harmonious by a shared interest in science, with the father at the centre of his excited brood, both outdoors and at home. Here and in *Madam How*, he 'shows' his readers landscapes and live creatures as if they were actually present, like his children, at the scene. Taking his readers to a shell bed, crammed with life, for example, he asks: 'What are they all? What are the long white razors? What are the delicate green-grey scimitars? What are the tapering brown spires? What are the tufts of delicate yellow plants, like squirrels' tails and lobsters' horns, and tamarisks and fir-trees, and all other finely cut animal and vegetable forms?' Prefiguring *The Water-Babies*, perhaps, he asks: 'What are those tiny babies' heads, covered with grey prickles instead of hair?'[28]

In *Glaucus*, he more explicitly aims to educate the father figure who will need to cope with all these questions, though like *The Water-Babies* it suffers from an uncertain intended readership. Whereas the later book was dedicated to Grenville but published in *Macmillan's Magazine*, a periodical for adults, *Glaucus*, which is dedicated to Kingsley's sister-in-law, 'Miss Grenfell', is usually classified as an introduction to natural history for children, but addresses its Preface (by inference) to a cynical and disillusioned father. Although the sex of the parent is not immediately evident ('You are going down, perhaps, by railway, to pass your usual six weeks at some watering-place along the coast'), the addressee soon resolves into a father who wastes his time in yachting, fishing 'and the consumption of many cigars'. In fact Kingsley opens with a picture of idle and pointless masculine activity: the sons take pot shots at birds ('the lads have nothing else to do'), while the father spends his evenings in a 'soulless *rechauffé* of third-rate London frivolity'.[29] In urging his fatherly readers to take up natural history and 'discover a few of the Wonders of the Shore' (p. 218), he cites Bewick's *History of British Birds* (1797) and Gilbert White's *History of Selborne* (1788) as positive examples and influences, White's *History* reading 'like any novel' (p. 220). This would have obvious appeal for Kingsley who, throughout his career, tended to merge genres and styles to make the educational process more entertaining. Instead of lying on the grass, dozing over a cigar, the manly father would, he suggests, do better 'to have walked quietly round the lake side, and asked of [his] own brains and of Nature the question, "How did this lake come here? What does it mean?"' (p. 226). In other words, the father must question himself before he is ready for the child to question him. The greatest difficulty for beginners, he argues, is how to 'learn the art of learning' (p. 244).

Moreover, in defining the physical and moral qualities of the ideal naturalist, Kingsley stressed the need for a combination of a strong body and a reverent mind, urging parents to pursue a rational and 'manful' system of education with their children: 'for, though it be impossible and absurd to wish that every young man should grow up a naturalist by profession, yet this age offers no more wholesome training, both moral and intellectual, than that which is given by instilling into the young an early taste for outdoor physical science' (pp. 240–1). Kingsley in fact identified a generational problem in the educational habits of Victorian families, in suggesting that the shift from country to town had in many cases confined the sons to the commercial outlook of the counting house: 'a frightful majority of our middle-class young men are growing up effeminate, empty of all knowledge but what tends directly to the making of a fortune' (p. 242). He was concerned, too, about girls spending all their time indoors gossiping over their needlework, when they could be outside collecting ferns. Kingsley always sees the study of natural history in moral terms, as a great safeguard against the social dissipations that might otherwise tempt young adult children into bad habits and drain their physical energies.

Kingsley's educational theories have been summarised by Brendan Rapple, who notes that though some of his ideas changed over his lifetime, he remained committed to a belief in state education for all, equal provision of fresh air and exercise for girls as well as boys, extended science teaching, and more opportunities for women to learn some branches of science, including medicine.[30] Kingsley insisted that women must educate themselves in order to educate others. Every woman, he argues in 'Thrift', an 1869 lecture to women on education, exercises an 'influence' on the minds of those around her, and 'the education of boys under the age of twelve years ought to be entrusted as much as possible to women'. As his lecture reaches its climactic ending, he tangles himself in a familiar contradictory plea for women to be the educators of men, but to do so in the name of self-sacrifice, and the performance of duty: 'Surely that is woman's calling – to teach man: and to teach him what? To teach him, after all, that his calling is the same as hers, if he will but see the things which belong to his peace. To temper his fiercer, coarser, more self-assertive nature, by the contact of her gentleness, purity, self-sacrifice.'[31] As John Hawley summarises, Kingsley saw women as 'saviors [sic] of men, transmitters of civilization, advocates of the heart working in conjunction with man's mind'.[32] However liberal and inclusive Kingsley's arguments about women's education initially sound, they always return to this concept of a higher duty towards others; and because he so often begins with the premise that men are essentially savage and need taming, he rarely shows girls and women being educated alongside male learners. His point is that they are already ahead of them: so that although Ellie in *The Water-Babies* joins Tom in his underwater world only mid-way through the book, she has nothing to learn. Indeed she is there to teach him, even if the text denies the reader any detail: 'She taught him, first, what you have been taught ever since you said your first prayers at your mother's knees; but she taught him much more simply' (p. 120). Although this teaching lasts for seven years, we never discover the substance of it: unlike those comic-grotesque passages where Mrs Bedonebyasyoudid punishes all the adults who have been cruel to children, and gives them a taste of their own medicine (Chapter 5).

Early in *The Water-Babies*, when Tom is being chased from Harthover Place after falling down the chimney into Ellie's bedroom, the narrator compares him with a 'small black gorilla fleeing to the forest' (p. 19). 'Alas for him!' the narrator continues, 'there was no big father gorilla therein to take his part; to scratch out the gardener's inside with one paw, toss the dairymaid into a tree with another, and wrench off Sir John's head with a third, while he cracked the keeper's scull [*sic*] with his teeth, as easily as if it had been a cocoa-nut or a paving-stone' (pp. 19–20). With his father in Botany Bay ('Tom did not remember ever having had a father'), he expects no miraculous rescue: but this strangely aggressive and primitive notion of fatherhood, based on recent discoveries of the gorilla in West Africa, accords with the brutal behaviour of his father figure, Mr Grimes, who is shown rousing Tom for the day by knocking him down. Moreover, Grimes intervenes in the flow of knowledge between Tom and the Harthover keeper, who is prepared – however gruffly – to answer his questions about bees:

> 'What are bees?' asked Tom.
> 'What make honey.'
> 'What is honey?' asked Tom.
> 'Thou hold thy noise', said Grimes. (p. 13)

In his children's books, Kingsley never exactly confronts the relationship between masculinity and fatherhood, which seems to underlie Tom's difficulty in finding an appropriate male role model. David Rosen, who sees Kingsley as having 'eventually reconstructed masculinity as a private, partially disclosed, substructure of self', derived from Rousseau and Carlyle, thinks he was driven partly by the developing feminist movement, which made him 'concentrate on devising a definition of masculinity that protected men against the possible intrusion of the new evolving femininity'.[33] Kingsley was a strong believer in the doctrine of separate and distinctive gender roles based on a clear distinction between the sexes themselves. His definitions of masculinity can be found throughout his writings, but a particularly marked example occurs in *Glaucus*, where he defends the naturalist as the reverse of effeminate. He should be 'strong in body; able to haul a dredge, climb a rock, turn a boulder, walk all day . . . ready to face sun and rain, wind and frost . . . to pull an oar, sail a boat, and ride the first horse which comes to hand'. If necessary, he should 'be able on occasion to fight for his life' (p. 238).

The challenge for Kingsley is to find some way of domesticating these energies, so that they can be channelled towards effective fathering. As Claudia Nelson has argued, grown men in Kingsley, especially *The Water-Babies*, are often destructive: 'Sir John bears responsibility for Tom's death and the professor for Ellie's.'[34]

The Water-Babies is full of men, but few of them are fathers. This absence of the father has been noted in a recent article by Laura Fasick, who observes that in his novels, Kingsley 'never shows a hero fulfilling himself through paternity'.[35] It was as if Kingsley was unable to communicate his own delight in being a father – evident in so many of his letters – in much of his fiction: possibly because he was troubled by the threat to masculinity implied by the father's need to show tenderness as well as exercise authority. The only father in *The Water-Babies* is Sir John Harthover, who bursts into tears when he thinks he is responsible for Tom's drowning, and all his household cry with him (p. 45). A contradictory figure, he is alternately admired for his down-to-earth heartiness, and exposed as an unintentionally clumsy buffoon. When he reappears in the text in Chapter 4, he is seen engaged in manly sports and activities typical of a rural squire: 'Four days a week he hunted, and very good sport he had; and the other two he went to the bench and the board of guardians, and very good justice he did' (p. 79). The narrator commends Sir John's sensible dining habits to his 'dear little man', and begins to offer him as a role model to his son, only to undercut his positive image with accounts of his snoring, and hopelessness as a domestic companion, which drives his wife away to the seaside for a few days' holiday with the children. Ellie's death in the rock pool is thus the indirect result of Sir John's insensitive behaviour as a father and husband. Perhaps there are echoes here of a passage Kingsley omitted from the book version of the text after it had first appeared in *Macmillan's Magazine*. In the deleted passage from Chapter 5, describing how water babies are made from neglected or cruelly used children,

the poor little children were there whom King Darius, like a passionate old heathen sultan as he was, threw into the lions' den along with their fathers (though he was quite right in throwing their fathers in, for that was according to the laws of the great fairy Madam Bedonebyasyoudid, which alter no more than the laws of the Medes and Persians).[36]

This surprisingly heartless statement derives from Daniel 6, when King Darius punishes not only the men who reported that Daniel had flouted the King's decree against direct petitions to God, but also their families: the fathers were here to blame for having Daniel thrown into the lions' den, so they deserve Mrs Bedonebyasyoudid's tit-for-tat style of punishment. Though their children are rescued and made into water babies, Kingsley perhaps thought this example was too frightening for children.

Instead of filling his texts, as he might have done, with exemplary fathers, Kingsley makes his narrator into the voice of the father, with all the quirks and peculiarities of the unregenerate male he thought needed smoothing by female influence. The voice of the father in *The Water-Babies* is essentially volatile and unpredictable. He gives the child misleading information, and at times fancies himself offended by the child's response, as an irritated father might: 'Now if you don't like my story, then go to the schoolroom and learn your multiplication-table, and see if you like that better' (p. 46). Indeed the father narrator's voice is so overwhelming that his relationship with his 'dear little man' drowns out Tom's with Mr Grimes, and the more emphatically he asserts himself, the more he is to be distrusted, as in the famous pun on the *hippocampus minor*: 'No, my dear little man; always remember that the one true, certain, final, and all-important difference between you and an ape is, that you have a hippopotamus major in your brain, and it has none' (p. 83). In order to make any sense of this passage, the child-reader would have to know that, in a heated debate about natural selection, Professor Richard Owen, President of the British Association for the Advancement of Science, had recently claimed that human brains could be distinguished from apes' because the former possessed a lobe called the *hippocampus minor*. Not only would the child need to know this, but also that Owen's anti-Darwinian argument was attacked as a specious denial of the evolutionary theory that man was descended from apes. In this passage, the pro-Darwinian Kingsley pretends to reduce complex and highly controversial ideas into 'the great hippo-potamus test', which he knows is wrong.

The father narrator is thus a thoroughly unreliable educator whose pleasure in confusing the child listener is evident throughout the text. He either refuses to give a straight answer to the questions he is always inviting, or else he satirises the adult worlds of Darwinism, medical science and social hypocrisy, in language no five-year-old child like Grenville could be expected to understand. Even towards the end of the book, when both Tom and Grenville must be wiser than they were at the beginning, he allows a page of allusions to 'backstairs' influence to go unexplained to the bewildered Tom and, by implication, the child reader: ' "But why do they want so to know about the backstairs?" asked he, being a little frightened at the long words, and not understanding them the least; as, indeed, he was not meant to do, or you either' (pp. 179–80). This parallels the allusion on the first page of the story to swearing – 'He never had heard of God, or of Christ, except in words which you never have heard, and which it would have been well if he had never heard' (p. 5) – except that here the middle-class child's innocence excludes him from knowledge that the streetwise Tom already possesses. In making the allusion, though, the narrator risks inciting questions about blasphemy that no good father should be encouraging. It seems as if, in passages like this, Kingsley positively relishes the teasing of well-bred children by spiking their curiosity about forbidden things: a philosophy that runs completely counter to the safe parameters of the Edgeworth world.

Kingsley's educational project is in fact full of mischievous traps for child readers, of which the most noticeable is the attempt whenever possible to sabotage the knowledge exchange from within. This is done using the female characters, even more dramatically than through the small boy's ignorance and scepticism. Although Kingsley gave 'Lectures to Ladies' (1855), his early lectures to adults (such as 'How to Study Natural History', 1846) often assumed an audience of young men seeking in shared study 'a ground of brotherhood with men'.[37] Rejected as human teachers and learners, however, female figures surface in his stories as quirky fairies and earth-mothers, fickle life forces and moral guardians. Moreover, they generally provide the vengeful or unpredictable element in the natural order. In this respect, they add another element missing from earlier examples of the educational dialogue book, where the woman educator is normally the earnest and gentle mother who has the utmost concern for her children's welfare, and not some mythological or supernatural being whose vengefulness is a natural instinct.

Essentially, Kingsley's is a gendered, sexually alive universe, composed of male and female presences. This is particularly the case in his educational writing (not necessarily for children), such as his 1869 lecture 'The Air-Mothers', which characterises the breezes as female, and the 'great sun' as their 'father'.[38] His children's books likewise divide up the natural and spiritual influences in a child's upbringing into father and mother surrogates. Thus the Father in Heaven is complemented by Mother Earth, both of them teacher figures, who in *Madam How* are supported by the two female figures of the title. Even Mr Grimes, Tom's master and substitute father figure, is complemented by his own mother, the old schoolmistress, who gives Tom some milk in his flight from Harthover Place. God himself is presented as a kind of father teacher, whose lessons ignorant mankind too often ignores. Madam How, in support, is 'the Housekeeper of the whole Universe' (p. 7), active and unpredictable, constantly rearranging things in order to test the mettle of humankind. She and Lady Why are repeat versions of the two female fairies, Mrs Bedonebyasyoudid and Mrs Doasyouwouldbedoneby from *The Water-Babies*, between them distributing punishment and spiritual enlightenment respectively. In turn, Madam How has two grandsons, Analysis and Synthesis (p. 134), while Mother Carey in *The Water-Babies*, 'the grandest old lady he had ever seen' (p. 148), makes millions of newborn creatures out of the sea water, and tells stories that prove she is 'perfectly right, as it is my custom to be' (p. 150).

In his progress through the underwater world, Tom is schooled largely by female teachers who alternately punish and soothe him into behaving more considerately to his fellow creatures. While Mrs Bedonebyasyoudid mechanically gives both adults and children a taste of their own medicine, Mrs Doasyouwouldbedoneby is the universal mother whose lap swarms with thumb-sucking babies. Though Tom watches foolish mothers being punished for strapping their children into uncomfortable clothes, Kingsley confessed himself heartened by the selflessness and heroism of the majority: 'this dark world looks bright, this diseased world looks wholesome to me once more – because, whatever else it is or is not full of, it is at least full of mothers'.[39] By splitting the mother figure into two schizophrenic halves, he separates the disciplinarian instincts normally associated with the father from the nurturing qualities of the idealised mother figure. It seems to be difficult for him to accept that the vengeful streak in Mrs Bedonebyasyoudid, symbolised by her extraordinary ugliness, may be a normal part of a mother's constitution.

If Mrs Bedonebyasyoudid is a wayward figure, still more is Ellie, despite being first introduced as a golden-haired princess asleep in an immaculate white bedroom. Even if she was once human, Ellie is like the other educating women in Kingsley's writing for children: essentially symbolic or mythical in a text that excludes girls from its readership and participation in an all-male dialogue. Perhaps because of her secure middle-class status as a 'lady', she has more power than Tom to cause havoc, just as Alice does in Carroll's Wonderland; and she does it – like Alice – by making unexpectedly subversive remarks. Ellie rebels in

Chapter 4 against Professor Ptthmllnsprts ['Put-them-all-in-spirits'] when he tells her about the flora and fauna of rock pools:

But little Ellie was not satisfied with them at all. She liked much better to play with live children, or even with dolls, which she could pretend were alive, and at last she said honestly, 'I don't care about all these things, because they can't play with me, or talk to me. If there were little children now in the water, as there used to be, and I could see them, I should like that.' (p. 82)

Ellie further irritates the Professor (thought to be based on Huxley) by asking the inadmissible question: 'But why are there not water-babies?' (p. 84), eliciting the ungrammatical, unscientific answer: 'Because there ain't.' When he catches Tom, he realises he has himself been caught: 'There was no denying it. It was a water-baby: and he had said a moment ago that there were none. What was he to do?' (p. 85). Though the narrator suggests that honesty would have been the best policy, and Ellie would have respected him more for telling the truth, the Professor not only remains in denial, but airily dismisses what she saw: 'My dear little maid, you must have dreamt of water-babies last night, your head is so full of them' (p. 86). It is left to one more subversive female figure – 'a very terrible old fairy' (p. 87) – to find him out, by her powers of prognostication, though Kingsley gives his fate a topical relevance by predicting that 'the old fairy will find out the naturalists some day, and put them in the Times; and then on whose side will the laugh be?' (p. 87).

In *Madam How and Lady Why*, Kingsley returns to the realistic world of *Glaucus*, and removes the more zany nonsense element from his educational dialogue with Grenville. This time they are there to learn some serious natural history, with Kingsley presenting himself as a father who urgently wants to be asked questions by his son, in a form of 'reverse interrogation'.[40] It was his view that God had made children naturally inquisitive, so that they would constantly seek for knowledge and come to understand the wonders of the God-created universe, but the questions needed to be asked, and not just of fathers, but of nature itself. 'If you want to understand Madam How', the narrator tells Grenville, 'you must ask her questions yourself, and make up your mind yourself like a man, instead of taking things at hearsay or second-hand, like the vulgar' (p. 19). By making question asking into a 'manly' activity, which stimulates an independent attitude of mind, Kingsley is reclaiming the educating role for fathers like himself, instead of allowing the occasional Ellie to reveal the truth. Indeed, he is still asking questions himself: he claims to have asked Madam How 'a hundred different questions ... in the last ten years' (p. 18) about how a chine might change into a glen, 'and she always answered them in the same way, saying, "Water, water, you stupid man"' (p. 19). Madam How is like Ellie, in that she can always see further into the heart of things than the male professionals, the Professor or Kingsley. Indeed the whole structure of *Madam How* is based on the idea of a father and son trying to fathom the elusive thinking of two quasi-mythological female characters cooperating to teach mankind both how and why things happen as they do in the universe.

Though the dialogue in *Madam How* tells children all about the causes of earthquakes and volcanoes, it has a subtext that dramatises the father's love of teaching. 'Ah! My dear child, that I could go on talking to you of this for hours and days!' the narrator exclaims in the midst of a history of volcanoes. 'But I have time now only to teach you the alphabet of these matters –' (p. 75). So far as he can, he points out landmarks for Grenville's inspection, and asks him to hold pieces of stone and observe their peculiarities. Their dialogue teases him into making guesses; riddles and conundrums are suggested until the child is exhausted and wants a straight answer.

Though all the questions are presumably invented by Kingsley himself, he needs Grenville's voice to ask them. In effect, he becomes a ventriloquist, making his son feed him continuous prompts: 'I would sooner answer one question of yours than tell you ten things without your asking', Kingsley urges at a point in *Madam How* when he has been carried away by his own eloquence (p. 76); yet of course these are his own self-questionings. This even happens in a lecture, such as 'The Air-Mothers', where a dialogue in the style of *Madam How,* with 'my little man', about securing clean water supplies, suddenly invades the address. Kingsley here presents himself as unable to stop giving information. Like King Midas's slave with his secret, he needs to tell someone what he knows and thinks but, like the Professor, he feels embarrassed by the risk of being found out as inadequate. 'I might have said more to him: but did not', he states in relation to a discussion of water wastage. 'For it is not well to destroy too early the child's illusion, that people must be wise because they are grown up, and have votes, and rule – or think they rule – the world.'[41] Having questioned himself as to how he should respond to the boy's questions, Kingsley is ready to proceed by drawing out the child's unsophisticated, common-sense attitudes to the need for a secure provision of pure drinking water. Once Grenville is satisfied, Kingsley next imagines the shade of an old Roman Emperor coming back to question him about the absence of public baths. The more awkward questions he is asked by children and ghosts, the more determinedly informative he becomes.

Within his portrayal of the questioning child, however, Kingsley includes a subtext of rebellion. If Ellie refutes the Professor's logic, Grenville is not always willing or able to ask a question, and sometimes he just feels tired of listening to the answers. In *The Water-Babies*, the narrator's prompts sound less hectoring, such as on the occasion when Tom first meets another water baby, and 'you will, no doubt, want to know how it happened, and why Tom could never find a water-baby till after he had got the lobster out of the pot' (p. 100). He also assumes that his child reader will be unfamiliar with hard words, such as 'amphibious', but gives a comic answer, referring him to 'the nearest Government pupil-teacher', who will provide a suitably dry definition (p. 47). In *Madam How*, which is more directly didactic, the narrator repeatedly prompts Grenville with phrases such as 'What do you want to know about next?' (p. 105), or 'You want to know then, what chalk is?' (p. 134); even a wishful 'What? You have a question more to ask?' (p. 23), or 'But you do not seem satisfied yet? What is it that you want to know?' (p. 42). Eventually, however, the child has had enough, and the narrator imagines him asking: 'This is all very funny: but what is the use of knowing so much about things' teeth and hair?' (p. 245), or commenting: 'I wanted to ask you a question, but you wouldn't listen to me' (p. 258). By inscribing the son's frustrations within the text, Kingsley seems to be acknowledging, however fleetingly, that his paternal urge to educate has reached saturation point. Indeed, his own allegory of the Isle of Tomtoddies in *The Water-Babies*, where all the people have been turned into turnips and 'mangold wurzels' because their foolish parents have made them work unremittingly at their lessons, was written only a few years before *Madam How*. When one of the turnips asks Tom: 'Can you tell me anything at all about anything you like?' his voice sounds suspiciously like a question from *Madam How* (p. 166). Kingsley revived the over-educated turnip caricature in a lecture given towards the end of his life, combining it with his ever-present fear of the wrong sort of education driving men to drink. In 'The Science of Health' (1872), which makes a case for setting up what he calls a 'public school of health', with lectures given by women as well as men, he warns that a child educated in ignorance of the laws of nature could end up 'with a huge upright forehead like that of a Byzantine Greek filled with some sort of pap instead of brains, and tempted alternately to fanaticism and strong drink'.[42]

Laura Fasick has argued that in working out the meaning and performance of fatherhood, Kingsley found it difficult to temper his instinct for 'hyper-masculinity' with the tenderness he thought men as well as women should cultivate. 'Despite his homage to gentleness and patience, Kingsley's real attraction is apparently to the displays of power and aggression with which he adorns his novels.'[43] Where his children's books are concerned, these hyper-masculine displays are diverted into a habit of intense questioning designed to trigger extensive demonstrations of his own knowledge. Nevertheless, in both *The Water-Babies* and *Madam How*, the male dyad of father and son is subservient to the superior wisdom of a pair of women who between them govern the moral and physical universe, in turn serving an invisible Godhead, whom Kingsley prefers to introduce to children via intermediaries. In this context, the omnipresence of the narrator's voice – fatherly and authoritarian like God's, but humanly tetchy and interventionist – more than makes up for his shortcomings. Perhaps because he saw God as *the* supreme father and teacher, Kingsley has no positive father figures or male teachers in his children's books, other than the paternal voice of the ever-present narrator.

Kingsley was clearly a pervasive presence in his children's lives, and continued to be so after his death in 1875, but it was his daughters, like their cousin, Mary Kingsley, rather than his sons, who most obviously continued their father's literary and spiritual legacy. All three daughters (including George's Mary) found themselves interacting in some way with their father's heritage, whether it was editing memoirs, finishing his work, or reminiscing about their upbringing. Rose, who was nicknamed 'Charles Kingsley in petticoats',[44] and had accompanied her father on his American travels, found the relationship the least problematic. She concealed her identity behind his 'editorship' of her travel book, *South by West; or, Winter in the Rocky Mountains* (1874), though a cited letter home in her narrative with the addressee's name removed sounds as if it might have been meant for him: '. . . every day I find some fresh puzzle or curiosity that I have not seen before, and long for you to see it too, and explain it to me'. Her liveliest chapters recount the time she spent roughing it with her brother Maurice in his Colorado Springs shanty, where she locked herself in at night with his revolver, and by day strolled about looking for 'seeds and stones' in true Kingsley fashion.[45] She later edited her father's *Glaucus* and *Water-Babies* for a 1908 Everyman edition, faithfully recalling the pleasure his children experienced when he shared his love of natural history with them. Comparing him with his own ideal of the natural scientist as a knight errant in *Glaucus*, she has nothing but praise for the unique qualities of a father whose 'listening ear, like that of the hero in the fairy tale, seemed almost to catch the growing of the grass and the opening of the shell'.[46] Her *Eversley Gardens and Others* (1907), inspired by her childhood home, included reminiscences of her father in his 'Study Garden', 'up and down which my father paced bare-headed, composing sermon or novel, lecture or poem'. His children, according to Rose, were trained 'by one of the keenest and most poetic of naturalists to observe every weed in the hedgerow or furrow, every pebble in the pathway or gravel pit, every bird in the forest or the garden'.[47] Though she clearly appreciates her legacy as his daughter, her prose here mimics his relentless thoroughness, which lets nothing pass as insignificant. She describes herself in later life going to 'mother earth' with her emotions: again, like her father humanising and gendering the natural world to provide solace for those who knew how to appreciate its wisdom.

The second daughter's experience was somewhat different. Having studied at the Slade School of Art, while Rose trained to be a nurse, Mary, who concocted the pseudonym 'Lucas Malet' from her mother's side of the family to distance herself from the Kingsley name, was married off to his curate, William Harrison, in what quickly proved to be a hopelessly incompatible relationship. Asked by an interviewer for a women's magazine in 1896 whether she wrote during her father's lifetime, 'Lucas Malet' said: 'No, I never wrote until some time after his death. And I am not altogether sure he would have cared about my working. He held the old-fashioned and chivalrous notion that women should be treated *en princesse*, should be provided for, worked for, not permitted to struggle with the world at first hand.'[48] How he would have reacted to Mary's completion of his novel, *The Tutor's Story* (1916), is anyone's guess. In her 'Prefatory Note' she claims to have been totally surprised by the discovery of this incomplete manuscript of 150 pages, written, she suggests, around the time of *The Water-Babies*. In deciding how to finish it and filling the gaps, she engaged in a kind of inter-generational dialogue, not just with her father, but with the bygone literary age with which he was associated. In her description of the novel's hybrid style, she defends its lasting appeal, while admitting that she personally holds 'no brief for that day either in its literary, social, or political methods'.[49] What must have made the text all the more problematic for Mary to complete was that it was written in the first person: 'I have often thought of writing the story of my life, at least of its most interesting portion' (p. 1). Though not her father's actual voice, it was certainly a male one, which *The Times Literary*

Supplement thought she had largely succeeded in imitating: even if this was not the book he originally planned, and the eponymous tutor did occasionally misquote Milton, 'he would be a bold critic who would vow that this or that could never have been written by Kingsley'.[50] Where reviewers could connect her otherwise hybrid and violent style with her father's legacy, they tended to feel more positive about it. Janet Hogarth, writing in the *Fortnightly Review* (1902), weighed Lucas Malet's 'taste for the abnormal' against the spiritual intensity with which she portrayed natural landscapes. In taking 'almost a sacramental view of life', she was, in more senses than one, 'a true daughter of Charles Kingsley', while Janet Courtney, summarising her achievement as 'A Novelist of the 'Nineties' after her death, agreed that she was at her best when she described scenery in attentive detail: 'its look, texture, even smell'. To Courtney she had already confessed: 'I merely, like the man of science, register the results of my observation and experience'.[51]

If Lucas Malet, however briefly, succeeded in imitating her father's writing, and elsewhere demonstrated that she had learnt from him how to record the minutest details of the natural world, she did not always relish being compared with him. According to Patricia Srebrnik, in interviews with newspapers and magazines, 'Mrs Harrison simultaneously asserted her personal affection for her father and her deviation from his values and philosophy.'[52] One senses her continuing to argue with him, and trying to establish her position as a literary daughter. A troubled *Fortnightly* article, 'The Threatened Re-Subjection of Woman', written by Malet in 1905, in focusing on the impact of the women's movement on the middle classes, seems to be disputing not just with John Stuart Mill (through the title), or the American President Roosevelt (whose views she is rebutting), but also with her father, who believed women could be doctors, but wanted his own daughter to marry his curate and keep house. Malet is, in fact, just as confused and uncertain about the future role of women as her father was. Her most interesting passage, arguably, is when she refers to women with a 'dual nature – a man's brain and ambitions, and woman's capacity of loving and suffering along with that most intricate and capricious piece of mechanism, a woman's body'.[53] John Martineau, a pupil of Kingsley's, famously described her father in rather similar terms: 'with all his man's strength there was a deep vein of *woman* in him, a nervous sensitiveness, an intensity of sympathy, which made him suffer when others suffered'.[54] The explorer Mary Kingsley was similarly remembered by an obituarist as combining 'masculine courage and intellect' with 'feminine heart, devotion, and true simplicity'.[55]

In writing George Kingsley's memoir as a preface to his *Notes on Sport and Travel* (1900), this Mary Kingsley, like her cousin and namesake, also found her own identity merging with her father's. Her biographer, Katherine Frank, cites her as saying: 'My life can be written in a very few lines . . . It arises from my having no personal individuality of my own whatsoever.'[56] While she glosses over the family characteristics of sexual energy and manic depression, Mary agrees with her father that the phrase '*Free* and *alone*' sums up what they both needed from life in order to be content, and compares him with Tennyson's Ulysses, bored at home and perpetually longing for further travel. Unlike her cousins Mary and Rose, however, this Mary was never eagerly taught at home, except in an inconsistent way when her father returned from his travels: 'I cried bitterly at not being taught things', she bewailed in an interview of 1899: ironically, she was given a copy of George L. Craik's *The Pursuit of Knowledge under Difficulties* (1831). Frank, however, doubts the honesty of her claim that she had pursued her research into West African culture as an act of filial piety, 'a desire to complete a great book my father George Kingsley left unfinished'.[57] The book, according to Frank, was never begun, and Mary was simply looking for a good excuse to explain her need to be 'free and alone' in an unexplored culture. 'I fancy I was wrong to have felt any irritation with him', she concludes forgivingly in her biographical sketch.[58]

When her own obituaries came to be written in June 1900, following her death in West Africa, she was inevitably linked with her father's legacy as an explorer-adventurer. 'Indeed, much that she tells us of her father', opined the *Athenaeum* writer, 'might literally be transferred to herself'; while a second obituary commented: 'She had, unconsciously, in part, great sympathy with her father's cast of thought, but, with stronger resolution, carried her convictions to more definite results.'[59] In a culture that valued large families and their connections, it was impossible for the two Mary Kingsleys to sever their public connection with their fathers, though it was perhaps only Charles's Mary who was anxious to do so.

The narrator of *The Tutor's Story* presents himself as a man with 'noble children for whom I live, growing before me day by day in beauty and in virtue' (p. 2) – an idealised image, perhaps, of how the novelist viewed his family of four. If the two Kingsley brothers, Charles and George, represented contrasting parenting styles, as fathers they could agree on the thrill of sharing the wonders of the natural world with their offspring. As children, these offspring could agree that their fathers had been remarkable, if difficult men, and the two-generational model used to open and conclude this chapter suggests that for both parents and children, the sense of what it meant to be a responsible father needed to be endlessly debated. Though Charles invites his children to participate in this process, they are conscripted learners, whose spontaneous curiosity needs to be prompted; and though his letters show that he was keen to interest his daughters in natural science, his literary model of educational fatherhood ultimately sidelines the female members of his family. Read in the context of his own 'gender trouble' – his uncertainties over whether mothers or fathers were the better teachers, and concerns about his own masculinity – Kingsley's children's books show him over compensating for his absent fathers with his own pervasive, fatherly-teacherly presence, which overrides the voices of women scientists and motherly fairies. In the next generation, the gender uncertainties of the father persisted more urgently in the daughters, who – all childless themselves – were seen by the public very much as their fathers' daughters, while the sons disappeared from public view. By a curious twist of fate, Kingsley's fostering of the manly dialogue of father-teacher and 'little man', excluding the distracting presence of the 'kind pussy mammas' of *The Water-Babies* (p. 114), and the 'little maid' whose fatal bump on the head is her reward and punishment for flooring the Professor, ended by developing a generation of daughters who wrote books on 'manly' subjects, and never became mothers.

CHAPTER 4

Matthew and son (and father):
the Arnolds

I am aghast sometimes when I think of bringing them up – but then I think of Papa, and the mountains that he managed to move so easily.[1]

Matthew Arnold was nineteen when his father died suddenly of heart failure in June 1842, at the start of the Rugby School summer vacation. This deathbed scene, with Arnold's wife, at his command, reading psalms and prayers, as he declared himself grateful for the pain of his angina spasms, remained ingrained in his son's memory: not because he was present at the time (he was not), but because he had often read the scene in Arthur Stanley's *Life* of his former headmaster (1844). Arnold regularly thought of his father in June, his contiguous birth- and death-dates (13th and 12th) providing a particularly poignant reminder each year of human mortality in general, and the congenital frailty of the male Arnolds in particular. In a letter to his mother of 14 June 1862, Matthew – by then in his fortieth year – tried to sum up what it was about this set piece of the Stanley biography that both attracted and repelled him:

[I]t is the part most in the style of an ordinary religious English middle class biography, with (for my taste) too much detail, and too bourgeois in its character: whereas the characteristic thing about Papa is the loftiness and fine ardour of his spirit and life, as in the great men of antiquity and Plutarch's heroes. A few pages of his letters, however, soon give one the right impression again.[2]

Arnold essentially *reads* his father as a text, and prefers him as a Greek classic to a Victorian 'philistine' (to use his own terminology for the middle class, from his later *Culture and Anarchy*, 1869). Moreover, he would rather read his father's letters, than Stanley's description of his father; he prefers him unmediated by an interpreter from outside the family. It was, how- ever, Dr Arnold's fate to be endlessly interpreted by outsiders, both those who did and did not know him when he was alive, with the nature of his death inevitably sanctifying him as a great man cut off in his prime.

His relationship with his mother – 'that central personage of our past', as he called her after her death – was much longer and fuller than that with his father, to whom he wrote only as a schoolboy and Oxford undergraduate.[3] Matthew wrote to Mary Arnold more or less every week of his adult life, telling her the details of his work as a schools inspector, his achievements as a poet, and the struggles of his growing family as they grappled with ill health and troubled schooling. The relationship was not without its difficulties, as she never seemed entirely to acknowledge his success as a poet, but it was not the demoralising reminder of non-achievement that characterised the relationship between father and son. The image of his formidable father moving mountains, cited above from a letter of 1857, suggests there was something overwhelming about Dr Arnold's masculinity. He was unnervingly virile, on an epic scale, whereas Matthew favoured a foppish dilettantism; fittingly, perhaps, fathered sickly sons; and was forced to define himself and his family in terms of a very different kind of masculinity. Swinburne cited a 'profane alien', who saw the Arnold father and son as Goliath and David; less flatteringly, Matthew towards the end of his life joked that he was like Mr Woodhouse in Jane Austen's *Emma*, especially in relation to his sayings about his daughters.[4] He was certainly a worrier, and with good cause: three of his four sons predeceased him, after he had spent years painfully amassing money to support them through their education; even his first lecture tour in America (1883) was undertaken to pay the debts of his last surviving son, Richard. In the end, it was his daughters – 'the little girls', as he persisted in calling them, long after they had passed 'little' girlhood – Lucy and Nelly, who gave him the greatest satisfaction and pleasure as a father, just as he had drawn most support not only from his mother, but also from his favourite sister, Jane (nicknamed 'K'). Though Matthew was close to his next brother Tom, and all his siblings, his female relatives – mother, sisters and daughters – seem to have provided more sympathy and congeniality than he found in the fraught and complex relationship of father and son.

At the heart of the problem was the issue of expectations. Dr Arnold was a demanding father, who hoped for moral and intellectual distinction in all his children, but especially his sons, while Matthew in turn awaited achievement of some kind from his own. Both worked hard at being fathers. They were intensely interested in their children's development (even though they adopted a partly satirical attitude towards them) and, as they were both educationalists, were acutely conscious of benchmarks for academic standards and behaviour. Their role was essentially didactic: to form the minds and moral principles of the next generation. Inevitably, their construction and interpretation of the father's place in home and society came under pressure from the public nature of their work, combined with its two-way overflow from the schoolroom into their domestic space. The two-generational, comparative model of the Arnolds creates a confrontational dialogue between a pair of mid-century Victorian fathers as they reinvented or 'customised' a mission for themselves in the family home. The fact that both were professionally employed in education – Thomas as a headmaster and Matthew as a schools inspector – emphasises the parallels and startling differences between them, especially in relation to their management of their own children at home and those of other people (as well as their own) in school. According to his great-grandson, Arnold Whitridge, Dr Arnold 'brought home and school into closer relationship than they had ever been in before', largely by constructing the school as a family.[5] This was no mean feat at a time when life in a public school was generally seen as inimical to the cultivation of homely feelings in boys exiled from their families at the age of eight. It also perhaps implies that he constructed his family as a school.

From the beginning, the Arnold sons had to share their father with a whole host of entranced Rugbeians, who proclaimed a spiritual kinship with him that seemed to transcend actual blood bonds. These honorary sons and brothers included Thomas Hughes, Arthur Hugh Clough and Arthur Stanley; William Charles Lake, who wrote several appraisals of Arnold, told Mrs Arnold after her husband's death that he considered himself as 'a kind of child of yours'.[6] As Terence Copley confirms, 'There was a second type of Arnold child, not the biological children of his marriage, whose educational influence was considerable, but his pupils at Rugby.'[7] For Hughes, author of *Tom Brown's Schooldays* (1857), he was simply 'the Doctor', whose death announcement Tom reads in a newspaper during a fishing trip. His impulse is to go to Rugby immediately, where he can only gaze at the empty spaces no longer occupied by his hero: the shuttered schoolhouse and vacant chapel pulpit. Hughes makes the point that schoolboy mourners had to share him with 'those yet dearer to him who was gone, who bore his name and shared his blood, and were now without a husband or father'.[8] There was almost a kind of 'bereavement-envy' or jealousy of the fatherless children, but the sibling rivalry was probably more pronounced in the opposite direction. Matthew's relationship with men like Stanley and Clough, while mostly cordial and friendly, was also awkward and uncomfortable. As Ian Hamilton puts it, 'Looking at Clough, the fifteen-year-old Matthew might easily have thought: so *that* is what my father wants from me'.[9] Nor was this collective boyish hero worship by any means forgotten with the passage of time. Addressing Rugby pupils in 1874 on the thirty-second anniversary of the fateful day, Stanley concluded: 'We are indeed all of us here, and in many a place besides, "the sons of Arnold".'[10] Thomas Mozley's Oxford *Reminiscences* (1882) recalls roomfuls of ex-Rugbeians repeating his great sayings, proliferating still further the ripple effect of the great father figure in the lives of his adult 'sons'.[11] In 1954, Frances Woodward devoted a book-length study, *The Doctor's Disciples*, to an examination of four of Arnold's pupils, including the son who was said most to resemble him, William Delafield Arnold, author of the Anglo-Indian novel *Oakfield* (1854). If not quite the father of the nation, Dr Arnold was quickly transformed by legend into a charismatic patriarch, a schoolmaster-father-hero, triply authoritative, whose spiritual sons would claim to understand and appreciate him better than his biological children, and carry his teaching beyond the Oxford colleges into the Empire itself.[12]

Though Arnold Whitridge portrays him as a straightforward character who was essentially 'a practical schoolmaster',[13] both Mozley and James Fitzjames Stephen saw Arnold's public persona as split between two contrasting types. If his persona in *Tom Brown* was magnified into that of the lofty and all-wise 'Doctor', Stephen, writing in the *Edinburgh Review*, claimed the real Dr Arnold as 'intense' and 'impatient', 'full of scruples', and scenting moral evil everywhere. Few men, thought Stephen, were 'less simple or unconscious'.[14] Mozley, characterising Arnold as living in a moral jungle, 'where every moving of the reeds was fearfully significant', saw him as a mixture of the dove and the hawk. Author of an anti-Tractarian article in the *Edinburgh Review*, 'The Oxford Malignants' (1836), which revealed his 'hawkish' side, Arnold was for Mozley something of an enigma. Was the 'true' Arnold, he asked, 'the dove assuming for the hour the sombre plumage and shrill screams of the hawk, or the bird of prey that as often as it found convenient, could glisten in the sun and coo like a dove?'[15] Even Charlotte Brontë, otherwise a stranger to this Oxonian world of church and college, felt he was 'not quite saintly; his greatness was cast in a mortal mould; he was a little severe, almost a little hard; he was vehement and somewhat oppugnant'. When she met Matthew Arnold in 1850 on a visit to Mrs Arnold's Ambleside neighbour Harriet Martineau, 'the Shade of Dr Arnold seemed to me to frown on his young representative'. Eight years after his death, she still felt the 'untimely loss of his Father' had been 'unfortunate' for him.[16]

Post-Lytton Strachey and Bertrand Russell, both critics of Arnold's schoolboy-flogging zeal, his image has hardened still further in the negative direction, the current fashion being to blame the elder Arnold, as W. H. Auden and Ian Hamilton do, for the gradual extinction of the younger's poetic inspiration. Auden's 1939 poem 'Matthew Arnold' characterises the son's poetic psyche as 'a dark disordered city; / Doubt hid it from the father's fond chastising sky.' This 'gift' would have developed in him, Auden continues:

> But all his homeless reverence, revolted, cried:
> 'I am my father's forum and he shall be heard,
> Nothing shall contradict his holy final word,
> Nothing.' And thrust his gift in prison till it died.

All he was left with was 'a jailor's voice and face', which denounced 'a gregarious optimistic generation / That saw itself already in a father's place.'[17] In becoming his father's apostle, the younger Arnold can no longer be a poet; but nor, as events proved, could he be a heroic patriarch. All he could do was try to understand the kind of man his father had been.

In his letters to his mother, as well as in his poems, Matthew repeatedly discusses his father, disputes the image handed down by non-family members, but still measures himself against him, as has been noted by his most recent biographers.[18] In 1858, shortly after complaining about Fitzjames Stephen's review of *Tom Brown's Schooldays* as inventing 'a physiognomy which no one who had ever seen him would recognize for his', he bought a print of his father to hang by itself over the dining room mantelpiece: the famous 1839 oil portrait by Thomas Phillips, which shows him in full doctoral regalia with open book and penetrating expression.[19] It was as if Arnold needed to be reminded, every day, over dinner, of his father's true 'physiognomy', and his tireless record as an example of what could be achieved in a short life span. Not that he could easily escape him anyway. On circuit in Norwich with his father-in-law, Judge Wightman, in 1861, Matthew found 'the memory and mention of dear Papa everywhere', as he did when he went on his first lecture tour to America in 1883. Preparing for a visit to Rome in 1865, where he used maps overwritten by his father ('You may imagine how I shall think at Rome of dearest Papa'); reading Arthur Hugh Clough's *Letters and Remains* the same year, with its eagerness to 'repel the charge against

Papa, of over stimulating, prematurely developing' his charges; even reading Plato and Aristotle on Christmas Day, 1867 – all reminded him of Papa. 'Then, I never touch on considerations about *the State* without feeling myself on his ground.'[20] Perhaps because his imaginary dialogue with his father so often incorporated the triple activities of writing, education and fatherhood – the three most significant of his own adult life – Arnold found it impossible to stop evaluating the intertwining of their parallel experiences. Discussing an old letter of his father's, which was written when he was a schoolboy, Matthew marvelled at the stilted language and the change in family relationships that had occurred between the two generations:

certainly if one of our boys now wrote such a letter we should call it prim, if not priggish: much is due, no doubt, to the greater formality of 60 years ago, but I imagine that it really was not till after he had grown up that Papa got that freedom of nature and humour which we all associate with him, and which were so charming.[21]

Dr Arnold's private papers indicate that he had only very gradually acquired the language of fatherhood, and even then he never attained the open expression of un-self-conscious warmth and devotion to his children that was characteristic of his son's letters to the next generation of Arnolds. Married to Mary Penrose in 1820, Arnold senior found himself a year later the father of a baby daughter. Having lost his own father when he was only six, he had no male role model from his own family to help him with his new responsibilities. Hence the day in April 1823 when he spent two hours trying to teach his daughter Jane (age 1½) to curtsey to her mother. 'She understands quite well what we want', Arnold told his friend, George Cornish, 'but looks as dogged and obstinate when we mention it, as a little child can look; – her little Heart swelling with Pride'. Inexplicably, she suddenly gave in, and as Arnold added to the letter, 'made her curtsey very obediently and was a very good child afterwards'.[22] It had been desperately important to him on this occasion to break the child's will, albeit to enforce respect for her mother rather than for himself, and his correspondence of the early 1820s shows him essentially feeling his way towards communication with his children. In keeping with the Arnoldian respect for the written word, he soon began exhorting them in letters. 'You are a good boy to take your weaning so well', he praised one-year-old Matthew, '– and so are you too, my dear little Tom, for doing so well, and making your dearest Mamma happy'. Tom was scarcely a month old, but his father enjoyed the fiction of addressing him before he could read.[23] His later letters to the children were sometimes in rhyme ('My dearest Tom Tit, / I love you a great bit'), or teased them in other ways, as when he wrote to four-year-old Tom:

My dear Prawn,
  You are a little boy, and here is a little letter to you from your very loving Papa,
  Thomas Arnold, Senior[24]

There is a stilted self-consciousness in Arnold's way of addressing his children, much as there is with Kingsley's 'dear little man' in his published writing, as if both fathers enjoy drawing attention to their 'ownership' of offspring, especially sons. For Arnold it triggered numerous kinds of experimentation in domestic writing very different from his formal style as historian, headmaster and cleric. In this he was supported by his wife, like him an amateur poet, whose main purpose in writing was to commemorate their children's individuality, reinforce good educational habits and create an extended group ethos within the family.

From the start of their joint experience of parenthood, Thomas and Mary Arnold saw it as something to be written about, and began a system of shared record keeping in a notebook that was ultimately intended for the children's use as an informal family history. Mary separately made notes of her husband's conversations, on topics such as British sovereigns, Latin verse, public affairs and history, perhaps in keeping with Thomas's wish that his children should have as many 'memorials' of him as possible: 'for I have always regretted having nothing of my own Father's'.[25] It was as if the legend of the father's early death and the children's lifelong engagement with his legacy had always been anticipated and prepared for. Calling the collaborative family notebook 'a little record to our children of their parents [*sic*] married life', Mary pointedly meant it to be different from a commonplace book in which people made copies of their favourite poems: it was to be both original and entertaining, a mutual diary of their children's lives, written by both parents, with frequent anxious breaks for the eleven childbirths Mary experienced between 1821 and the arrival of her last child Walter in 1835.[26] The narrative was about everyone: parents, children, godchildren, aunts, uncles, grandparents and friends. While Mary's contributions are often overshadowed by fear that she might not survive the next child's arrival, her husband's are more concerned with life outside the family home. Highly sensitised to danger, she describes domestic accidents – Matthew's fall from a sofa, little

Mary's knee penetrated by a broken needle – while her husband focuses on his career and takes on the heavy responsibility of running Rugby School. He also inscribed poems (his own and others') exhorting his growing family of children to be active and busy, and when little Tom fell dangerously ill in 1828, both parents treasured a mini-biography recording his change from 'Tom of Laleham' to 'Tom of Rugby': 'His father is very fond of this fragment', Mary recorded, '& wishes it to be preserved so that perhaps in his manhood he may stumble on this record of his infancy – written when we scarcely ventured to hope he would be preserved to us'.[27] Even at five, little Tom was potentially beginning an exemplary life; a comment of his at eight – 'I think that the eight years I have now lived Mamma, will be the happiest of my life' – prompted a poem urging him not to pine for vanished joy (fo. 64), while two years later, verses inspired by an attack of measles gently reminded the child of his 'better Parent' in Heaven (fo. 65). On the whole, it was the frailer-looking Tom, rather than Matthew, whose experiences gave rise to this kind of memorialising; Matthew – foppish and posturing – was to shine more as a poet in his own right once the family magazine was launched in 1838, and he had the opportunity to respond to the daily rough-and-tumble of sibling mockery. Meanwhile, as they grew older and began to fall short of the ideal, both Tom and Matthew were singled out for an extra reminder of their purpose in life, and the reward of appreciating both now and later that they had been a lasting 'delight' to their parents.

At one point in her narrative Mary rests contentedly in her husband's study, the focal point of their domestic happiness, surrounded by mementos both of his work and his children, foremost among which was 'Bacco the Doll' named after the second daughter, Mary. Like Dickens, Arnold, who referred to his children as 'the Dogs' or 'the Fry', gave them all nicknames, many of them eccentric and unflattering. Matthew's was 'Crab', Tom's 'Prawn', and Mary's first 'Wild Cat' and then 'Bacco', a name shared with the 'droll little Doll with the curly wig, bought at the Bazaar by your dear Papa and treasured by him for its likeness to his little daughter' (fo. 62). Mrs Arnold's chief underlying purpose in contributing most of the notebook narrative seems to have been to foster the children's admiration for their father as a kind of domestic hero, setting a fine example of aspiration, firmness and piety. It fell to the children, in their writing, to challenge this ideal and tease him as a father with characteristic poses and activities that all could recognise and find amusing.

The *Fox How Magazine*, begun in 1838 as a multi-authored family journal, and issued twice a year when the Arnolds were on holiday, took their recording habit a stage further, as all the children who were able to write or draw became regular contributors. As Christine Alexander has shown, the collaborative writing of mock periodicals was practised in several Victorian literary families, including the Brontës, Lewis Carroll's (the Dodgsons), and Virginia Woolf's (the Stephens), functioning as a form of play that allowed them to experiment with adult voices and mimic the sophisticated tones of print journalism.[28] The two eldest Arnold children, Jane and Matthew, had already tried their hand at autobiography, as their mother's notebook recorded; and Edward, the third son, described how he was nearly killed ('and [would have] been *food for the Ravens, as* Papa said'; original emphasis) when he fell off an overhanging rock on a family walk in the Lakes.[29] This near disaster was commemorated in the *Fox How Magazine* in mock-classical verse, 'The Cliffiad' ('Didu hangs in Air suspended / By his Hands not Neck sustained'), which was followed in turn by 'The Wansfelliad', 'The Lakiad' (when eight children broke the pier by all standing on it at once), and several tales of uncomfortable and overcrowded epic coach and rail journeys made by the whole family between Fox How and Rugby.[30] Dr Arnold both contributed to the journal himself, and featured in it as one of the *dramatis personae* – going round the bedrooms in the morning to wake them up, not in the 'common way', as a poem of 1840 explains, 'But on us does bestow a spat / Rather hard with a hair brush flat' – a ritual mentioned again in an article called 'A Day at Fox How', where Papa is otherwise described reading and translating from the classics.[31]

The print culture of the Arnolds was boisterous and satirical, as befitting a production assembled by a family of growing children in the school vacations. All are mentioned by name (usually nickname), mostly for some characteristic piece of behaviour that affords entertainment to the others, and Jane supplied sketches which showed (among other things), skaters falling over on the ice, and eight Arnold children sinking the fragile pier with their weight. While the *Fox How Magazine* conveys a sense of family values in holiday mode, it reveals the multi-faceted nature of Thomas Arnold's management of his role as father. He believed equally strongly in work and play for his children, leading them in dangerous hill walks and brook-swimming, while also anxiously overseeing their academic and moral education. Noticeably reluctant to send his boys away to school, as Matthew was with his own sons, Arnold created an 'Arnoldian' tradition in his home life that persisted for at least another two generations. This was characterised by a moral earnestness about all things educational, garnished by his rather heavy-handed style of humour. His son Tom felt that his father was neither witty nor humorous; he did, however, have a taste for the droll: 'the comic and grotesque side of human life attracted him strongly'. As his Oxford associates noted, Arnold's dual nature was difficult for his friends and family to negotiate. Tom claims that although his children were 'very much afraid' of being discovered in any wrongdoing, they recognised that he was trying to make them 'good and happy'.[32]

This aim is revealed more directly in his domestic letters, where his desire to improve the 'Fry' emerges in his habit of involving them in disciplinary rituals. To his aunt Susan Delafield in 1829, for example, he explains how he carries out occasional spot checks of their listed personal possessions: 'and when any Thing is missing I take some other Thing away as a Pledge, and do not give it back till the lost Article is found'. These unannounced raids could produce surprising demonstrations of honesty that Arnold found gratifying: as when 'Matt' not only helped Tom find a missing article, but also owned up to a lost item of his own, thereby forfeiting the shilling reward for a full set.[33] He even invented a list of house rules for 'the Dogs', requiring the younger ones not to 'go on walks without the elder Dogs' and show respect to their eldest sister, 'Dog K' – 'not barking, biting or otherwise molesting her, under pain of heavy judicum with many smites'.[34] There is a solemnity about all these moral games and comic rules with their lurches back and forth between self-incrimination and heroic self-sacrifice that is echoed in Arnold's heavily jocose letters to Matthew urging him not to be depressed by his struggles with Greek grammar. Comparing the boy's education with a pilgrim's progress in which he must learn to fight against setbacks 'as with great & bloody Giants', Arnold assures his son his letter was meant 'to pat you on the Back, and say to you, "Never mind, Crabby," "To it again, Crabby:" and get through your Work well'.[35] There is a physicality about his version of tireless fatherhood that turned the children's efforts into a battle against mythologised enemies or, on their Lakeland walks, against a strenuous landscape that somehow symbolised their father's rugged masculinity as their moral leader.

As the eldest son, Matthew was driven the hardest, beginning with the leg irons he wore for two years to straighten an apparent defect (hence his nickname of 'Crab' or 'Crabby'), and the home lessons and Sunday evening Bible examinations, which all the children started with their parents as soon as they were old enough. Mary Arnold's notebooks contain domestic timetables personalised for each of the older children. The day began with Bible study and hymns; Jane took Greek before breakfast, and the slot for Tuesday 'After dinner' prescribes 'Sums done at every opportunity.'[36] As a professional educator, Arnold's role as Head-master of Rugby – where he did eventually send his four eldest boys – clearly overlapped with his role as father. Stanley observed in his 1844 *Life* that he 'was not only the father and guide, but the elder brother and playfellow of his children'.[37] He was the boys' teacher and disciplinarian as well as their parent, and his suspicion of boys' tendency to mutual corruption at school was hardly likely to be forgotten when he returned to his own sitting room. Stanley notes that his 'gentleness and devotion' as a family man at home were very different from his stern manner at school, but both, he claims, were entirely natural to him. 'Nor again, was the sense of his authority as a father ever lost in his playfulness as a companion' (p. 190).

His sons, meanwhile, attended their father's boarding school, but boarded at home, further blurring the distinction between times of being on and off duty, at leisure and under school rules. Chapter 7 of *Tom Brown's Schooldays* includes a scene where Tom is summoned to the Doctor's study and finds him chiselling a toy boat with some of his children looking on; similarly, Stanley famously depicts him at work in his study, 'with no attempt at seclusion, conversation going on around him – his children playing in the room –' (p. 188). It is common to describe the working habits of nineteenth-century women writers such as Jane Austen and Elizabeth Gaskell as being exposed to regular inter-ruptions from the daily business of the household, but Arnold clearly positioned himself at the hub of both school and home, and allowed incursions from both directions. Sometimes these were invited, as when he encouraged boys to visit him in his study whenever they had a problem; Norman Wymer notes: 'As a father might talk to a son, he discussed their future, inquired into their home life, and displayed an intelligent interest in their hobbies.'[38] Arnold also invited his 'Praepostors' or sixth-form prefects to dine with his family, as a way of civilising their manners and integrating them into domestic life. Stanley felt that for all his pleasure in family life, Arnold invested it with a solemnity, an 'almost awful happiness', which made the upbringing of his children no light matter. Moreover, Arnold saw his identity as inextric-ably bound to the experience of being a father. 'I do not wonder', he said, 'that it was thought a great misfortune to die childless in old times, when they had not fuller light – it seems so completely wiping a man out of existence'. The effect of this view, according to Stanley, was that he regarded his children essentially as a continuance of his own life and identity, which, taken to its extreme, entailed 'the blessing' of 'a whole house transplanted entire from earth to heaven, without one failure' (p. 191). On earth, meanwhile, the whole valley around Fox How 'became consecrated with something of a domestic feeling' (p. 197). In Stanley's portrayal of the spreading Arnold influence, 'the Doctor' constructed around himself a holy family whose moral example was intended to improve the homely tastes of his neighbours, before being elevated en masse in a state of perfection, to the next world.

This was perhaps less surprising in view of yet another variation on Dr Arnold's role: that of school chaplain, which he took over in 1831 when the previous chaplain left Rugby. Rather than appoint someone new, he himself became the boys' spiritual guide, through the delivery of a weekly sermon in the school chapel, where he repeatedly reminded his hearers of the need to keep up the 'struggle against nature', as he put it in an 1841 sermon on 'The Necessity of Christian Exertion'. 'We eat and drink, work and play, and the end of these things is death', was his bleak warning; while at Rydal Chapel, in a message to himself and all other parents, he argued that a parent's example is far more influential than a schoolteacher's: 'he uneducates much more than the schoolmaster educates'.[39] Significantly, he sees the father, rather than the schoolmaster, as the more dangerous moral role model, especially in terms of religious education and behaviour. The underlying message of these and all his other sermons, many of them at least partially concerned with the insouciance of the young, was that life was not designed to be anything other than a continual struggle against the temptations of an indolent and careless world beyond home and school, or within both locations of the child's upbringing.

His spiritual role notwithstanding, Arnold also inflicted physical punishments on miscreants who were unable to respond to his moral advice. Though he flogged boys reluctantly, and only for serious breaches of the regulations, especially lying and bullying, he sometimes found there was no alternative to corporal punishment other than expulsion, or what was known as 'superannuation' for boys who were over fifteen and gaining nothing from staying on at school. His mission as chaplain therefore meshed awkwardly with his role as ultimate judge and disciplinarian, though both could be seen as having godlike qualities.

Thomas Arnold's relationship to Matthew was therefore much more than that of father to son. He was Matthew's spiritual guide as well as his biological parent, his teacher as well as his playmate, and the embodiment of a particular model of masculinity that was physically as well as

mentally omnipotent. All Arnold's biographers comment on his
tremendous energy as a man, and he could, if he wished, punish his
Rugbeian sons by various means extending well beyond those of a
'normal' parent. No part of his son's life while he was at home could
easily be enjoyed in privacy, without his father having some kind of
jurisdiction over it, and for much of the year his home was scarcely
separated from his school. Even when he was boarding at Laleham
(a school run by his 'uncle Buckland'), letters from his father seemed aware
of every disgrace 'Crabby' had accumulated. When Matthew escaped to
Oxford during the last year of his father's life, Dr Arnold reappeared, this
time in the guise of Regius Professor of History, and the family travelled up
en masse to hear his inaugural lecture in December 1841.

The withdrawal of such an omnipresent influence from Matthew's life
in 1842, when he was still under twenty, created both a vacuum and an
opportunity. It was something commentators at the time noted with
curiosity, concern and interest. Dr Arnold was already dead when Harriet
Martineau moved into her new house in 1846, but she became great
friends with his widow and youngest daughter 'Fan'. Although her
relationship with Matthew was never exactly warm and congenial, she felt
he had been done an injustice by his father. 'I dare say you are aware that
discernment of character was not Dr Arnold's *forte*', she told Lord Carlisle
in a letter of 1857. Above all, she observed,

his actually expressed 'contempt' for the 'character of mind' of his eldest son,
who has turned out so gloriously, & his expectations from Tom, are very striking
to all to whom he imparted them. His withdrawal from his sons so early may
have been so far good for them as that they have gained a freedom of will &
action which they could hardly have enjoyed while settling in life under his
superintendence; but it is in other ways very sad. He thought & willed for all the
family; & the sudden transition from this to perfect self management has been a
misfortune to, perhaps, four out of the five sons, – Matt: (the eldest) being the
exception.[40]

Making due allowance for Martineau's love of gossip, and her limited
external knowledge of the dynamics of the Arnolds' family circle, this
analysis of Dr Arnold's legacy to his children identifies the perceived risks
of his absence, even fifteen years after his death. Her comments suggest
Dr Arnold controlled the family so closely that their freedom of will was
suspended while he was alive. In fact, far from being the only one to
manage himself successfully, Matthew was actually seen by many as the
most overt rebel: cultivating a frivolous and unmanly image in clear
opposition to his father's virile energy, neglecting his opportunities at

Oxford, taking a sinecure of a job as Lord Lansdowne's secretary, and generally idling through his twenties with no apparent direction in life. 'He was everything which his father would have disapproved', Lionel Trilling affirms, '– jaunty, indolent, debonair, affected'. Wags called him a 'Jeremiah in kid gloves'.[41]

Even Matthew's reception as a poet in the public world of the man of letters was dogged by his father's legacy, as many of his first reviewers behaved like his father's friends in identifying him as Dr Arnold's son and measuring the overall health of his philosophical outlook against his father's. Initially, reviewers felt some sympathy for Matthew because of who he was. Several belonged to the extended circle of colleagues and acquaintances, such as John Duke Coleridge, whose 1854 review in *The Christian Remembrancer* announced: 'The appearance of the name of a son of Dr. Arnold on the title-page of a volume of poems, can not but excite a kindly interest in all those who admired, even when they could not agree with, his well-known father.'[42] In fact, Matthew's first volume of poetry appeared under the pseudonym 'A' precisely for this reason, and his brother William initially published his novel *Oakfield* (1853) under the name of 'Punjabee', wanting both to avoid unmerited kindness from reviewers because of the Arnold name, and bringing shame upon it by falling short of the expected standard. Being Dr Arnold's son created expectations of a philosophically healthy outlook, which Matthew's poetry failed to satisfy, chiefly – so far as his early volumes were con-cerned – because of its persistent gloom. Coventry Patmore, for one, was disappointed that the poems of 1853–4 'so little recall, either in subject, form, or sentiment, the works of the late Dr Arnold, that they will derive small favour from hereditary association, but must stand or fall by their intrinsic merit'.[43] Reviewers of the 1850s often referred to the so-called 'teaching' of his poetry, as if didactic instincts came naturally to an Arnold, and they had a right to expect something uplifting from it, but what he was teaching seemed self-absorbed, morbid and unwholesome. Even at the end of his life, in the critical overviews of the major journals, Matthew was found wanting as the moral leader his public expected of his father's son. Rowland Prothero, writing a long summary of his achieve-ments for the *Edinburgh Review* six months after his death in 1888, berated him for his 'impotent and profitless' teaching; while R. H. Hutton complained that the 'lofty didactic impulse' that Matthew had inherited from his father had 'sadly dwindled in the descent from father to son'.[44] The word 'teaching' obviously made readers think of the other Arnold, who was associated with a whole new reforming philosophy of education. Even in his farewell speech when he retired from his career in schools inspection in 1886, Matthew referred somewhat ruefully to his father's example. Wondering why his professional associates had placed so much confidence in him over the years, he assumed that 'one cause of it was certainly that I was my father's son', which the text records was greeted with 'cheers'.[45]

His poetry was frequently – if only incidentally – about fathers and sons. This was one of several themes, and probably an unconscious one at that, which allowed Arnold to explore the nature of father–son relationships in a context very different from the actual cultural conditions in which he was living. One notable exception to the obvious caveat against reading the poems biographically is 'Rugby Chapel' (1857), where he talks directly about his father, and enters the public debate about Arnold in the wake of *Tom Brown's Schooldays*.[46] The Headmaster's family rarely participated in the continuing re-evaluation of Arnold's contribution to public life, especially school reform: this poem, coming as it did when the nature of Arnold's legacy was being freshly and more critically evaluated, unusually makes a personal and emotional intervention, in favour of the heroic stature of the great Headmaster as leader of men. Beginning with images of November dusk and the school room lights, contrasting with the gloom of his father's tomb in the school chapel, the poem insists on Dr Arnold's 'radiant vigour' and 'buoyant cheerfulness' in his son's memory (lines 18–22). Continuing the opening imagery of light and darkness, the poem then circles around the notion of 'shade': essentially the protecting shelter of a 'mighty oak', which the father represented to his children, but implicit in the word is also the sense of a ghost (as in Charlotte Brontë's reference, cited above, to 'the Shade of Dr Arnold'), as well as the suggestion of his legendary status keeping his children 'in the shade'. Auden's 'Matthew Arnold', also previously cited, similarly plays with the light and darkness imagery, in imagining the younger Arnold's mind as 'a dark disordered city'. Even in death, Matthew never sees his father as weak or vulnerable. In 'Rugby Chapel' he portrays him essentially as a leader, finding it difficult to believe that his 'strong soul' is now idle: 'Somewhere, surely, afar, / In the sounding labour-house vast / Of being, is practised that strength, / Zealous, beneficent, firm!' (lines 39–42). Matthew imagines his father, in effect, as still exhorting boys to be on the watch for backsliding and indolence.

In language that anticipates Yeats's images of aimless crowds – for example in 'The Second Coming' ('The best lack all conviction, while the worst / Are full of passionate intensity'), Arnold distinguishes his father from the non-achievers and represents him heading the march through life, just as he led his children on their walks around Fox How.[47] Already depressed by the banality and mediocrity of British middle-class life in the middle of the nineteenth century, Matthew salvages him from all association with the bourgeois narrative he objected to in Stanley's biography: hence his insistent need to imagine his father as belonging to some more ancient civilisation, befitting Dr Arnold's own passion for classical history and literature, rather than as a mid-Victorian moral hero of middle-class schoolboys. 'Yes! I believe that there lived / Others like thee in the past', Matthew proclaims, as he envisages 'souls temper'd with fire, / Fervent, heroic and good, / Helpers and friends of mankind' (159–61).

By the time he wrote this poem Matthew had already set back his longest and best-known father–son explorations into a more heroic period within poems written in a classical epic style. Arnold often complained that he lived in an 'unpoetic' age, and seemed to blame this for the gradual decline of his own career as a poet; he was therefore strongly attracted to a past in which there were apparently more opportunities for great deeds, and men achieved fame not through writing poetry but by fighting battles. One of his earliest long poems in this mode was 'Cromwell' (1843), which Park Honan describes as 'oddly entangled with memories of his father . . . One feels that a very gigantic paternal shadow darkens an otherwise lucid historical sketch.'[48] This is true, inasmuch as Cromwell's initial energy and then his exhaustion at the end of his active life will have reminded Arnold of his father's unresting zeal in the causes of education, history and religion. The Lord Protector's life is evoked in the poem as 'A life – that wrote its purpose with a sword, / Moulding itself in action, not in word!'[49] All the soldiering images with which Dr Arnold is associated in his son's poems might seem oddly chosen, given Arnold's distinctly bookish and civilian habits as a headmaster, but even the *Christian Remembrancer*, reviewing Stanley's *Life*, compared him with one of the Greek heroes of the Trojan war: 'A phantasmagoric halo of truth accompanied him, and the flame played upon his helmet, as it did on that of Diomede; he was invulnerable; his armour was proof against sword-cut and thrust.'[50] Matthew Arnold later took lessons in military drill with the Westminster Rifle Volunteers (1859), as if to prove something about his own middle-class masculinity.[51] The point was, perhaps, that Dr Arnold's clear purpose lent itself to military imagery; the legend of a long and active life of service suited Matthew better than memories of a father who died prematurely of an inherited heart condition that he was already able to trace in himself and his eldest son Tommy.

Alongside the many versions of his father that he read, Matthew began writing alternative legends of his own. The most recurrent entailed the death of the son, not the ironclad father, who is made to feel remorse and regret for actions carried out in impulsive ignorance. It was perhaps a rather masochistic portrayal of the father–son relationship, which stopped short of killing the father, but heaped guilt on his head, either for not recognising his son until it was too late, or for ruining the son's potential by inconsiderate behaviour of his own. It was as if Oedipus was killed by a guilty Laius, instead of the other way round, and is then made to suffer for it for the rest of his life. Another related theme was the difficulty of disputing with a father by any other means. While an ordinary father demanded respectful obedience, the headmaster of a top public school expected to give unquestioned orders and not to be challenged by other views. As *The Times* noted in 1844, it was in the nature of schoolmasters to be obeyed, rather than argued with, and Dr Arnold was an extreme version of the model: 'Accustomed to communicate his own ideas without receiving others in return, and to measure his own intellect by a standard far below it, he was wholly unable to appreciate the force of reasoning which ran counter to his own opinions.'[52] If Matthew spent the rest of his life, in effect, arguing with his father, either by counting, theoretically, on his approval, or educating his sons very differently from the way he had been educated himself, this purely suppositional or abstract way of maintaining the dialogue was less satisfactory than an outright physical battle.

The best-known of these father–son poems is 'Sohrab and Rustum' (1853), in which Rustum the father unknowingly kills his own son in an inversion of the Oedipus myth.[53] The fight is in fact preceded by an obstructive dialogue in which the father stubbornly rejects what his son tells him of his search for Rustum. He also suspects him of a devious plan to avoid single combat: 'But he will find some pretext not to fight, / And praise my fame, and proffer courteous gifts, / A belt or sword perhaps and go his way' (lines 352–4). At the heart of the poem is the son's longing for recognition and acknowledgement, but Rustum, believing his one child is a 'slight helpless girl' (line 230) can only wish ironically that he had such a son as Sohrab. Rustum's disavowal of both his own and his son's identities is the main cause of their tragedy, in the face of his son's repeated claims for recognition from the man who even in old age is 'a giant figure planted on the sand, / Sole, like some single tower' (lines 336–7). Rustum declares himself as 'vast, and clad in iron' (line 325); as in 'Rugby Chapel', he is contrasted with the small mediocre people who never achieve any kind of distinction, and taunts his son as effeminate: 'Girl! Nimble with thy feet, not with thy hands! / Curl'd minion, dancer, coiner of sweet words!' (lines 457–8). It is hard not to see in this some allusion, however unconscious, to Matthew as the unmasculine poet he had seemed in his posturing adolescence. Sohrab, meanwhile – positioning himself as the smaller, inferior man, in every sense – seems incomplete without this climactic reunion with his father: yet the avowing of his true identity, cemented in kisses and embraces, comes too late to save Sohrab or establish a meaningful relationship between the two men. Two of Arnold's most recent biographers have been anxious to play down the biographical implications of the poem. Park Honan suggests that 'Arnold in writing perhaps made no conscious autobiographical connection, but drew on a very rich experience of filial love, mixed, as it was, with anxiety about his identity and aims'; while Nicholas Murray denies that the poem should be read as an encoding of 'a suppressed resentment at how his way of life was hampered by having to grow up in the shadow of a famous and powerful personality, and how his father, oblivious, had crushed some of the life in him accordingly'.[54] Whether or not a biographical reading is useful here, it does fit Matthew Arnold's preoccupation with father figures as dangerous and daunting presences, whose influence could just as easily be destructive as nurturing. It also suggests that a damaged father–son relationship is impossible to repair, given the ingrained pride of both parties, without tragic emotional wastage.

A much simpler variation on this theme occurs in 'A Picture at Newstead' (written 1863), an angry and indignant poem about a painting at Byron's Nottinghamshire home, which shows Lord Arundel beating 'the child he loved so well.'[55] The exact identity of this picture (assumed to be a Van Dyck) is still disputed, as the beaten child may actually be a grandson, rather than a son, of the first Earl of Arundel, but the speaker is unequivocally angry and upset at what he sees, and finds the father's cruelty infinitely more tragic than any woe suffered by Byron himself. Again, the father is presented as a physically powerful man, a warrior venting his uncontrolled fury on a mere child: 'Behold the stern, mail'd father, staff in hand! / The little fair-hair'd son, with vacant gaze, / Where no more lights of sense or knowledge are!' (lines 9–11). In this case, the father has literally beaten his son senseless, and the poem's speaker remembers it with a swelling heart.

'Mycerinus' (1849) is also full of anger against an unjust father who cared nothing for his son or his people, and somehow escaped unpunished. The speaker declares uncompromisingly: 'My father loved injustice, and lived long; / Crown'd with gray hairs he died, and full of sway'.[56] By contrast, Mycerinus himself is doomed by the gods to die just seven years later, which time he intends to spend in wild revelling in the hope of making his short life seem twice as long. This is another resentful, bad-tempered poem, which rails both at the gods and Matthew's father. The usual critical reading is that he blames his father for passing on the inherited heart disease that numbers his own days as well as his father's. His letters are full of references to the short time he probably has left, and the little he has to show for it. What again characterises this poem, as well as the others about fathers and sons, is the notion of the son as a helpless victim of fate or circumstances, in which the father lives, but suffers agonies of remorse. Moreover, the father has (unlike Matthew's own) enjoyed a long life as well as a powerful one. He seems to have had all the advantages, while his son, following in his wake, can be nothing more than a feeble shadow with no opportunity to achieve any grandeur or fulfil any social purpose.

A common theme of most analyses of Matthew Arnold's life is his difficulty in finding a meaningful career to match his father's, or his father-in-law's: both in terms of his creative life as a poet, and his worldly life as the husband of a judge's daughter, and also as father of six children. Like his brothers, he seemed inevitably drawn into a career in education, but whereas Dr Arnold had become the most famous of all Victorian headmasters, credited (inaccurately, according to most commentators) with achieving a massive culture-shift in educational and moral attitudes, Matthew eventually settled into a relatively humdrum life as an inspector of state schools, interspersed with journeys on circuit as marshal to his father-in-law, Judge William Wightman. Both of these could be seen as passive roles. His own father dead, he was now serving his wife's father as a semi-ceremonial attendant (he was paid £75 per circuit), while as schools inspector he was a visitor and commentator, whose ability to change anything was confined to what he wrote in his reports. The children who came under his inspectorate were mostly what we would now call primary school pupils, and they were from the lower social classes. In neither situation could he shine as an innovator or charismatic leader. As an inspector, particularly, his appearances were too intermittent to inspire the kind of devoted following his father enjoyed as a head-master-chaplain, regularly haranguing the whole school in an emotionally charged appeal to their better selves.

As a young man, Matthew Arnold had seen himself as superior to those around him, exaggerating his fastidiousness in self-parodic gestures of disdain for his younger siblings as travelling companions or at the meal-table. In his thirties, he projected his psychological life away from the real world of London dinner parties and train journeys to village schools, into a distant and legendary epic past, where fathers and sons argued out their position on the battlefield. In his forties, as a schools inspector con-demned to read countless essays and write endless reports, he also established himself as a particular kind of father: unlike his own, a weak disciplinarian who adored his children, and had to plead with his sons to study and to think of their future purpose in the world. His efforts mostly ended in tragedy and failure. Whereas Dr Arnold successfully raised nine out of eleven children (the other two dying as babies), Matthew's six dwindled gradually to three; after parting with his last surviving son Richard to Australia in 1878, he was left with just the two 'little girls', until his elder daughter Lucy left him to marry and live in America.

He never found it easy to be a father. When his first, frail little son Tommy was born in 1852, he vowed never to have any more: 'The baby (he is now squalling upstairs) is my first & last, remember. The alarm they give one for their mother's sake, & then the plague of their nursing & rearing is more than the pleasure of their society can ever repay one for.'[57] This is the language of the bachelor-at-heart who finds the arrival of animal-like children a noisy intrusion on his relationship with his wife. Within a few weeks, however, Matthew had become not only a proud and doting father, but an unashamedly sentimental one, entranced by his children's talk and physical appearance. Though the tradition of giving them ugly nicknames continued – his second son Trevenen William was always known as 'Budge', and his second daughter Eleanor was 'Gorilla' before she settled into homely 'Nelly' – many of his letters expatiate on their ephemeral aesthetic beauty. The most famous is what might be called the 'Dover Beach' episode of 1859. Though not published till 1867, the poem was probably written in 1851, eight years before the day when the Arnolds took their three boys to bathe, and Matthew told his mother: 'You should have seen that lovely little figure of Dick's laid down flat on the bright shingle with his sweet face upwards and his golden hair all floating about him waiting for the wave to come up and wash over him.'[58] Whereas 'Dover Beach' refers to the withdrawing sea of faith, Arnold here toys decadently with the thought of his child in his fragile beauty inviting engulfment from the vast impersonal waters. As it was, he dreaded change for his children, especially Dick, whose 'beautiful infantine roundness'

(Vol. 1, p. 489) seemed likely to leave him 'any day', as he warned his mother. When the child appeared in proper trousers for the first time at ten, Arnold reported: 'it breaks one's heart to think of his changing the dress that one knows him so by' (Vol. III, p. 52).

Arnold's comments in his letters show him strongly attuned to the physicality of his children. He particularly admired them in fancy dress for the various children's balls and parties they attended around Christmas. 'The duck he will look in his blue satin and point lace you may imagine', he enthused over Dicky as a miniature Van Dyck Charles II (Vol. III, p. 104), while Nelly in just her stays and petticoat was 'a delightful vision' (Vol. III, p. 158). He and Fanny Lucy – or 'Flu' – his wife, frequently shared their bedroom, and even their bed, with a child, as Matthew reveals in his letters without a tinge of embarrassment. 'Nelly insisted on being close to me, kicking me like a young colt', he reported on the eve of Basil's birth, when he and Flu were in separate rooms, and he was sleeping with his younger daughter (Vol. III, p. 65); while on another occasion, Budge lay on the bed next to him, 'with his head on my shoulder, asking me from time to time if I love him, and assuring me 'ur [*sic*] do love Papa' (Vol. 1, p. 349). When his first grandchild was born – Lucy's daughter, Eleanor, nicknamed 'the Midget' – Arnold enjoyed holding her, remembering her 'sweet, fresh, midgetty smell', and wishing he and Fanny Lucy could have her in bed with them (Vol. VI, pp. 234, 241). Arnold comes across as a warm, demonstrative, amused father, who never wanted to punish his children or discipline them in the way his own father had done. Though Dr Arnold had enjoyed some physical rough-and-tumble with his 'Dogs' it tended to be of the vigorous Lake District walking and swimming kind. Matthew had to be more cautious with his children because of their greater fragility, especially with Tommy as he weathered one crisis after another, until he died at sixteen. As a father, Matthew developed a tragi-comic style of narrative in his letters, which alternated between sickbed and deathbed details of the very kind he had disliked in Stanley's description of Dr Arnold's death, and an amused reportage of his children's sayings, sometimes said to him directly, and some of which he heard from the classic Victorian father's vantage point, the study.[59] When each of the boys died, he responded to them aesthetically. He had a photograph taken of Basil, and wrote of Budge: 'He looks beautiful, and my main feeling about him is, I am glad to say, what I have put in one of my poems, the "Fragment of a Dejaneira".' (Vol. IV, p. 98). This was a poem probably written as early as 1847–8, but published in his 1867 collection. It was therefore pure coincidence that it expressed his feelings about Budge's loss – 'him, on whom, in the prime / Of life, with vigour undimm'd, / With unspent mind, and a soul / Unworn' (lines 25–8) – which acts as a wholesome warning against oversimplified biographical readings; but it shows that Arnold's mind was continuously preoccupied with the difference between the unthinking majority and those (often represented by family members) whose short lives were distinguished by a certain spiritual nobility. Unlike many of the other bereaved fathers mentioned in this study, Arnold avoided religious explanations for the deaths of his sons, but in his letters dwelt instead on their last days, what treatments were prescribed, and how he had tried to keep on working. He had been starting the Preface to *Culture and Anarchy* when Tom was taken ill, and told his mother: 'I remember turning round from the table where I was writing to look at him dozing.' It was hard for him to continue the Preface in the same tone ('there was some persiflage in what I had written and I could not go on in that strain' (Vol. III, p. 303)): thus his children's frail lives created a contrapuntal interplay in his writing with the contrasting references to his own father's more rugged values. In his allusion to the 'great dangers in cramming little boys of eight or ten and making them compete for an object of great value to their parents', he was perhaps thinking of his decision to spare his own sons, especially Tommy, the stresses he had undergone in Dr Arnold's unforgiving regime.[60]

While his mother was alive (until 1873), Arnold told her about all the coughs and colds that plagued the family every winter; he noted numerous anecdotes about his children, and gave each a distinctive character. If Tom was the most fragile and Dick the most beautiful, Budge was an affectionate, if volatile, 'fat old duck'; Nelly a red-cheeked 'jolly' tomboy; and Lucy a valued walking and travelling companion. His youngest child, Basil, who died before his second birthday, came as something of an unwelcome afterthought, whose death prompted some uncomfortable thoughts about his own encroaching middle age: 'And so this loss comes to me just after my 45th birthday, with so much other "suffering in the flesh"', he noted sadly (Vol. III, p. 211). Inevitably, his thoughts slipped back to his own father, whose lifespan was by then only two years longer than his son's. Ever sensitive to anniversaries, and none more so than Dr Arnold's 13 June birthday, Matthew responded to major family milestones by referencing back and forth between his own life and his father's. Thinking aloud to his mother in 1868, the year both Basil and Tommy died, Matthew found it hard to place his father in the context of his own current life. It was as if he was both redundant and obsolete, but also ever present and needing to be accommodated somehow in a world that had moved on from the debates about church and scripture that had so preoccupied him. Matthew, however, still needed his approval: 'I think of the main part of what I have done and am doing as work which he would have approved and seen to be indispensable', he tried to convince himself and his mother, claiming her endorsement as well (Vol. III, p. 259).

Unsurprisingly, perhaps, Arnold's comments on his own work often show him looking anxiously over his shoulder, or using the language of moral guidance that was second nature to his father. In the Preface to his 1853 volume of poems, for example, where he deplores 'the confusion of the present times', with its 'multitude of voices counselling different things', Arnold longs for a dependable mentor, with a clear set of values. As he describes the best guide for a young poet, it begins to sound like a reliable father figure, a Dr Arnold who never doubted that he was right about certain things, such as the wisdom of the great classical authors: 'a hand to guide him through the confusion, a voice to prescribe to him the aim which he should keep in view, and to explain to him that the value of the literary works which offer themselves to his attention is relative to their power of helping him forward on his road towards this aim'.[61] As no such guide exists, all the modern poet can do is look towards the great models, such as Shakespeare and the ancients, among whom he finds the 'only sure guidance, the only solid footing' (p. 663). The language of guidance and sure footing, of being helped forward, prefigures that of 'Rugby Chapel', where Dr Arnold is the leader of a straggling family on the march through the Lakeland landscape, and may have reminded Arnold of the letters he received from his father at school, urging him ever onward with his Greek grammar.

So far as his own children's schooling was concerned, there was little to hearten the son of the most famous Rugby Headmaster. Tommy was too frail to be sent to boarding school, and Budge repeatedly slid towards the bottom of the class at Rugby after running up a bill of £160. Arnold tried Budge and Dicky at one school after another, wept with them over their departure from home, and finally moved the whole family to a house in Harrow so that they could be day boys. Nothing, however, produced lasting results, and Arnold noted ruefully: 'it is curious how I am destined to receive through my own child a confirmation of my instinct that the old English school system has served its time' (Vol. III, p.165). Budge died in 1872, after settling with his father that he would join the army and go to India. When Dicky finally made it to Oxford, where his grandfather had been Regius Professor of History and his father Professor of Poetry, all he seemed to do was run up debts, and he left without a degree. Arnold's instinct, as with Budge, was to send him away: this time to Melbourne, where he worked for a few years as a bank clerk before asking for permanent employment back home. In wondering what to do with well-meaning and likeable sons who were lifelong non-achievers, Arnold, like Dickens and G. H. Lewes, in effect deported them, hoping the extended employment opportunities of the empire would somehow absorb them and solve the problem of their long-term subsistence. The truth was, as Arnold complained, 'they do not throw their heart and interest into any part of their work, and are therefore passed by all the boys who do, and sink to the bottom of their form or thereabouts' (Vol. III, p. 445). After all the zeal and dogmatism of Dr Arnold and his premature 'burn-out', the sight of his own sons' inert indifference to ambition and achievement was hard to take; it was as if his determination to avoid over-stretching their brains and bodies had returned to mock him. Instead he was strenuous on their behalf, undertaking a lecturing tour of America in 1883, largely to clear Dick's debts, but he clearly lacked his father's oratorical skills: *Punch* reported that he was often inaudible, and his delivery was 'ineffective'.[62] On Dick's return home from Australia, Arnold humbled himself to ask the Home Secretary William Harcourt for help in procuring his one remaining son a factory inspectorship. It was still necessary for Dick to take a qualifying exam (which he passed), but Arnold was beside himself with gratitude for such help as he had received: 'He is the only boy we have left, and we owe it to you that we are able to keep him with us in England.'[63]

Even his girls were by then beginning to lead mildly dissolute lives. They were much in demand for house parties and balls, and though his letters are reticent on the subject, the question of their eventual marriage must have concerned him. Nevertheless, it was ultimately as a father of daughters that Matthew was happiest and most successful, in the process breaking the complex and painful pattern of association between fathers and sons that otherwise marked two generations of his family. Lucy and Nelly amused and entertained him throughout their lives; he enjoyed their company as children, often quoted their sayings, and admired their appearance. As young adults, they consoled him for the loss of his sons, and accompanied him on theatre visits and walks. Though he took it as a general truism that 'after 10 a child ceases to be much pleasure to anyone except itself and its parents', he made an honourable exception for his girls, 'whose company is more and more pleasant to me'

(Vol. III, p. 167). Even here, though, he was destined for further distress. Lucy, who accompanied him on his American tour, found herself a husband, and after her marriage settled there. He reported always crying when her letters home were read out to him, but even before she had gone, he told her: 'I like telling you how fond I am of you, though that is not necessary.'[64] His new nickname for her, ironically in view of her marriage, was 'Miss Lu', as if trying to retain some part of her schoolgirl self for teasing references to the home life she had left behind, especially the family dogs who became for Lucy 'the gentlemen' or 'the boys'. Always in need of a correspondent with whom to discuss his domestic news, Arnold replaced his mother, and to some extent his sisters 'K' and Fan, with Lucy, who in the last four years of his life became his chief confidante. As he waited for news of Lucy's first baby in 1885, he confessed to being haunted by the spectre of Laura Lyttelton's traumatic death after childbirth: 'the two cases joined themselves together in my mind, although the chances, one might say, were against both of them issuing so unhappily' (Vol. VI, p. 146). Arnold's last letters suggest that, at the end of his life, Lucy was the child with whom he had the most emotionally satisfying relationship, but whose daily presence he missed acutely: she was increasingly 'my Lucy', as he held tight to all connection with her. Ironically, it was in going to meet Lucy at Liverpool docks on her return from the United States in 1888 that he collapsed in the street and died.

'Never was a man more deeply beloved or more loving' (Vol. VI, p. 364), his sister Fan commented in tribute. The same might have been said of his father, Dr Arnold, but it was a different kind of love, much as their characteristic types of fathering were diametrically opposed. Both were strongly domestic men who largely avoided homosocial or professional bonds with their own sex, preferring their wives' and children's company to that of other men; but whereas Dr Arnold was loved by his disciples as well as his biological family, Matthew never attained that symbolic adoration of the nation. Caricatured in W. H. Mallock's *New Republic* (1877) as the supercilious 'Mr Luke', whose poems are 'a wail of pain', he maintained a lifelong distance from both the general and literary public, and never had the opportunity to build a following of devoted acolytes as his father had done.[65] Indeed, though both Arnolds have been the butt of caricaturists – especially Lytton Strachey, who made fun of the son as well as the father – Matthew was the more heavily mocked of the two. This is partly because of a shift in cultural attitudes, encouraged by publications such as *Punch*, which fostered a habit of jeering at authority figures, but it was also because Matthew Arnold stood for an unpopular kind of elitism, which it was easy to satirise. As a father, however, he was an essentially modern, forward looking figure, who fully enjoyed his children's company. The two Arnolds together neatly exemplify the transition from a patriarchal model of fatherhood – by which the children feared and revered their father, while acknowledging his deep, almost overwhelming love for them – to a much more recognisable up-to-date version, whereby the father provides, the children take, and the two generations interact on the understanding that there is little the father can do to make his children behave any differently.

Unlike his own father, Matthew Arnold was no disciplinarian. There were no inspections of possessions, no waking his children with the flat end of a hairbrush, and none of the fear instilled in them of 'being found out and punished', which Matthew's brother Thomas describes as characteristic of the feelings Dr Arnold inspired in his own family.[66] It is hard to imagine the elder Arnold being treated with the friendly disrespect shown to Matthew by one of his great-nephews, who insisted on calling him 'Matty': 'he had heard me much talked about as "Uncle Matt who was fond of children"', Matthew noted with more amusement than offence, 'and he shows his regard by dropping the *Uncle*' (Vol. vi, p. 345). Compared with his father, who had insisted on his toddler daughter Jane's curtseying to her mother, Matthew wrote to Lucy of his pleasure in seeing 'the Midget' wriggle at him in the morning; as for picking up the notorious American habit of spitting, Arnold was delighted that his granddaughter had succumbed: 'That dear little dirty thing, the midget; how I should like to see her spitting' (Vol. vi, p. 208). The Midget, in fact, restored the comic dimension to Arnold's experiences as a father, which had been lacking in recent decades and needed to be narrated to be fully appreciated. When his mother was alive and the children were small, his letters were full of comic anecdotes about the sayings of Budge and the tomboyish behaviour of Nelly, diverting him from the more anxious undercurrent of commentary on little Tom's fragility. Now that Lucy was in America and the Midget a new character to be shared and enjoyed, Arnold was back in his element participating in her adventures, albeit more passively than with his own children. For all his superior aloofness as a critic, and lofty distance as a poet, he is the most domestic of all the fathers discussed in this study, and the one best able to adapt to misfortune. Though the critical consensus is that he became more subdued and despondent after Budge died, and his letters certainly reveal an underlying tiredness, he came to regard fatherhood as something that sustained him through his disillusionment with contemporary middle-class life. Less buoyant than his father, and with considerably less energy, Matthew nevertheless writes fluently of the intimacies of domestic life: something he never explored either in his poems or his essays, and which conflicted with his public persona of the world-weary critic offended by the vulgarity of the age.

CHAPTER 5

'A fine degree of paternal fervour':
scientific fathering

'Children are one's greatest happiness', wrote Charles Darwin in 1862, 'but often & often a still greater misery. A man of science ought to have none, – perhaps not a wife.'[1] This blunt statement, coming when Darwin had already fathered ten children, establishes a clear conflict between the professional calling of a 'man of science' and the demands of a family. If a man had no one to care about, he argued, there would be nothing to stop him working 'like a Trojan', something Darwin recognised as early as 1838, when he drew up his famous list of arguments for and against marriage. The possibility of having children was entered in both columns, as a crucial, if equivocal consideration. Heading the 'Marry' case is 'Children – (if it Please God)', while the 'Not Marry' list includes 'not forced to have the expense & anxiety of children ... if many children forced to gain one's bread'. In other words, Darwin was from the start unsure whether the advantages of being a father would outweigh the disadvantages, which he identified as mainly entailing 'expense & anxiety'. He concluded, however, that 'One cannot live this solitary life, with groggy old age, friendless & cold, & childless staring one in ones [*sic*] face, already beginning to wrinkle.'[2]

In the event, he was a devoted father, lovingly recalled by his children, but he was astute in recognising as a bachelor exactly how they would encroach on his need for time, space, tranquillity and freedom from anxiety – whether about money, their future careers, or their physical wellbeing. Darwin was also arguably a selfish father, whose chronic ill health and reclusive habits permanently constrained his household's activities. When his stomach problems and daily vomiting became intolerable, even for him, he would decamp to the water cure at Malvern, Moor Park or Ilkley, taking his family with him, or else leaving them to manage as best they could without him. Where possible he avoided all public appearances, and created a domestic laboratory away from London, training his children and friends to work for him, whether as amanuenses, data-collectors, illustrators, or specialist advisers. Like his friends Hooker and Huxley, the children became loyal supporters of the evolutionary cause, though (ironically) underlying his relationship with them was the fear that they might have inherited his feeble constitution. As one after another sickened with weak pulse or queasy stomach, Darwin blamed himself as the source of their physical frailty. Fatherhood therefore emerges in his correspondence as predominantly a matter of intense anxiety; moreover, the cross currents of pleasure and pride in his children were inseparable from his preoccupations as a scientist with the impact of heredity, family determinism, inbreeding and the struggle for existence. He was not, however, alone in his concerns about the conflict between his professional life as a 'man of science' and the demands of a family.[3]

This chapter will explore Darwin's (1809–82) experience of fatherhood alongside that of his two closest friends and scientific colleagues, Thomas Henry Huxley (1825–95) and Joseph Dalton Hooker (1817–1911). All three men had large families – nine children (from two marriages) in Hooker's case, and eight in Huxley's, compared with Darwin's ten – and all can be said to have founded influential dynasties, not just of scientists, but of scholars, artists and writers in various fields. All, however, experienced the loss of at least one child. Two Huxley children predeceased their father – Noel (1856–60) and Marian (1859–87) – as did Hooker's second daughter, Maria (known as Minnie) (1857–63); while Darwin lost two babies – Mary Eleanor (born and died 1842) and Charles Waring (1856–8) – and, more traumatically, his ten-year-old daughter Anne Elizabeth ('Annie': 1841–51). While childhood death was by no means uncommon in large Victorian families, as we have seen from earlier chapters, in the scientists' case it was more directly implicated in their developing research on evolution, and concomitant loss of religious belief. It was also something that intensified the three men's intimacy, as was their anxiety about their wives' pregnancies and childbirths, and the future of sons who seemed less hard-driven and passionate than their fathers. While this, too, was in many ways a familiar story, for Darwin, Hooker and Huxley, the emotionally draining business of life and death in their own families assumed an even more acute resonance than it did for many of the other fathers in this study. At the very least, as scientists with basic medical training, they felt they should have been able to do more to save their children from premature suffering and death. Both Huxley and Darwin broke down under the strain, and Hooker sought sympathy from Darwin in his daughter's loss. Beatrice Webb, who met Huxley in 1887, the year his artist daughter Marian died, went further in diagnosing overall emotional exhaustion and frustration caused by children who lacked any real intellectual kinship with him. Noting both his 'warm, indulgent, loving nature', and the commonplace personalities and behaviour of his children, she commented: 'There is a strain of madness in him; melancholy has haunted his whole life.' The blame for this she laid firmly at the door of providing for 'a large and indifferently dutiful family. He suffers in his old age from the melancholy of true failure; from the wearing anxiety of unself-controlled [*sic*] children.'[4]

As with all the other middle-class male professional groups of the period, Victorian scientists struggled to find a way of developing a home life alongside their intellectual work, which in this case might entail long absences from their families, and/or experiments carried out in greenhouses and gardens; high-profile disputes; and the risk of public notoriety, especially when the moral implications of their discoveries became common knowledge. One comment often cited in relation to Huxley was Catharine Tait's surprised 'And yet I hear that he is a devoted husband & an affectionate father.'[5] Scientists like Huxley and Darwin who abandoned orthodox Christianity were under particular pressure to demonstrate their impeccable moral standards and exemplary family lives.[6] Paul White further argues that Huxley, for one, developed a particular kind of domesticity and associated male professional community that closely reflected the values of his vocation. As White illustrates, Huxley saw his research as essentially unworldly and driven by an honest desire for the discovery of truth. He resented the fact that he needed to secure a reliable salary before he could marry his fiancée of eight years, Henrietta Heathorn, but was confident that his altruistic motives would provide a solid domestic foundation. As White puts it, 'the virtues of scientific genius – its perfect transparency, its honesty and integrity, its purity of purpose – these were the virtues of the happy home'.[7] As Henrietta wanted him to prioritise financial gain so that they could marry, their respective value systems had to be carefully negotiated before they could establish a comfortable home and family life. Huxley's closeness to his mother, fiancée and sister Lizzie, whose letters he received while he was on board the *Rattlesnake* from 1846 to 1850 on a voyage of discovery around New Guinea and Australia, had already perhaps compromised the assertion of his own masculinity in all-male communities, whether of sailors or scientists. Hence the somewhat confused impression we have of Huxley as a man who both supported the cause of female higher education and his daughters' careers as artists, while maintaining a popular conservative stance on women's emotional instability and physical weakness as obstacles to career advancement.[8] White adds that 'scientific work had no significance for men of science without a domestic community – a realm of sociability, affection and sympathy that was in many ways an affront to their faith in reason and meritocracy'.[9] This 'domestic community' can be seen both as the family at home and its extension in the all-male professional community that existed in the various public places where Huxley and other scientists aired their discoveries.

The alternative to a wife and children was a 'family' composed of adult men. While the Arnolds provide a father-and-son model of fatherhood, and Gladstone and Benson that of a Prime Minister and his Archbishop as 'fathers' of the state and church, the three scientists can be viewed as a kind of asexual homosocial group, who interacted interchangeably like brothers, fathers and sons. At its most neutral, the term 'homosocial' has been used to describe 'social bonds between persons of the same sex', and is both close to, and distinct from, notions of the homosexual. While there is no suggestion of any homosexual feeling among them, or erotic triangles over possession of women, as in the original model of homo-sociality proposed by Eve Kosofsky Sedgwick, her terminology of a 'continuum' of male homosocial desire in mid-eighteenth to nineteenth-century culture (she focuses on the novel) is applicable in certain ways to the type of relationship enjoyed later in the nineteenth century by Darwin, Hooker and Huxley. Kosofsky Sedgwick associates the term with 'the emerging pattern of male friendship, mentorship, entitlement, rivalry, and hetero- and homosexuality [that] was in an intimate and shifting relation to class'.[10] The homosocial model can be adapted, and in some ways further complicated, by reference to Sara Ahmed's *The Cultural Study of Emotion* (2004), which argues that the Darwinian model, based on works such as *The Expression of the Emotions in Man and Animals* (1872), suggests that the emotions, already culturally associated with women rather than men, are 'a sign of an earlier and more primitive time'. For Ahmed, 'the story of evolution is narrated not only as the story of the triumph of reason, but of the ability to control emotions, and to experience the "appropriate" emotions at different times and places'.[11] This group of scientist fathers will therefore be discussed in relation to a form of homosocial bonding that both fostered the sharing of intimate feeling, while also problematising its expression and 'appropriateness' in men committed to objective scientific research.

There were crises in the lives of all three men when they needed to unburden themselves emotionally outside their immediate family.

Darwin, by virtue of his seniority, both in age and tragic experience, became a 'father-confessor' to the two younger men but, flinching from a recurrence of his own despair when his children died, he tended to discourage their expressions of grief, sometimes by claiming he felt too ill and exhausted to deal with them. His answer to everything was that time was the best healer, yet the intrusion of other men's misery tended to reawaken his own. In this respect the model described in this chapter is very different from that associated with the Arnolds, which was essentially the dialogue of a son with his dead father, exacerbated by rivalrous pseudo-sibling relationships with his father's protégés. While Matthew Arnold was extravagantly emotional in his response to his own children, he seems not to have shared his paternal feelings and experiences to any great extent with other 'men of letters', his key correspondents being his mother and sisters. 'Men of science' depended more on bachelor-like social and professional groups, sometimes taking holidays together, and sharing moments of crisis in their personal lives. Their correspondents number far fewer women than Dickens's or Matthew Arnold's, and the scientists' wives formed a subculture of their own, bringing their children to the Darwin home at Downe in Kent to weather family crises by placing themselves under Emma's motherly protection. For however often Darwin appeared to fail as a father – largely by retreating into a state of distinctly un-masculine self-absorbed anxiety, hypochondria and illness – Emma (whom Darwin sometimes addressed as 'Mammy') never faltered as a mother, becoming her husband's mother when necessary, as well as her children's.

Within this two-way emotional structure (homosocial and hetero-sexual), Darwin functioned as the father figure to his friends, while Huxley and Hooker acted both as sons and younger brothers. As a young man, however, Darwin had needed father figures of his own: both his biological father, Dr Robert Darwin of Shrewsbury (1766–1848), and his Cambridge Professor, John Stevens Henslow (1796–1861), who had helped him join the voyage of the *Beagle*, after mentoring him through his university career. Henslow subsequently became Hooker's actual father-in-law, which cemented his continuing connection with this circle, and when Darwin excused himself from attending his old mentor's funeral, his guilty feelings were distinctly filial. So far as his biological father was concerned, Darwin wrote about him extensively in his *Autobiography*. A huge man, whose weight peaked at around twenty-four stone, Dr Darwin was in every sense a towering presence in his son's life, his main skills being sharp perception of character and ability to win people's confidence. Darwin asked his advice on the health of his young children and cited his opinions in his *Notebooks* of 1836 to 1844, where he aired his ongoing thoughts about hereditary characteristics in mankind as well as in animals and plants. In 1838, for example, he noted: 'My father has seen innumerable cases of people taking after their parents, when the latter died so long before, that it is extremely improbably [*sic*] that they should have imitated.' More ominously, he added a few pages later: 'Verily the faults of the fathers, corporeal and bodily are visited upon the children', a thought that troubled him throughout his life, and which he said should motivate a man to do all he could 'to improve his organisation for his children's sake & for the effect of his example on others'.[12] Though Darwin, rather oddly, denied having gained much from his father intellectually, he relied on his continuing presence well into his own adult life.[13] Unlike Huxley, who declared himself the son of his mother so completely that he could find hardly any trace of his father in his personality or appearance, Darwin and Hooker were strongly 'father-identified' in terms of both professional and emotional connection. While Darwin considered and rejected his father's profession of medicine, Hooker eventually succeeded his father, Sir William Jackson Hooker (1785–1865) as Director of the Royal Botanical Gardens at Kew, having already attended his lectures at Glasgow University where he was Regius Professor of Botany. Within the second generation of scientists roughly contemporary with Darwin, familial terms were often used to designate close personal bonds; when, for example, the geologist Sir Charles Lyell (1797–1875) died, Hooker told Darwin he felt his loss 'most keenly, he was father and brother to me; and except yourself, no one took that lively, generous, hearty, deep, and warm interest in my welfare that he did'.[14] According to James Secord, when Huxley and Hooker mixed in the bachelor society of the Geological Survey, its director Henry De la Beche conceived of it as a large extended family with himself as father. He discouraged his junior recruits from marrying young, and though 'Survey wives' and children provided useful sketches or fossil samples, De la Beche in effect formed a dedicated male brotherhood of researchers under his own paternal leadership. A song sung at Survey dinners included the rallying cry against disloyalty or dilution: 'We'll work with Daddy De la Beche; / And stick to one another.' 'Continue to think of me as a kind of daddy', De la Beche counselled one of his young geological recruits, Andrew Ramsay: 'the more you do that the better I shall be pleased'.[15] Huxley's 'X' Club of scientists, founded in 1864, provided another opportunity for men of science to eat and talk together, their 'Yves' (jokingly so-called) mostly banished to their separate sphere of home and children.

Selectively, however, the men transplanted their fatherly-brotherly network into the domestic world as well. Not only did the three scientists stand godfather to each other's sons, despite a common lack of Christian belief, but one of these (god)sons, Leonard Huxley, subsequently edited both his father's and Hooker's *Life and Letters*, thereby performing a filial literary role for one of his father's closest friends.[16] Successive generations of Huxleys commented on their illustrious forebear, while the Darwin family became a veritable memoir industry.[17] Darwin, meanwhile, wrote a brief 'Autobiography' (1876–81), and still briefer memorial notes of his dead children Annie and Charles. Though not quite so intensively self-analytical as the Bensons, who wrote about themselves and each other obsessively for the best part of sixty years, the Darwin circle loyally memorialised their father, not just as the father figure of modern science, but also the progenitor of a band of professional 'sons', each with his own troubled experience of fatherhood.

Darwin dominates this chapter, almost inevitably, because, as recent commentators have noticed, there are today 'myriad biographical Darwins', but only one modern biography of Huxley, and not even that of Hooker.[18] Yet both Huxley and Hooker led far fuller and more active lives than Darwin, who quickly settled into a semi-invalid's existence at Down House except when travelling around the country for his own or his children's health. Scientists' lives remain problematic for biographers because of the difficulty of explaining their achievements to readers without scientific knowledge. An early reviewer of Francis Darwin's edition of his father's *Life and Letters* suggested that 'The biography of a man of science generally presents no aspects of interest to the general public', though, in Darwin's case, he was prepared to make 'a remarkable exception'.[19] Not the least of Darwin's appeal as a biographical subject is the contradiction between the global historical impact of *The Origin of Species*, and the timid domesticity of its author. Because much of his post-*Beagle* research was done, in effect, in his own backyard, understanding of his research is inseparable from a knowledge of his home life and its crises, in the midst of which Darwin was formulating his most influential ideas. His daughter Henrietta was dangerously ill with diphtheria (a disease little known in Britain before the mid 1850s) and his youngest child Charles Waring dying of scarlet fever in the midsummer of 1858, when Darwin was being urged to publish his species theory in order to forestall a pre-emptive strike from Alfred Russel Wallace. A reading of

Darwin's letters shows how complex and precarious was this balancing act between the pressures of his home life as a father and husband, and those of his professional networks. Huxley and Hooker, who had long been participants in the scientific debate, could hardly avoid becoming Darwin's more personal confidants, just as they increasingly turned to him for advice on sick or errant children. It was not unusual for the letters exchanged between them to follow a paragraph on a highly specialised scientific question with concern about a son's schooling or a daughter's physical frailty.

Darwin first encountered Hooker in 1839 in the street in London, but did not get to know him properly until 1843. Huxley was a later acquisition, first met in 1853 at the Geological Society.[20] Recalling the nature of each of these relationships years later when he was composing his *Autobiography*, Darwin used the same word, 'intimate': 'At a somewhat later period I became very intimate with Hooker, who has been one of my best friends throughout life', he said of the botanist (p. 62); while of Huxley he explained: 'A little later I became intimate with Huxley' (p. 62). By contrast, he felt he could not 'easily have become intimate' with Herbert Spencer, whom he found 'extremely egotistical' (p. 64). Intimacy was therefore not something that came easily or automatically to Darwin when he found an intellectual compeer, and, even with Huxley and Hooker, he thought his feelings for them declined in old age – a view not necessarily borne out by a reading of their correspondence.[21] Of the three, he was the first to have children, beginning with William Erasmus in 1839, whose birth he announced in the ambiguous, half-proud, half-jocular terminology adopted by many of the fathers in this study. 'Perhaps you have not heard, that I am become a Father', he appended to a letter of early 1840 to T. C. Eyton: 'the event occurred last Friday week: it is a little Prince'.[22] By the time of George's birth in 1845, he was sounding distinctly less pleased: he had intended to write a few days earlier, he told Hooker in July, 'but on Wednesday an upsetting event happened in the fact of a Boy-Baby being born to us – may he turn out a Naturalist'.[23] Darwin always found the births of his children an emotional strain, but this last comment indicates his increasing concern about their future careers. As with Dickens and Matthew Arnold, the arrival of daughters was more welcome, presumably because they would either marry and be supported by someone else, or they would remain single and look after their ageing parents. Nonetheless, when Huxley's second child and first daughter, Jessie, was born in 1858, Darwin warned him that where babies were concerned, 'enough is as good as a feast'.[24] Huxley, in turn, phrased procreation in terms of other kinds of productivity. The children, even as young adults, were often described as 'the chicks', but sometimes they became an expanding library: 'I received another important publication yesterday morning', he informed Darwin in 1865, 'in the shape of a small but hearty son, who came to light a little before six'. Later he referred to his family as 'the seven volumes' who were, by 1874, 'growing into stately folios', while Darwin, conversely, called William Erasmus his 'little animalcule of a son', and *The Origin of Species* his 'child', a term repeated in 1867 when he was nurturing his theory of 'pangenesis', 'an infant cherished by few as yet'.[25] Darwin, however, remained doubtful about the appeal of large families. When his youngest son, Charles Waring, was born in 1856, he initially forgot to tell his highly prolific cousin, William Darwin Fox. 'It was a complete oversight that I did not write to tell you that Emma produced under blessed Chloroform our sixth Boy almost two months ago', Darwin finally admitted. 'I daresay you will think only half-a-dozen Boys a mere joke; but there is a rotundity in the half-dozen which is tremendously serious to me. – Good Heavens to think of all the sendings to School & the Professions afterwards: it is dreadful.'[26] As shown in Darwin's later letters to his sons at university, with their litany of reminders about avoiding debt and asking for help on money matters, this was no passing anxiety.

Fox was to father twelve children by two wives – hence Darwin's wry joke about his own mere half-dozen boys – but Darwin's own family was hardly small. As it happened, baby Charles, who was born with some form of mental impairment that delayed his walking and talking, spared him the expense of a college education by dying of scarlet fever the following year. Taken in a scientific context, Darwin's family seemed at times to be testing the full implications of his theories about inheritance, survival and adaptation: all the more so in relation to contemporary scientific evidence that fatherhood in the animal world was largely an act of impregnation, and then the father's purpose was completed. This kind of instinctual behaviour was clearly inimical to the interests of the family, given that the father had no compunctions about starting again with another female, and abandoning each brood as it was born. According to Claudia Nelson, Victorian scientists 'could discover no paternal instinct akin to the maternal drive'.[27] Inevitably, periodical writers drew comparisons between the animal world and the human, sometimes joking and sometimes arguing seriously that there was something odd about a man who wanted to spend much time in the nursery. Huxley's own research on parthenogenesis in aphids (1857–8) convinced him that the male of certain species was redundant in the reproductive process. He was still taking issue with Richard Owen on the matter as late as 1894, when he insisted that 'The young, which these animals produce with such wonderful fertility in summer, are all fatherless. So are the drones in a hive of bees.' Far from seeing this as the exception in the lower animals and plants, he argued, 'we might just as well have been led to think sexless proliferation the rule, and the other the exception'.[28] Leonard Huxley remembers him declaring over lunch 'that until you come as high in the animal kingdom as monkeys the male parent has no affection for his young'.[29] Doting father as he was in his own private life (he claimed that 'children work a greater metamorphosis in men than any other condition of life'), Huxley used to call himself 'the lodger' at home because he spent so little time with his family.[30] When the eldest daughter Jessie published an article in the *The Nineteenth Century* (1889) on the 'Mental and Physical Training of Children', she claimed that 'The men cannot be troubled about babies . . . they leave all that to the women.'[31]

   Though Darwin's children had to compete for their mother's attention with their chronically invalid father, Darwin himself closely observed his first two children as if they were scientific studies, making notes on their facial expressions and behaviour from the first few days of their lives. As James Sully subsequently argued, the observation of children by fathers gained a certain credibility, and was recommended as a means of investigating the primitive psychological origins of human emotion. Darwin's semi-professional notes on his own babies, as scientist-father, can be said to have inaugurated a new, pre-Freudian way of examining the physical and verbal development of infants.[32] His observations of William and Annie form the basis of his article 'A Biographical Sketch of an Infant', published in *Mind* (1877), a quarterly review of psychology and philosophy, having previously featured in *The Expression of the Emotions in Man and Animals* (1872). The title of Darwin's article suggests something more akin to life writing than a scientific study; indeed, at the end of the article he refers to 'the infant whose biography I have here given', even though the thrust of his argument was to demonstrate the similarities between babies and the lower animals in terms of their early learning. There was potentially a conflict here between the objective scientist and the proud father, as the editors of the Darwin *Correspondence* have noted, but in this instance his 'deep scientific curiosity transcends his obvious pride and joy in his first-born' – to such a degree that he sometimes refers to William as 'it'. His notes on crying may seem uncomfortably detached for a parent: 'NB. I find bad crying, chiefly connected with resperative

function. – convulsive movements of chest? is sobbing abortive crying &
shouting?'[33] As for himself, Darwin as the scientist-father appears in the
guise of a benevolent trickster, hiding and reappearing, ambushing him
with strange and sudden noises, and generally testing his children's ability
to cope with the unexpected. William's alarm was not always generated
by actual tricks played on him, but merely by changes in his routine,
which in themselves give us a clue to Darwin's domestic behaviour as a
father. He was clearly not normally involved in bath time, as one
observation indicates: 'Three days ago when he was being washed & was
naked I took him gently in my arms which made him scream violently,
which could only have been caused by the novelty of the situation producing fear.'[34] On other occasions the baby comes across as indignant and
foolish in his undignified responses, as when Darwin made a loud
unaccustomed snoring noise, and William 'instantly looked grave and
then burst out crying'.[35] Nearly twenty years later, Darwin was still
experimenting casually with his youngest child, the mentally and physically retarded Charles Waring, on whom his father nevertheless seems to
have lavished his investigative attention. In a short commemoration of his
last son's life, Darwin describes how the baby 'often made strange
grimaces & shivered, when excited; but did so, also for a joke & his little
eyes used to glisten, after pouting out or stretching widely his little lips'.
These are intensely physical descriptions, indicating a concentrated study
of the baby's mysterious psychology, often in relation to himself as father.
Before he died, Darwin had 'just taught him to kiss me with open mouth
when I told him'. 'He would play for any length of time on the sofa,
letting himself fall suddenly, & looking over his shoulder to see that I
was ready.'[36]

   This is an intimate piece of writing, which focuses on the relationship
between the two Charleses, father and son – as if to compensate for the
other children's more clinging response to Emma. Whenever she is
mentioned in the 'Biographical Sketch', it is as a source of food and
comfort, a more reassuring presence than their father with his observa-
tional notes. Darwin records that whenever pleasurable smiles appeared
on his babies' faces in their early days, they 'arose chiefly when looking at
their mother, and were therefore probably of mental origin'.[37] Emma,
indeed, appears to have had a much less complicated relationship with the
children, judging by Darwin's reports here and in his voluminous correspondence: she existed primarily as the ever-present comforter and
nurse of the whole family, Darwin included. When she later joined him
in making notes of the children's amusing sayings, it is unclear from the

'Observations' whether she decided to do this spontaneously with Darwin then taking over, but he subsequently encouraged mothers to become his unofficial field workers in observing the early gestures and behaviour of their children. For her part, Emma focused on the children's language, phraseology and peculiarities of pronunciation, as when 'Betty' (Elizabeth) added an 's' to the end of every word, and said things like 'No, I'm not a drop old' (p. 425). Emma's different interests may well have sent Darwin in a new direction in his child observations, as the rest of the document abandons the physical details and records his children's peculiar expressions and mode of reasoning. On the other hand, most of the children had by then outgrown babyhood, and the next stage was logically an investigation of how their thought processes and speech patterns were developing.

What his reported interactions with the children in the 1850s suggest is that his relationship with them by then had become relaxed and informal. They were unafraid of answering back and defending themselves, even when they had done something wrong, and much of the chaffing that goes on between father and sons is about kissing – whether kisses withheld for bad behaviour, or kisses bargained for, even sensuously, by boys relishing both gesture and language: 'Lenny lying in bed – You may have a sweet kiss – Oh so sweet – (as he continued kissing) Don't they come sweeter & sweeter?' (p. 428). Lenny indeed is the star of the 'Observations', as Darwin records one unguarded saying after another. One of the last shows just how unafraid of his father Lenny must have been: '1856. May 21. Lenny lying on my lap, coolly said "Well you old ass" & being very slightly shocked, remarked "Really, I did not mean to spurt that out".' (p. 430). By this stage of the 'Observations', although an interest in the curious logic of children is maintained, one senses that the main driver is amusement at the children's sayings, especially their unawareness of the gap between their own and their father's understanding of their comments.

Outside the 'Observations', Darwin's letters in the early stages of fatherhood show him eager to watch and describe his children's most trivial activities. Nevertheless, this interest competes with his own self-preoccupations, especially when he is away from Emma and her motherly care. A classic example occurs when Darwin is absent visiting his father in Shrewsbury on 1 July 1841, and tries simultaneously to report on William (who was already there), himself and his father. 'I was very very desolate & forlorn without my own Titty's [Emma's] sympathy & missed you cruelly', he confesses after opening with an account of his own upset stomach and headache on arriving at his father's. This soon gives way to his description of 'Doddy' (William), whose response to himself is recorded in intense detail: 'Doddy's reception of me was quite affecting – He sat on my knee for nearly a quarter of an hour, gave me some sweet kisses, & sniggered & looked at my face & pointing told every one I was pappa.' 'Dear old Doddy', he concludes, 'one could write for ever about him'. The rest of the letter, less reassuringly, lists all the advice given by Darwin's father about the child's inappropriate diet: he was to have more meat and less cream, with a glass of water at his bedside at night. 'I tell you all these disagreeablenesses; [*sic*] that you may feel the same necessity that I do', Darwin advised Emma, after completing his catalogue of mistakes, 'of our own selves looking & not trusting anything about our children to others –.'[38] As middle-class parents the Darwins inevitably delegated much of the daily childcare to servants; being gently reprimanded by his father for misjudging the management of his own children, Darwin did his best to cope with the partial undermining of his authority as father of the next generation.

Inevitably, the deaths of vulnerable children in all three families caused a crisis of conscience that was akin to, but also very different from that of Dean Tait, discussed in Chapter 1. While Tait had 'failed' as a father because of his fruitless intercession with God to save his five daughters from dying of scarlet fever, the three scientists 'failed' because even their medico-scientific knowledge combined with psychological empathy was not enough to pull their children through life-threatening illness. Moreover, as men who understood, and indeed propounded, the theory of the struggle for existence, they knew that emotion had no place in this competitive environment, where survival of the species was dependent on successful production of progeny. As their wives buckled under the strains of loss (Henrietta Huxley was devastated by Noel's death, and Emma Darwin heavily pregnant when Annie died), the fathers had to discover reserves of strength and a language capable of expressing grief that avoided primitive emotionalism (to return to Sara Ahmed's Darwinian terms). Given the nature of the fathers' relationships with each other, much of their grieving had to be done by letter, rather than by personal interaction. Indeed, as the Darwins were apart when Annie died, the management of her illness and death as a narrative exchanged between parents placed an additional burden on Darwin as the one present at the sickbed. He wrote about it copiously at the time, but apart from occasional allusions to Annie's death when Huxley or Hooker needed comforting about a similar loss, he was then reticent on the subject, confining his feelings to the 'memorial' he wrote after her death. Each father's management of his child's tragic narrative had to be carefully mediated, to balance paternal tragedy with a sense of audience – whether the audience was his wife, his male friends or the wider public. In each case, it failed to save the father from projecting his despair on to his scientific theory, and ultimately on to his view of the mental and physical resilience of the species.

Annie Darwin's death was in many ways an exemplary child's death of the period, though a secular one, judging by Darwin's reports. She remained polite and grateful throughout her ten-day gastric fever, thanking her attendants for everything they did for her, and making only the occasional gracious objection. As with Darwin's own condition, it was never exactly clear what was wrong with Annie, though, as she had been failing for some months before she died in April 1851, Randal Keynes suggests it was most probably a tubercular condition, culminating either in a form of peritonitis or meningo-encephalitis (p. 200). When the decision was made to move her to Malvern, where he had profited from the water cure, Darwin and his second daughter Henrietta went with her, while Emma stayed at Down because of her advanced state of pregnancy. The letters he sent to Emma record a daily fluctuation of hope and despair: a classic version of the long Victorian illness that features in so many novels and letters, and turns parents into narrators of suspense and sentimentality. This type of letter feeds the recipient's craving for information, but also problematises the narrator's freedom to talk about his own feelings. Darwin's narrative, which had to spare Emma any dangerous shocks, oscillates between careful accounts of food taken, treatment applied and symptoms that have alleviated or worsened, with brief references to his own feelings as he tries to control them. 'She does not suffer thank God', he insisted, resorting several times in this one letter to the traditional Christian terminology of desperation and comfort. 'It is much bitterer & harder to bear than I expected – Your note made me cry much – but I must not give way & can avoid doing so, by not thinking about her.' He adds guiltily: 'Her case seems to me an exaggerated one of my Maer illness.'[39] Over the next few days he wrestled with the image of Annie before and during her illness, finding the only way he could cope was by not seeing her as she currently was. 'I could only bear to look at her by forgetting our former dear Annie. There is nothing in common between the two', he told Emma as another day went by (p.15). Unmanned by his child's suffering, he found it a 'relief' to write to Emma, 'for whilst writing to you, I can cry' (p. 18). Emma's calm and rational responses show that she constantly feared for his own wellbeing, while Fanny Wedgwood, the Darwins' sister-in-law, who stayed at Malvern to oversee the burial, added her hopes that Charles would avoid being ill: 'I cannot be surprised at yr fears for him it will be hardly possible that he should not be ill', she told them both (p. 28). While there is no evidence that Darwin intentionally drew his wife's concern away from Annie and towards himself, the whole episode exposed his emotional susceptibility as a father, and his own need for motherly care.

Once Annie was dead, she took on, for Darwin, the conventional symbolism of the perfect child. 'Thank God she suffered hardly at all, & expired as tranquilly as a little angel', he told his cousin Fox only a few days after her death; his language possibly tailored to suit Fox's religious outlook, otherwise it seems surprising. 'Our only consolation is, that she passed a short, though joyous life. – She was my favourite child; her cordiality, openness, buoyant joyousness & strong affection made her most loveable' (p. 32). 'Joyous', along with 'sensitive', in fact became his favourite words for Annie, whose brief life he commemorated in a 'memorial' written a week after her death. 'From whatever point I look back at her', he recalled, 'the main feature in her disposition which at once rises before me is her buoyant joyousness tempered by two other characteristics, namely her sensitiveness, which might easily have been overlooked by a stranger & her strong affection'.[40] Mildly flirtatious with her father, she pleased him with her 'pretty coquettish manner' (p. 541); he regretted that in losing her, they 'lost the joy of the Household, and the solace of our old age' (p. 542). There was a Wordsworthian ring to Darwin's laments for the spirit of Down House, whose future he had hoped would be infinitely tied to his own.

When Huxley and Hooker subsequently faced the loss of their own ideal children, they turned to Darwin as a source of agnostic support. As Hooker put it, in his grief, 'your affection for your children has been a great example to me, & there is no other, living soul with whom I can talk of the subject'. He added: 'it would make my wife ill if I went on so to her'.[41] Noel Huxley's birth as a 'Christmas child' of 1856 promised professional as well as personal fulfilment for his father, even before it occurred, as Huxley linked it with the achievement of his own scientific ambitions. 'I seem to fancy it the pledge that all these things shall be', he noted in his journal as he waited for the birth. Prone to waspish anger, Huxley wanted this first experience of fatherhood to elevate his moral outlook to new levels of 'abstinence from petty personal controversies, and of toleration for everything but lying'.[42] When Noel died in

September 1860 after a sharp attack of scarlet fever, Huxley inevitably felt that more than the loss of a child was at stake. As Pat Jalland has argued, 'Noel's death was for Huxley a crisis of faith', which suggested that the case for human immortality was a delusion. As he explained to Charles Kingsley, who – despite their profound religious differences – offered understanding support, Huxley could see no evidence of genuinely fatherly concern, as he understood it, in the operations of the universe.[43] Noel's death was in all senses a test of what Huxley understood as the true feelings of a father – both his own, and God's. All it did was prove to him that his own concept of fatherly care for his children was very different from the Christian notion of God's paternal relationship with creation.

Like Annie Darwin, Noel Huxley was an easy child to idealise. Huxley's wife, Nettie, in writing her own reminiscences, described him as 'a lovely child with large blue eyes golden curls clear fair skin & regular features'. Writing more emotionally than her husband, who tried to accept Noel's death without bitterness, she recalled: 'I was almost out of my mind – my head was one hot patch of pain –.'[44] For Huxley, Noel's death recalled him to the journal entry he had written about his own scientific ambitions on the eve of his birth: 'My boy is gone, but in a higher and a better sense than was in my mind when I wrote four years ago what stands above – I feel that my fancy has been fulfilled. I say heartily and without bitterness – Amen, so let it be'.[45] For Darwin, the news inevitably recalled Annie's death and his own desperate search for comfort. With no traditional Christian consolation to fall back on, he offered only the most rational and secular support to Huxley and, in effect, assured him that time would prove the best healer:

I know well how intolerable is the bitterness of such grief. Yet believe me, that time, & time alone, acts wonderfully. To this day, though so many years have passed away, I cannot think of one child without tears rising in my eyes; but the grief is become tenderer & I can even call up the smile of our lost darling, with something like pleasure.[46]

When Hooker's daughter Maria, or 'Minnie', died three years later in 1863, at the age of six, apparently of a bowel obstruction leading to a strangulated hernia, he turned immediately to Darwin for comfort: 'My darling little 2^{d}. girl died here an hour ago, & I think of you more in my grief, than of any other friend.' Although Darwin's response has been lost, Hooker clearly gained encouragement to confess that Maria had been his favourite child, 'the first who has shown any love for Music and flowers, & the sweetest tempered affectionate little thing that ever I knew'.

Taking no comfort from the spiritual side of the funeral, he dwells instead on his own failure, despite his medical training, to recognise how close to death she had been. Darwin, writing from Malvern, where Annie had died, responded with another reiteration of his promise that time alone would soften his friend's grief: 'Trust to me that time will do wonders, & without causing forgetfuless of your darling.'[47]

By 1863, therefore, the three friends had been drawn more closely together by the common experience of being unable, despite their scientific, quasi-medical training, to save a favourite child from premature death. Nor could any of them find any solace in the usual forms of Christian consolation that their wives still accepted. All the experience did was reinforce the sense of a competitive universe that not only eliminated the weakest of the species, but unfairly discriminated against the most sensitive. This was what Huxley argued in his Romanes Lecture of 1893, 'Evolution and Ethics'. Like Thomas Hardy, he saw the inevitable by-product of evolution as mankind's superior susceptibility to pain and suffering, and the destruction of those who were weaker physically, but morally more highly developed. 'The struggle for existence tends to eliminate those less fitted to adapt themselves to the circumstances of their existence', Huxley argued. He used his public platform on this occasion to plead for the kind of social progress that would foster the survival of 'those who are ethically the best.'[48] By 1893 this lesson had acquired a sharply personal resonance for Huxley, whose talented artist daughter Marian had died six years earlier after a long battle with mental illness. Increasingly disturbed by the implications of applying the 'survival of the fittest' theory to human society, he commented: 'I sometimes wonder whether people, who talk so freely about extirpating the unfit, ever dispassionately consider their own history. Surely, one must be very "fit", indeed, not to know of an occasion, or perhaps two, in one's life, when it would have been only too easy to qualify for a place among the "unfit".'[49]

Unlike the other lost children, Marian Huxley was a complex character to memorialise, nor did Huxley attempt to do so in the way Darwin had with Annie and Charles. Indeed, he found it very difficult to talk about her at all, outside the safe confines of his private letters. No innocent and loving child like Annie, Minnie and Noel, Marian had been a complicated and moody adolescent who went on to experience in her twenty-eight years the full gamut of late-nineteenth-century female cultural trauma, ranging from New Woman radicalism to postnatal depression and hysteria, before she finally died of pneumonia. As Beatrice Webb put it rather brutally, 'his brilliant and gifted child has sunk into hysterical imbecility'.[50] Huxley's emotional connection with her was all the stronger in that he had long been keenly interested in the practice of drawing and its underlying aesthetics. As a young man he had sketched not only the sections of biological specimens needed to illustrate his scientific papers, but also people, animals and buildings seen on his *Rattlesnake* voyage. In his off-duty moments he was a spontaneous cartoonist, of himself and others: prefiguring Marian's later sketches of her middle-aged father reading, Huxley drew himself at the age of twenty, glasses on nose, mouth tensed in concentration, and his long legs on the fender as he studied a textbook by lamplight. Leonard Huxley recalls that his father would delight the children with 'drawing all manner of pictures for us', including the serialised history of a bull terrier family visiting the sea-side.[51] He was also known as a creative peeler of oranges, sending even the newly married Jessie an example of his Christmas dinner handiwork, entitled (in the style of Whistler), *Piggurne; or, Harmony in Orange and White*.[52] As he developed his aesthetic theories more seriously in the 1870s and 1880s, partly through dialogue with Matthew Arnold, and also in after dinner toasts at the Royal Academy, he increasingly argued that art and science were inseparable disciplines, with Art the 'elder sister'. Joking in 1871 that the public were unlikely to appreciate the kind of art produced by scientists as much as that of Academicians, he insisted nevertheless that 'We both seek truth, and we both seek beauty'.[53] 'The greatest men of science have always been artists', he elaborated, adding that there was 'hardly a great artist who is not in the broad sense of the word a man of science'.[54] In 1887, the year of Marian's death, he developed the connection further, by seeing men of science and artists as practitioners who 'speak in symbols . . . symbols by which we are constantly recalling the order and beauty of Nature . . .'[55] As Charles Blinderman has commented, Huxley was obsessed with a sense of structure, seeing science and art as working towards the same end: that of building a reconstructed society: 'the structuring of chaos' can 'almost be said to have been an element of his personality'.[56] Within his extended household, however, art brought about the collapse of the family and of his own emotional resilience and mental stability.

Huxley never classed himself with Marian as a creative artist, but he followed her career proudly and, inspired by her example, pondered the relationship between artistic genius and the art of self-discipline. 'Artists are born, not made', he observed, the year after her death, adapting an earlier saying of his: 'Artists are not made; they grow.' In fact he had argued five years earlier, in a lecture to the Liverpool Institution, that he would make it absolutely necessary for everybody to learn to draw. Strongly committed as he was to giving children an aesthetic as well as a scientific education, he thought drawing taught attention and accuracy.[57] In other words, he regarded it as a discipline as much as a creative outlet, and began to link it with the wider subject of girls' education as a means of restraining emotional imbalance. Seemingly liberal, in that he argued for a broadening of the curriculum for girls and an open field for careers, he was sure that biology, especially the inevitability of motherhood for most women, would prove an insuperable disadvantage in a competitive marketplace. Marian was only six when he declared in 1865 that:

Women are, by nature, more excitable than men – prone to be swept by tides of emotion, proceeding from hidden and inward, as well as from obvious and external causes; and female education does its best to weaken every physical counterpoise to this nervous mobility – tends in all ways to stimulate the emotional part of the mind and stunt the rest.[58]

Huxley presumably thought he was counteracting this tendency when he supervised his daughters' education. Like all her sisters, and many other middle-class daughters of her generation, Marian attended the Slade School of Art, but quickly progressed beyond schoolgirl competency to take the 1877 composition prize for her 'Death of Socrates'. There was every sign that she would turn into a brilliantly successful artist. She exhibited at the Royal Academy between 1880 and 1884, but suffered intermittent physical and psychological collapses, including near blindness. Adrian Desmond describes her as a 'skittish beauty', a highly strung 'New Woman', who flirted with men and liked to cause a sensation wherever she went.[59] The Darwins disliked her when she visited Down and lounged about reading the paper instead of engaging sociably. 'It is clear we need never invite her again', Emma decided, tolerating her presence only because her husband was painting Darwin's portrait.[60]

By then Marian had made what seemed a highly suitable marriage in 1879 to the society portrait painter, John Collier, but their careers quickly developed in opposite directions. While he produced a succession of monumental oil paintings of great men, including Darwin and Huxley (the latter standing full square, holding a skull), she pencilled light, relaxed sketches of the two scientists and other men of the period, in 'off duty' poses, catching them unawares. Two sketches of her father focus on his face as he concentrates on a book, his eyelids lowered, as if for a moment oblivious to his surroundings and anyone who might be observing him,

Figure 3 Thomas Henry Huxley reading: pencil drawing
by his daughter Marian Collier.

while another, more formal oil painting shows him in profile gazing thoughtfully into the distance. Her image of a father figure is of a man engrossed in intellectual work, apart from his family, benevolently pre-occupied. She mostly reserves her grander oils, paradoxically enough, for what might seem more trivial subjects. *The Trinket-Box* (*c.* 1884) shows two girls kneeling down before a jewellery box and examining the contents, while *The Rehearsal* (1882) presents another two girls in black rehearsing dance steps, and *A Coming Tragedian* (1882) a girl posturing before a tall mirror in an attic. There is a suggestion of secrecy about all these activities, combined with a self-conscious love of performance, further symbolised by her painting of her husband painting her: his job apparently done, he looks away from the easel, a brush gripped between his teeth, other brushes and palette knife in his hands, the artist's eyes and his subject's at oblique angles, avoiding each other's gaze. Essentially, Marian portrays herself here as an artefact created by a man; her shape stands out from the white paper on the easel, the only light part of an otherwise dark domestic interior.[61] It is hard to tell what she meant by reducing herself to a picture created by her husband. It may be a tribute to his achievements as a portrait painter, or it may be making a serious point about her subordinate position as 'Mrs John Collier', wife and exhibited object emerging from the private space of their home. Her most controversial painting, however, alluded to a different relationship: two of her younger sisters, Nettie and Ethel, modelled as a gambler's daughters for *The Sins of the Father*, exhibited at the Royal Academy in 1880. *The Times* describes them as 'intent on a game of cards, which they have come upon in a chest of drawers, marked as the father's property by his pipe left on the top of it'.[62] The painting was sold before the exhibition opened, and after Marian's death was given a place of honour over the Huxleys' drawing room fireplace. *The Illustrated London News* revived the story when it marked Huxley's death in the summer of 1895, commenting 'She was not only beautiful, with a strong likeness to her father, but she had genius.'[63]

When her underlying condition was exacerbated, first by a miscarriage, and then by the birth of her daughter Joyce in 1884, the Huxleys sought help from Jean-Martin Charcot (1825–93), an expert in hysterical diseases at the Salpêtrière hospital in Paris, which Freud visited in 1885–6, to observe Charcot's use of hypnotic treatment. 'The daughter's disease', as Elaine Showalter calls it, hysteria was read as a form of protest against exclusion from the professions, while Charcot himself believed that 'hysterics suffered from a hereditary taint that weakened their nervous system'.[64] Neither of these views, if Huxley was aware of them, would have offered much comfort. In fact, as he had always strongly supported 'Mady's' career, the finger pointed more to the effects of 'hereditary taint'. Like Darwin, convinced that the physical sufferings of so many of his children were ultimately his fault as their progenitor, Huxley took his daughter's tragedy personally: it was difficult for him after her death to accept anything like a benevolent view, either of evolutionary theory, or of the Christian tradition in which he had been raised, and which his wife still accepted and practised.

Already an agnostic, he became obsessed with the miracle of the Gadarene swine in the Gospel of St Mark, Chapter 5, as a preposterous story that Christians were expected to take at face value; but there was also a more personal sense in which it recalled his daughter's sufferings. According to the story, when Jesus meets a man 'with an unclean spirit . . . crying and cutting himself with stones', he is able to remove the devils tormenting the man and transfer them to the swine, who stampede over a cliff and into the sea. Huxley returned to the story again and again, whether in disputations with Gladstone or Henry Wace of King's College, or just as a neat example of how Christianity encouraged a credulous state of mind. If Huxley drew a mental parallel with his own daughter's problems, he would have noted the implication that hysterical states like Marian's were attributed to demonic possession; moreover, if he read to the end of the chapter of Mark, he would have encountered Jesus' miraculous restoration of the apparently dead twelve-year-old daughter of a synagogue official. This biblical teaching was just too close to the bone, and Huxley wrestled angrily with it for the rest of his life.

Nor was the Bible the only place where Huxley found stories of possessed and recovered daughters. Several of his essays on the relationship between Christianity and science reflect on the history of religious credulity through the ages, among them 'The Value of Witness to the Miraculous' (1889). Here Huxley explores the myth making around the Emperor Charlemagne, derived partly from an obscure work, *The History of the Translation of the Blessed Martyrs of Christ, SS. Marcellinus and Petrus*, written in the ninth century by Eginhard, a former courtier. Among Eginhard's stories was that of 'a possessed maiden' of sixteen, brought to the basilica of the martyrs to be exorcised, and who speaks 'not in the tongue of the barbarians', but in Latin, a language she has never used before. According to the story, the voice coming from within her is a demon's, but the episode ends when 'the girl, by the power of Christ and the merits of the blessed martyrs, as it were waking from sleep, rose up quite well, to the astonishment of all present'.[65] Nor were all Huxley's examples ancient and obscure: the Quaker George Fox's autobiography provided another instance of 'a distracted woman, under a doctor's hand, with her hair let loose all about her ears'. Fox tells how he intervened to prevent the doctor from forcibly bleeding the woman, 'for they could not touch the spirit in her by which she was tormented'; he spoke to her, bidding her be quiet and still: 'And the Lord's power settled her mind and she mended.' It was clear to Huxley that certain kinds of illness – 'classes of disease in which malingering is possible or hysteria presumable' – had been particularly responsive to the restorative powers of Christian healers.[66] 'Hysteria' was Marian's disease, but the Huxleys had called in Charcot, not a priest; the near miss with Freud is one of those tantalising historical moments that could have created rich intellectual fusion. If it had, Marian Huxley Collier might have preceded 'Anna O' and the other early cases of hysteria on whom Freud collaborated with Josef Breuer, and Huxley's evolutionary science and attacks on Christianity taken a new turn from their collision with the experimental science of psychoanalysis. Marian exhibited many of the same symptoms as Anna O, including paralysis and visual disturbances; Anna was also said by Breuer to be 'passionately fond' of her father, whom she nursed through his last illness.[67] As it was, Marian's own failed motherhood – first through the miscarriage, and then from inability to bond with her daughter Joyce – points to a likely diagnosis of postnatal depression, at least for the later and more intensified stage of her illness. Huxley's devoted, if anguished, fatherhood forms a poignant contrast with his daughter's complete rejection of her role as mother; while his 'grandfatherhood' of Joyce was performed with the delight and care he had shown towards his own children. Two years after Marian's death, Huxley accompanied his youngest daughter Ethel to Norway so that she could become John Collier's second wife, in breach of the Deceased Wife's Sister legislation back home. Even in death, Marian was making extraordinary demands on her father and causing domestic upheaval, though this second marriage to a Huxley daughter was at least stable and successful.

The deaths of these four children – Annie Darwin, Minnie Hooker, Noel Huxley and Marian Collier – caused the worst emotional crises of each scientific father's experience of fatherhood. Their home lives afterwards were a matter of retrenchment, self-repression, resigned agnosticism and new directions in their work. They remained interested in their surviving children, but with lowered expectations: the special genius of each family seemed to have gone, and the excited, irrational hopes that were pinned on exceptional children were now more subdued. Narrowly missing Freud, both Huxley and Darwin were distressed by evidence of a family determinism driving the destinies of their children, but they saw it predominantly in evolutionary rather than psychological terms. Together with Hooker, they exchanged ideas about good and bad inheritance as it affected the children they had left. If daughters like Annie, Marian and Minnie had seemed too fragile for this world, the sons raised concerns of another kind in their state of motiveless lethargy. While Darwin's cousin Francis Galton confidently asserted his theories of hereditary genius in families like the Darwins and Hookers, the reality seemed somewhat different: in fact more akin to the problems experienced by other energetic fathers such as Dickens, Macready, Thomas and Matthew Arnold, and Kingsley, whose sons appeared to lack their fathers' drive and ambition.[68] Hooker, with self-conscious humour, overtly made the link between his paternal concerns and Darwin's evolutionary theory. 'My boy Willy is back from school, a standing protest against the "Origin of Species"', he complained to Darwin in 1862. 'I do not know one quality of my wife's or my own that he inherits.' What upset him most was his son's lack of passion for anything; even the others, in whom he could trace more family likeness, had no talent for music: 'The most wonderful thing to me is that not one has an atom of ear, & whereas I could sing in tune at 3 years old, I do not find that these have the smallest ear for music, or care – to hear it.' Darwin had already tried to reassure him when Hooker first raised his concerns about this eldest son (only nine in 1862): 'A child from such ancestry must lose the too great volatility, which seems the sole failing', Darwin insisted.[69] William Hooker eventually had a successful career as a civil servant in the India Office, and his father recovered his faith in the logic of heredity, except as it surfaced in fiction. Discussing Gaskell's *North and South* (1855) with Darwin he asked: 'How could such imbecile parents have such a child as Margaret?'[70]

A similar story unfolded with nearly all the sons in the three families. 'When you & I were five and twenty, my pet, there was a sort of go in both of us, which I do not observe in any of our children', a disappointed Huxley reminded his wife.[71] In fact two predominant patterns of behaviour seemed to emerge in the next generation: male inertia on the one hand, and female exhibitionism on the other. Nor was Marian the only one of the Huxley children to act unpredictably: his fourth daughter Nettie, who had once modelled for her sister, was painted by John Singer Sargent sharing a punt and an umbrella with Joseph Comyns Carr, gazing intently into his downcast eyes. Having married a picture restorer, she sang her way round Europe with her daughter, another Marian, in tow. As late as 1922, her nephew Aldous Huxley still dreaded the noise and tumult of her visits, relieved that for once 'she is in a very calm and piano mood, so that she is quite an agreeable companion'.[72]

So far as Darwin was concerned, the 'hereditary' argument could be used both ways: either as a scourge to blame himself (as with his weak stomach), or as a means of comfort – that good ancestry will 'out' – though this was a line he took more often with his friends than with himself. Although he avoided blaming Emma for any constitutional defects in their children, he worried intensely about the genetic implications of their cousin marriage. Given that so much of his research was concerned with reproduction of the strongest 'individuals' (as he often calls animal and plant species in *The Origin of Species*), it was inevitable that he would look inwards and worry about his own contribution to the family gene pool. His son George, pursuing his own research with inmates of lunatic asylums, and citing his father's experiments on the inbreeding of plants, cautiously concluded that there were some grounds 'for asserting that various maladies take an easy hold of the offspring of consanguineous marriages'.[73] Gwen Raverat's observations of life at Down as a grandchild confirm a mixture of hereditary and imitative behaviour as being responsible for the generally debilitated atmosphere in the Darwin household.

A corrective form of education was their best hope. With so many sons to place in public life, the three fathers shared their concerns about the available educational opportunities, and deplored the emphasis on rote learning of the classics. While Huxley tried to turn his daughters into artists, Darwin employed Henrietta as a critic and proofreader of his work, and Hooker urged his youngest daughter Grace to read Huxley's *Elements of Physiology* and acquire useful nursing skills (his other daughter Harriet became a botanical illustrator), Darwin encouraged his sons to become scientists. The challenge was to find a school and a university course that would lead to a career without forcing their sons into a programme of alienating dry study. Darwin alternated between allowing his eldest son William to do what he wanted, and directing him to take up the offer of a bank position in Southampton before he had completed his Cambridge degree. As a father he clearly had considerable power in deciding his son's destiny. 'The more I think of it, the more clear I am that you had better go to Christ Coll. so I will write & enter you tomorrow', he announced in February 1858.[74] Darwin often sounds tired, puzzled and faintly irritated by the available forms of educational training for his sons, and was gratified if they took an interest in something else, such as butterflies or heraldry. After reading a pamphlet (1860) by educational theorist Dr Neil Arnott, which became *A Survey of Human Progress* (1861), Darwin agreed with him about 'the dreadful waste of time, on the dead languages', but somewhat disingenuously added:

I really have no suggestions or criticisms worth giving it would indeed be presumptuous to think that I had, for I have never thought much about Human Progression or on the all important subject of Education – I can, however, say from my own personal experience with my five Boys that it is surprising how very early in life they take *vivid* interest in & understand something of Natural Philosophy.[75]

His sons were employed at an early age in helping Darwin with his experiments, mostly by collecting specimens or reporting on phenomena they had seen. While William was asked to look out for striped horses in Norfolk, and sent home camera lucida drawings of Lythum twigs and pollens, the younger ones began pursuing their own interests in plants and insects. By 1859, Darwin was boasting that he now had 'five Entomological sons! For Skimp [Horace] has begun with great energy to collect Beetles'.[76] Four years later, Horace was 'the Natural Selection Hero',[77] because of an astute remark he had made on the behaviour of adders. Unlike Huxley, however, Darwin never felt the need to proselytise about education. Avoiding public confrontation here as in all other aspects of his life, he quietly encouraged his sons in small-scale scientific research at home in a form that would advance his own work, and guide them towards worthwhile careers.

Hooker's experience as a father of a growing family was different again. Widowed in his fifties, when his first wife Frances Henslow died in 1874 leaving him with six children aged between twenty-one and six, Hooker felt unable to manage the children on his own, and married a widow, Hyacinth Symonds, with whom he had two more sons, Joseph (1877–1940) and Richard (1885–1950). Fathering his last child at sixty-eight, Hooker thus returned to the early stages of childcare at an age when his friends were engaging with their first grandchildren. While Darwin and Huxley could afford to be more relaxed with children at one remove from themselves, Hooker continued his policy of earnestly educating his two youngest offspring about natural history. At his children's parties he had already enjoyed masquerading as a lion ('and a very fine lion he made', Leonard Huxley remembers); the lion games continued with his second family, his beard representing a shaggy mane, 'whence their pet names for one another, the Old Lion and the Little Lion, regularly used in the letters'.[78] The so-called 'Lion Letters', typed transcriptions of which are preserved in the Library of Kew Gardens, read like gentler versions of Charles Kingsley's attempts to educate his children by making them look at everything around them. Lacking Kingsley's hectoring energy, they are nevertheless the persistent efforts of an ageing father to encourage an enquiring frame of mind in the next generation.

Addressing his son by variants of 'My dear little Lion', and signing himself 'Most affectionate OLD LION', Hooker assiduously tells him all the facts and figures, history and geography of the places he visits while his son is at home or school. Joseph is ten when his father informs him of the Roman origins of Cirencester, and the way Roman houses were heated: 'the underneath space for hot air was called the hypocaust, a word I will explain when we meet'. From his home in Sunningdale, Berkshire (known as 'The Camp') he educates Joseph about rainfall averages, telling him that the amount falling that month 'is more than twice as much as last year when only 1.03 fell and in 1886 1.14 fell'. A concern for accuracy and close study characterises these letters, perhaps recalling Hooker's anxiety about his eldest son William's lack of dynamism as a teenager. When Joseph duly responded with accounts of the 'big trees at Pendock' – the home of his maternal grandfather, the geologist William Symonds – Hooker sent back more facts and figures: 'The Elm must have grown very fast to have been so big as 23 feet in girth in 145 years; for, as only one ring of wood is formed every year, the tree must be 145 years old. Hence it was a seedling in Queen Anne's reign! did you think of that?'[79]

When the inevitable happened and Joseph did less well at school than his father hoped (a letter of 1890 condoles with him on narrowly missing 'an A–'), understanding remarks followed. These can be compared with Gladstone's disappointment whenever one of his sons missed a first at Oxford, or Matthew Arnold's with his sons' persistent failures at school. Hooker was decidedly more philosophical: 'I was so often disappointed at School or College at not getting so high a place as I hoped & looked for, that I can well sympathise with others in this respect', he told his 'dear Cub' (as he was now calling the overgrown little Lion). 'Such disappointments teach us patience & resignation . . .' (30 October 1890).

It would be inaccurate to generalise too sweepingly about the experiences of Darwin, Hooker and Huxley as fathers. Their personal circumstances were, for a start, significantly different. While Darwin and Hooker came from privileged, gentlemanly backgrounds, Huxley had to make his own way into a profession and a class that he was instrumental in creating even as he was trying to enter it. While Darwin married a cousin, and Hooker the daughter of a well-known scientist and father figure, Huxley found his wife in Australia. As their lives and careers developed, Darwin became more reclusive and Huxley more visible and vocal, campaigning not just on Darwin's behalf but also for changes to the school curriculum, or the questioning of biblical miracle. As fathers within each family, their roles similarly adjusted and fluctuated, in keeping with the extended age range and changing priorities: 'the lodger', 'the old Lion', the scientific observer, the invalid and recluse, 'Pater' (pronounced 'Patter' by the Huxley children), or simply the 'F' by which Emma Darwin referred to her husband in letters to her children. All these names signify not just a relaxed self-mockery in the fathers, but also the full spectrum of behaviour allowed by their position in the family. As a group they stand out in distinctive ways from the other fathers discussed in this study. Mild and tolerant with their children, if not with scientific opponents, they began with lower expectations than Thomas Arnold, Gladstone or Benson – perhaps because religious idealism was never part of their make-up. They were no great disciplinarians in the home, leaving the details of domestic management largely to their wives, with whom their children appear to have enjoyed a steady and unproblematic relationship. Huxley with his drawings, and Hooker with his lion games, come across as preferring to be playmates with their children, while George Darwin recalls noisy games of 'roundabouts' and punting about the drawing room using 'microscope chairs' from the study and walking sticks: 'However hard my father was at his work we certainly never restrained ourselves in our romps about the house.'[80] For all their emphasis on the altruism of scientific research and their pursuit of 'truth', the three fathers could also be self-absorbed, emotionally and physically volatile, and often too busy or distracted to focus for long on the growing children who bustled and scrambled outside the closed door of the study.

Undaunted by the mostly negative example of paternal behaviour in the animal kingdom, the scientists were nevertheless some of the most well-intentioned and kindly fathers of their generation, the conscientious upbringing of their children an integral part of their wider pursuit of truth, integrity and self-improvement.[81] Their own fatherly-brotherly alternative family survived the traumas of their real families, and proved a supportive resource for the balancing of objective research with mutual affection. If evolution worked on a personal scale, their discussions of fatherhood imply, the next generation would benefit from the mistakes and insights of their parents. 'We shall try to make him a better man than his father', Huxley said of his first son Noel at fifteen months old.[82] The tragedy for the fathers discussed in this chapter lay in their inability to guarantee that these special children of the next generation would live and thrive as their evolutionary perfection suggested they should.

CHAPTER 6

Death comes for the Archbishop
(and Prime Minister)

We were all together as a happy family, at the Altar.[1]

This final chapter is about the Bensons and Gladstones, two families of adult children whose struggles towards emotional independence were at least partly exacerbated by their relationship with their fathers. Still less were the fathers able to let go of their children, whether in death or life, and so we return to the agonising grief of two fathers whose attempts to rationalise their relationship with God were severely challenged by their inability to come to terms with a child's loss. Because of the father's dominant personality and high-profile position in public life – as Chancellor of the Exchequer, Prime Minister or Archbishop of Canterbury – the family revolved around his needs, and became part of his working household. As H. C. G. Matthew argues, 'The Gladstone family was an integral part of a Gladstone administration'; while A. C. Benson commented that Benson's family life 'played so large a part in his whole career that it is difficult to imagine him without it. He always wanted as many as possible of his family to be with him.'[2] Most of the Gladstone children took on secretarial work for their father, and the daughters helped run the various offices and households at Downing Street, Carlton House Terrace and Hawarden. Even at ten, his third daughter Mary promised 'that if please God I am alive when you are old I trust I shall be your help and comfort'.[3] Attempts to leave the family fold were discouraged; those who married did so in their thirties and forties, and most continued to live with, or close to, their ageing parents. Even Henry Neville Gladstone, who worked in India for fourteen years, was employed by family business connections, and became Gladstone's Private Secretary and Lord of the Manor at Hawarden. Only Agnes made a clean break by marrying the Headmaster of Wellington College, though she remained in regular contact with affairs at Hawarden. In the family of Archbishop

Benson, where there was a similar prioritising of the father's needs, none of the children married, and there were no grandchildren.

Although Benson's sons were sent away to school and university, and eventually found places to live away from their parents' home, their compulsion to keep retelling and reassessing their childhood and family life in one auto/biography after another suggests that while they might have left home physically, they never did emotionally. A. C. Benson, in his *Memories and Friends* (1924), published the year before his death, recalls the very specific 'emotional pulse agitating the atmosphere' when he first left for boarding school in 1872, 'as though I were passing out of a sheltered nest into something adventurous and even perilous, which might blur the old innocence and diminish the familiar loyalties'.[4] As young adults, all the children experimented for a while with more independent and adventurous lifestyles, but they also suffered from depressive illness inherited from their father, and returned to wrestle in different ways with his emotional legacy. Benson's relationship with his children was intense and anxious, and even after his death he over-shadowed the lives of Arthur and Maggie as they edited his work, and compiled a *Life and Letters*. His youngest son, Robert Hugh, who became a Roman Catholic priest, remembered: 'He dominated me completely by his forcefulness, and I felt when he died . . . as if the roof were lifted off the world.'[5] Though the children's friends were welcomed as guests at the official residences, the composer Ethel Smyth recalled that even as a permitted visitor, 'the sight of [Benson's] majestic form approaching the tea-table scattered my wits as an advancing elephant might scatter a flock of sheep'.[6]

With these last two fathers of my study – both of them dying within the final five years of the century – we therefore return to the Victorian patriarchal stereotype I have been trying to dismantle. Both men were towering personalities whose dominance was buttressed by their religious faith and total commitment to the ideal model of the Christian family, albeit through a sexuality they found disturbing and at times uncontrollable. Benson selected his future wife when she was only twelve, and Gladstone notoriously recorded having talked to between eighty and ninety prostitutes in the course of his reforming night time promenades around London, besides forming strange friendships with women such as Laura Thistlethwayte, the exact nature of which continues to puzzle historians.[7] Neither man was exactly a conventional father figure – an underlying sense of guilt and unworthiness disturbed their relations with other people – though both strongly upheld the hierarchical structure of the traditional upper-middle-class patriarchal family. The difference between the two family stories and the way they were managed by the next generation lies in the sharply contrasting responses of the two sets of children. While the Gladstones closed ranks to defend their father from all allegations of domestic tyranny, the Bensons endlessly probed the reasons for their fear of a father they all acknowledged had cared deeply about them.

Both men had been eager to marry and father families. Gladstone's (1809–98) 1839 marriage to Catherine Glynne (1812–1900) produced eight children, of whom six outlived their parents: William Henry, known as 'Willy' (1840–91); Agnes (1842–1931); Stephen, known as 'Stephy' (1844–1920); Catherine Jessy (1845–50); Mary (1847–1927); Helen (1849–1925); Henry Neville (1852–1935); and Herbert John (1854–1930). As Catherine's sister Mary (1813–57), who had married George (1817–76), Fourth Baron Lyttelton, died in 1857, some weeks after giving birth to her twelfth child, the Gladstones in effect became surrogate parents for this additional family of nieces and nephews. Edward White Benson (1829–96) married his younger cousin Mary Sidgwick (1841–1918) in 1859, when she was eighteen. Their six children were Martin (1860–78); Arthur Christopher (1862–1925); Mary Eleanor, known as 'Nellie' (1863–90); Margaret, known as 'Maggie' (1865–1916); Edward Frederic (the novelist E. F. Benson, 1867–1940); and Robert Hugh (1871–1914). Gladstone recommended Benson for the preferment of Archbishop of Canterbury in 1882, and it was while the Bensons were staying with the Gladstones at Hawarden in October 1896 that the Archbishop suddenly collapsed in church and died shortly afterwards, curiously fulfilling Gladstone's own notion of the ideal death, which was 'To die in Church', though 'not', he added conscientiously, 'a time to disturb worshippers'.[8] Although the two families' lives were so closely intertwined only in the final tragic stages, they had known each other for many years; Benson respected Gladstone's 'Churchmanship', as his son Arthur put it, and while he often disagreed with him politically, their friendship 'was a very deep-seated sentiment in my father's mind'.[9] Their children's experiences of being raised by an intense father and a somewhat more relaxed and lenient mother reveal how each household struggled to accommodate the ramifications of the father's high-profile role, private grief and dramatic outbreaks of personal self-doubt.

Each family had more than one spokesperson in the next generation, but whereas the Bensons repeatedly analysed their own childhood and wrote memoirs, biographies and autobiographies evaluating what they all saw as a disturbed and uneasy upbringing, the Gladstones wrote far more sparingly and positively of their parents, and sound ungrudging of the amount of time devoted to their care. Negotiations among the siblings as to who took over from whom, especially when a daughter married, were carried out by letter, away from the public eye. The children who struggled most with their parents were also the most reticent: Willy, Stephen and Helen all made significant personal sacrifices, as did Mary, the 'home daughter', but only Mary published recollections, and declared it a privilege to have lived with her parents both before and after her own marriage.[10] Stephen was less easily consoled, making more than one attempt to become a missionary in India, but his father persuaded him to stay on at home. 'The whole idea of severing you from the charge, let alone the House, is a wrench, and a rend; and separates bone and marrow', Gladstone told him in 1893, when his son was nearly fifty. Instead, he offered Stephen responsibility for establishing a 'Clergy House' through the St Deiniol's Trust, which he hoped to set in motion. While accepting that Stephen must ultimately be guided by God, Gladstone nonetheless pleaded: '*Could not you* perhaps undertake the quiet & cautious modelling of all this? Could not you become the first head of my Trust?' Looking forward to much 'sweet Counsel upon it', Gladstone threw in a promise of 'not *less* than £300 a year', which Stephen dutifully accepted.[11]

By contrast, all the Benson children wrote about their family, except Nellie and Martin, who both died young, and their memories were embedded in a variety of genres, from the formal *Life* of his father by A.C. Benson, to relaxed and entertaining recollections.[12] Each family subsequently faced the anti-Victorian backlash in the early twentieth century against the great names of the period, and the 'debunking' trend established by Samuel Butler's *The Way of All Flesh* (1903), Edmund Gosse's *Father and Son* (1907) and Lytton Strachey's *Eminent Victorians* (1918). While the public developed an appetite for thrilling stories of paternal bullying, and in the Bensons' case the surviving children wanted to communicate what they saw as a damaged upbringing, the Gladstones presented a united front to protect their father's reputation against libel, and to endorse his good relationship with his children.

Though the differences between the two families will be fully explored later in this chapter, the first thing to establish is how these two monumental public men managed to find space for fatherhood in Downing Street and Lambeth Palace, or indeed in the numerous other houses they inhabited during the year, such as Hawarden or Addington.

One of Gladstone's earliest biographers, G. W. E. Russell, claimed that 'In order to form the highest and the truest estimate of Mr Gladstone's character it is necessary to see him at home.'[13] The symbolic importance of Gladstone's homes was complicated by the fact that he never actually owned Hawarden Castle, which passed from his brother-in-law Sir Stephen Glynne directly to the eldest Gladstone son, Willy. Although he lived there as 'an honoured guest' and his brother-in-law presided at the head of the table, everything about Hawarden was ordered to suit his habits, and its key features acquired names associated with him. His special library, for example, was known as 'The Temple of Peace', and the so-called 'Weg Walk', designed by him as a scenic route from the castle to the church, was marked by a doorway bearing his initials. By contrast, his passion for tree felling (a gift to political cartoonists), symbolised by an expanding collection of axes, publicised his image as a performer of manly labour. 'His grand maxim is *never to be doing nothing*', proclaimed an anecdotal biographer.[14] Even at meals, as a relative commented, dialogue over the breakfast table could mimic 'the weighty argument, the incisive repartee, of a miniature House of Commons debate', while in the evening, once three people had emerged for dinner, Gladstone called 'Quorum' as the signal to go in and eat.[15] As for his other houses, he never seemed to settle in them, shifting from 13 to 11 Carlton House Terrace in London, and for a time owning a lease on a house in Harley Street, before moving out to Dollis Hill. As four-times Prime Minister and Chancellor of the Exchequer (he was both between 1800 and 1882), Gladstone was constantly changing residences; with their mother often away from London – at Hawarden or the Lytteltons' home, Hagley Hall – the Gladstone household was essentially decentred and in transit for much of his active political life.

The Benson family home was also frequently on the move, following the father's promotions from schoolmaster to high-profile churchman. From Wellington College, where he was Headmaster, they moved first to Lincoln (1872), then Truro (1877) and finally to Lambeth Palace (1883). His son Arthur recounts each move into a larger and grander residence in terms of his father's making a personal imprint – a makeshift tennis court, rescued furniture, an enlarged room or more pictures on the walls. At his official country residence, Addington, the bedrooms were named after places personally connected with him, such as Wellington, and his Christmas sermons incorporated stories of family life. Arthur recalls his father's appearance in the pulpit on these occasions as 'the most perfect mixture of fatherliness and dignity'. At Lincoln, being in a more subordinate position, as Chancellor, he seemed less dominant: 'He did not originate, control, and sway the destinies of the place; and this I think we subtly or unconsciously felt.'[16] As John Tosh observes, Benson's increasing eminence in itself changed the atmosphere of his households: 'The Benson family is a striking instance of how the Victorian father's exclusive access to the public domain made him seem larger than life within the home.'[17] After Benson's death, 'Tremans', his wife's first private home since her marriage in 1859, was also notably a female house, dominated by Mary Benson, her companion Lucy Tait, Maggie, and Beth, the loyal family nurse.

The notion of active domestic fatherhood happening in an official residence may be less alien to us since the birth of Leo Blair (the first baby for 150 years to be born to a serving Prime Minister) and the advent of the Gordon Browns, but as Stuart C. Aitken has noticed, 'Fathering histories remain hidden because they are awkward, rarely fitting the geography of public ventures and power.'[18] Gladstone's children were mostly grown up by the time he became Prime Minister, but his granddaughter Dorothy Drew was remembered as creating 'a charming note of juvenility amid the official dinginess of 10, Downing Street'.[19]

His relationships with his children are of course mentioned by his biographers, but they function mainly as minor interruptions to the more important flow of political analysis. This was something Herbert Gladstone recognised when he published his memoirs of his father in 1928. Dissatisfied with John Morley's official biography (1903) because it 'left little room for the domestic life, which in the matter of time far exceeded the days given by Mr Gladstone to public affairs', Herbert boasted of having lived in his father's house from his own birth until Gladstone's death.[20] Aitken claims – not entirely fairly – that the narrative of Gladstone's care for his dying daughter Jessy in 1850 tends to be relegated to a footnote or take second place to discussion of political issues. 'Gladstone the father is hidden from his lauded public history', argues Aitken, 'because masculinity, as a symbolic and mythic form of identity, is overtly determined for its coherence upon external public discourse'.[21] Aitken's argument is influenced by Thomas Laqueur's self-confessedly 'grumpy, polemical' essay, 'The facts of Fatherhood', which, in also citing the displacement of Jessy Gladstone's story, comments: 'Fatherhood, insofar as it has been thought about at all, has been regarded as a backwater of the dominant history of public power.'[22] In fact one of Gladstone's best known biographers, Roy Jenkins, suggests that Jessy's death 'was certainly a major contributing cause of

Figure 4 W. E. Gladstone with his granddaughter Dorothy Drew, remembered for creating 'a charming note of juvenility amid the official dinginess of 10, Downing Street'.

Gladstone's being around the middle of the century in a state of what Morley described as "extreme perturbation", and what others might regard as nearly unhinged'.[23]

There is no doubt that Gladstone's middle decades, in which he agonised over Jessy's death and the illnesses and moral development of his other children while he began scourging himself for impure feelings inspired by his conversations with prostitutes, form more than just a colourful interlude in his developing political career. Gladstone's diaries and letters show that care for his children was closely interwoven with the political business of the day. When Willy was just four months old, Gladstone prided himself on being able to work with the baby in his room: 'I was thinking today how well I could look at baby when my head is at work, & feel the love to him as warmly as when unoccupied, yet without distraction.'[24] Once Willy could read, Gladstone sent him brief letters signed 'your loving Fa-ther', spelt so as to break up the big words. 'I went yesterday to Wind-sor where the Queen lives', he explained on one occasion; on another, he was 've-ry sorry to leave Agnes naughty'.[25] Gladstone was nothing if not a vigilant father, who always had one eye on home concerns. He regularly found time to teach the older children Latin and what he called 'H.S.' (Holy Scripture); he coached them for confirmation, and wrote special 'papers' to help Willy with his Latin and religious self-examination, or exhort his sons on the eve of going to Oxford. When Willy broke down in his Eton interview, Gladstone noted: 'his sorrows cut me to the soul'.[26] If family commitments clashed with political business, Gladstone did his best to manage both. On Stephen's christening day in May 1844, when 'Business pressed hard upon the sacred Office', he still attended the House of Commons, saw Sir Robert Peel, dined at Count St Aulaire's to celebrate King Louis Philippe's birthday and 'worked on papers at night'.[27] In their childish letters to their father, the small Gladstones respectfully thanked him for finding time for them in the midst of his work. If the relationship between public and private was strained for all the fathers previously discussed in this study, the difficulties of sustaining the father's role in public office were magnified on a massive scale for Gladstone and Benson, as Prime Minister and Archbishop: the one the human embodiment of British Parliamentary democracy, and the other the Church of England.

Gladstone and Benson were alike in upholding two core values in their upbringing of their children: those of Christian self-discipline and hard work. These clearly derived from their roots in the ethos of 'Christian manliness', endorsed both by Evangelicals and Anglicans, through developing permutations over the middle of the century. For both men, this was best demonstrated within the family, where they assumed a fatherly guidance of at least one sibling; both also idealised a dead sister who became their model of perfect womanhood: chaste, pure, feminine and saintly in Gladstone's case, more vivid and fairy-like in Benson's. As the first Wellington College Headmaster, Benson preached sermons with themes like 'Escaping the Average', 'Strength of Will' and 'No one else can do our Duty'. In a particularly revealing sermon called 'Thanking the Father', he shows how closely his notion of fatherhood was bound up with his image of the Deity. Although the 'Father' referred to here is God, Benson compares the kind of thankfulness one feels to Him with that felt for a human father in response to his kindness:

Anyone who has experienced that in his youth, who knows the evils from which it has kept him, the confidence with which he could confess sins to him, the assurance that nothing which concerned him would be uninteresting to the father, or the fatherly friend; who knows how he has turned back in thankfulness for unlooked-for, unexpected, gifts, provisions, arrangements, to find that the father had never once imagined that he was doing anything but what came quite naturally to do; such a one knows what is meant by "giving thanks to the Father".[28]

As an indication of the way Benson envisaged both fatherliness and the normal duties of a father, this statement shows how invasive an interest he thought the father should take in his child. In its reference to confessing sins, being protected from evils and having nothing to say that would be 'uninteresting' to the father, Benson's sermon maps out a role as confessor and intimate counsellor that he certainly attempted to perform with his eldest son Martin. It was perhaps hardly surprising that he wooed his future wife, Mary Sidgwick, in the manner of something between a schoolmaster and an elder brother, urging her towards active '*Self-Formation* in earnest'. In 1849, when she was only eight, he noted that she 'passed a good examination with me in Latin Grammar, to the end of Pronouns'. A much later, but undated, letter, reminding her of a promise to 'get up' marked parts of 'Blunt's Reformation', is signed 'Ever Your Most Harsh Taskmaster'. As John Henry Blunt's *A History of the English Reformation* was not published until 1868, Mary must have been a married woman with a family of children when she was still taking instruction of this kind.[29]

Gladstone's father lived into his late eighties in 1851, but following the deaths of his favourite elder sister, Anne, in 1827 and his mother in 1835, Gladstone appointed himself his younger sister Helen's moral and spiritual guardian. As Leonore Davidoff and Anne Isba have shown, this was a long and troubled relationship that culminated disastrously for Gladstone when Helen, after years of mental and emotional instability, formally converted to Roman Catholicism. So far as he was concerned, she seemed to embody the full spectrum of temptations open to women who were not properly integrated into a family.[30] By the time he had children of his own, he had therefore, like Benson, developed a habit of giving orders at home and expecting to be obeyed. His letters listed points for consideration, and he gladly proffered detailed advice on all difficult decisions about jobs and careers. Finding a God-given vocation was the burden of his advice to his children, with birthdays (including his own) an occasion for moral stocktaking, blessing and encouragement to further effort.

Gladstone was admired and recognised in his own day as an exemplary father figure, but often with a hint of incongruity: for example by the journalist W. T. Stead who, in a lengthy two-part review of Gladstone's achievements for the *Review of Reviews* (1892), described his family life as 'one of the most beautiful domesticities of our time'. Stead added that 'he is not in any way overbearing or domineering. He is very freely criticised in his own family, and, although his children agree with him in the main, there is abundant scope for divergence of views and details.' The article, intended to highlight the 'heroic Mr Gladstone', is illustrated with a mixture of photographs, prints and cartoons, including a serious portrait of Gladstone holding his baby granddaughter Dorothy, contrasting on the opposite page with a cartoon from *Judy*, headed 'An Improvised Nursery Rhyme'. In it, a jovial-looking Gladstone gives Dorothy rides on his foot (as Herbert Gladstone attests to his having done with his own children), while promising her in a song written in baby language, 'Grampa soon will fro' away / His pesky politics, / An' 'pend his Easter holiday / In teaching petzy tricks' ('Petz' was the name of his dog, also shown in the cartoon). Stead's commentary insists that far from being obsessed with his own career, Gladstone had repeatedly 'striven to rid himself of political embarrassments, and he is never so happy as when he is romping with his grandchild'.[31]

Benson was similarly admired for the quality of his domestic life, knowledge of which emerged with the publication in 1899 of his son Arthur's *Life*. He was already known, like Gladstone, to be what the *Saturday Review* called a 'remarkable personality', and other periodicals picked up on his handsome good looks and general charisma. F. W. Farrar, writing in the *Contemporary Review*, recalled his 'sunny charm and geniality of fatherliness and brotherliness which characterised his demeanour to all with whom he was thrown'. The weighty biography, bursting with letters and diary extracts, reinforced the sense of a man who sought and enjoyed his children's company, as well as his fellow churchmen's. 'He was devoted to his family', the *Saturday* confirmed, noting how often he referred in his diaries to the deaths of his children. 'He loved no society better than that of his family, and even under the pressure of the Primacy found time and thought for intimate fellowship with them.' In the reviewer's opinion, his domestic life had not only given him the strength to do his work, but had also been 'a most salutary influence on his character'.[32]

Whereas earlier chapters have shown that many fathers felt guilty about their genetic or economic legacy to their children, Benson and Gladstone often felt unworthy of their office, of their families' respect or of God's mercy. Their religious belief, though heartfelt, was found wanting when faced with family tragedy, and compounded the natural grief of bereavement with the additional strain of spiritual inadequacy. Like Thomas Arnold, both men searched their children continually for signs of moral backsliding or failure, but found it difficult to understand the cutting short of promising young lives of active service. Both men typically measured their children's worth at least partly in terms of the kind of work they could contribute to the improvement of society; 'nor is any life worth living that has not a purpose, or that is not devoted from day to day to its accomplishment', Helen Gladstone was reminded on her twenty-first birthday.[33] While Gladstone impressed on Willy his weighty responsibilities as owner of the Hawarden estate, Benson's eager identification with his eldest son Martin, and his attempts to turn him into a model of modern Christian manhood, became the passion of his life in the 1860s and 1870s. Both fathers drove their eldest sons hard, by a barrage of letters fired at them through school and university, in response to every detailed circumstance of their lives. Gladstone even discouraged the morning reading of newspaper reports on the Crimean War as being 'like eating a quantity of marmalade before dinner'.[34] As it happened, both fathers outlived their eldest sons, who each died of a brain disease. What emerges most strikingly from a mountain of earnest letters is the fathers' overwhelming need for their sons to distinguish themselves by an exceptional dedication to meaningful work, and to become the moral and intellectual leaders of their generation. In the event, however, it was Gladstone's loss of a four-year-old daughter that nearly pushed him over the edge.

WORK UNFINISHED: MARTIN AND NELLIE BENSON

Benson's memoir of his dead eldest son irrupts suddenly into the humdrum rhythm of church affairs noted in the pages of a T. J. and J. Smith's official octavo diary for 1871. When Martin died, his father abandoned the normal mode of diary entry and began a kind of written stream-of-consciousness that exposes the tortured nature of his thwarted ambitions interwoven with his yearning love for his son. As prophetic afterthoughts occurred, he interleaved them on the facing pages. The chronology therefore jumps about, like Margaret Oliphant's autobiographical narrative of her sons' deaths, and goes into reverse as he remembers signs of Martin's precociousness as a child and a young man whose companionship in the holidays became increasingly essential to him.[35] There was a memorable scene when Martin walked alone in the fading light, and another (recorded elsewhere in the same diary) when father and son shared prayers on horseback in the rain at Gwennap Pit, famous as a preaching place for John Wesley. The need to turn Martin's life into a series of symbolic scenes contends throughout the diary narrative with the intrusions of reality: the knowledge that Martin never quite made it as the top scholar that his father wanted him to be.

Opening with a statement of his death on 17 February 1878, and a tribute to his nature as 'all sweet and without reproach', Benson then swings immediately into a defence of Martin's failure to come first in the Goddard scholarship competition, 'the chief honour of Winchester College'. Dr Ridding, the Headmaster, 'told me that he had come out all but first, – "first with one examiner actually, and only after revision placed a 'little second' ".'[36] Even in the raw early stages of grief, such things mattered intensely to Benson. Nor was academic success enough: he noted that as a volunteer in the Rifle Corps 'at Xmas [Martin] was 5th or 6th in the Prize Shooting, gaining 47 marks against the Winners [*sic*] 53' (fo. 104). Benson as a father sounds like the Headmaster he had been at Wellington: he entered into all the details of boy life at school, and its tests and rankings engaged his emotions far more than they did the somewhat languid Martin's.

The diary then proudly recounts anecdote after anecdote in which Martin says or does something remarkable for his age. At two he could identify Jesus in a painting by Raphael; at seven or eight he was incredulous at the notion of 'idle boys' ('but *why* are they idle?' he asked his delighted father: fo. 103). The climax of the diary memorial, however, is the deathbed scene, which Benson restarts and retells, lingering over his conviction that he saw Martin greeting 'a circle of holy ones' in the next life who were invisible to his father. 'Some time after that', he remembered, 'he again pointed intelligently towards the middle of the cieling [*sic*] of his room – and motioned me to look – my boy, I could see nothing' (fo. 123). At the crucial moment, Benson's special powers as a spiritual leader failed him and he was left earthbound and bewildered.

Figure 5 Edward White Benson, Archbishop of Canterbury; a striking profile
taken by the Queen's photographer, William Downey.

The increasing desperation of Benson's narrative isolates him from the
more accepting and practical response of the nurse and the boy's mother
('My dearest wife understood it all more quickly – better – more sweetly
than I': fo. 125). With only his son's school possessions to remind him of
his bodily existence, Benson is left turning over Martin's blotting case and
books, and sorrowing over the promise of good work lost. Like Archibald
Tait's for his daughters, his prayers had proved fruitless, and Benson
mulls over his presumptuous belief that it was 'inconceivable' that Martin
would not be spared to fulfil his promise. 'Among all the forms of broken
hope none is so recurrent as the thought of work unfinished – unbegun,

so beautifully prepared yet untouched', he lamented (fo. 137). He had presumably forgotten George Arthur's passionate speech in *Tom Brown's Schooldays* where he too laments that 'there is no work in the grave', only to be granted a vision of the dead toiling 'at some great work', which will be his too when he comes to die.[37] Instead, Benson noted other instances of local sons lost or gone to the bad, such as 'the ghastly wreck of a clergyman's son' encountered in Boscastle that June (fo. 280), and a Hamlet-like dialogue with a bereaved stonemason working on Martin's grave at Winchester: 'He was exalted & refined by his sorrow so that I looked on him with reverence – And how slow am I to learn what he had learnt at once' (fo. 322). Everyone appeared to understand and accept their loss more willingly than Benson did himself, despite his professional qualifications for rationalising death and giving it meaning. If Martin had been destined to do God's work on a scale unavailable to lesser mortals, Benson remained completely baffled by such a pointless waste of opportunity.

As David Newsome first noted, the family correspondence tells a rather different story.[38] The pressure to succeed began as soon as Martin was shipped off to Temple Grove in September 1870, even his mother – who was generally more concerned about his overall welfare – urging him: 'Mind you tell me what your *place* is – & mind you get to the top as soon as possible.'[39] When the first bad report came through in October, showing that Martin was placed only sixth out of eleven, and had no 'good' grades, she warned him of a disappointed letter winging its way from 'Papa' who will 'dwell on the details' (fo. 19). Papa duly underlined a '<u>poor</u>' in mathematics, and began a series of exhortations to pay attention in class. A week later he heavily underscored '<u>continual inattention in class</u>' (fo. 23). Bribes and sarcasm followed, by way of carrot and stick: if Martin's next report was better they would request an exeat for a home visit (he duly moved up to fourth place); a visit to the zoo must be deserved by hard work, as must a good Christmas box. In still harder mood, Benson jeered unkindly at Martin's spelling mistakes: 'Appareuntly you think it [the word 'apparently'] has something to do with <u>eo</u> "to go"!!!'. The irritable underlinings and multiple exclamation marks engrave Benson's anger into the page. While it would be easy to overstate his repeated outbursts of disappointment in his son, which eventually gave way to a more equal dialogue about the classics and which public school Martin wished to try for, nevertheless what one notices most in this correspondence is Benson's unremitting pressure on his eldest boy to fulfil his own paternal ambitions. In comparison, Mary

Benson's letters must have come as light relief as she chats about the younger children's passion for magnets, and her own attempts to make armour for the family's Christmas charades. When Martin moved to Winchester, she entered anxiously into all the details of initiation rituals, such as the 'kicking down stairs' (fo. 73), perhaps all the more for being a stranger to schoolboy lore, except vicariously, as a headmaster's wife. When both parents ruminated on the symbolic moment of leaving Martin at the school gates, they interpreted it very differently. 'It seems so long since we left you at that green gate, and I do so want to hear from you', his mother yearned as soon as they had deposited him at Temple Grove (fo. 3). Even the gate sounds harsher in his father's message of March 1871 – 'It seems a long time since I left you at the iron wicket' (fo. 32) – with its obvious reminder of Bunyan's *Pilgrim's Progress*, and 'the beginning of a pilgrimage of Truth & Love & Goodness. Don't be afraid of Lions by the way . . .' Though Benson afterwards sanctifies everything associated with him, and the other children – especially Arthur, the closest in age – testified to Martin's apartness and difference, it is clear from the letters that he was no saint, but an intelligent and sensitive boy with normal human failings.

When Benson lost another child, Nellie, who died at the age of twenty-seven during a random outbreak of diphtheria at Addington in 1890, he was distraught, but calmer than at the time of Martin's death. As a girl, she had never embodied her father's messianic hopes for the future, and he identified with her less closely than he did with Martin. Though she too still had useful work to do, it took the form of social care of the poor, not whatever philosophical or 'manly' advances he had expected Martin to make as a leader of the next generation. The terms by which he refers to her are humbler, almost demeaning. 'She was to me really such an unobtrusive instance of a little saintly spirit using *all* its capabilities to help others and to love us with the most daughterly dearness', he explained to a friend, making her into the quiet domestic treasure the rest of her family knew she was not.[40] Her brother Arthur describes her as 'the only one of us, I think, who had no awe of my father. She knew exactly the sort of talk and companionship that he liked, and gave him exactly the sort of open and outspoken affection for which he craved.'[41] Because her manner reflected back to him what he wanted to see, Benson Senior's 'Brief Memoir', appended to her *Streets and Lanes of the City* (1891), which he had privately printed after her death, portrays her as the ideal daughter: capable and energetic, performing voluntary work in the local communities of Lambeth and Addington. Unlike his long memoir of

Martin, which remained unpublished, this is short and formal: a father's admiring recollections of a daughter he can think of sadly but peacefully. Her deathbed farewells to the family are recalled as a series of practical and sensible messages, rather than the spiritual transfiguration that suffused Martin and left his father unenlightened and earthbound, stranded on heaven's threshold. She looks forward to seeing Martin again, and adds, 'with the same eager look of interest in great things which was so familiar to us, "I wonder what it will be like."' Curiosity about the lives of other people was perhaps one of her hallmarks. 'There was no shadow of self-assertion', her father notes approvingly. 'It seemed as if there were no self to be asserted.'[42] This was hardly the view that her surviving brothers took of her, though even Arthur admits that she never seemed to express strong wishes of her own.

In return, Benson himself experienced a mysterious sense of what he called 'self-obliteration' in Marseilles the year after Nellie's death, when Fred was reading aloud from *In Memoriam*, and Benson listening to his children's discussion of the poem, which had been a favourite of his own since the deaths of his mother and sister. 'It was strange to be in, and not be in the least felt to be in my children's tender thinkings', he mused in his diary.[43] It was late in his life and relations with his children to begin withdrawing his influence from scenes of this kind, and the sense of self stubbornly returned when he least wanted it. In Switzerland in 1893, and still pondering God's purpose in removing Nellie, Benson regretted that an act so obviously directed against himself had had 'so little power to change me', while it had permanently altered his response to the mountainous landscape where Nellie had been active and well.[44]

'COME PAPPY COME': GLADSTONE'S LOST CHILDREN

Gladstone learnt rapidly how to be a father. He was moved by his wife's suffering in childbirth, but was pleased by her acceptance of its religious meaning and eagerness for formal thanksgiving. 'Her first wish after it', he observed in a long entry on his eldest son's birth, 'was that I should offer a prayer.'[45] When his second son Stephen was born on Maundy Thursday in 1844, Gladstone prayed that the 'child born on the day of the foundation of the Holy Eucharist be himself from the womb a thank offering to God'.[46] Every important stage of his children's lives was marked by anxious prayer, of which, like Benson, he often felt an unworthy mediator. As the opening quotation of this chapter shows, Gladstone was at his most content when he was engaged in acts of worship with his family around him, sharing Holy Communion at the altar.

Gladstone faced his first serious tussle with God for a child's survival in 1847 when his eldest daughter Agnes (nearly five) became seriously ill with erysipelas, the disease that had killed his mother. In his diary entries on the progression of her illness, he compares Agnes's readiness for the afterlife with his own refusal to give her up with the good grace of a Christian father. 'Her dear and pure and gentle soul wants nothing as it were but to be in the presence of its Lord', he notes at the height of the crisis. By contrast, 'my heart is hard & unquiet & not willing to give back my child'. If the torment of a suffering child was what finally destroyed a father's faith in God – as it was for Huxley, Hooker and Darwin – for Gladstone it was more a trial of his obedience, his willingness to submit to God's will. Unable to blame God, aware of Catherine's calmer acceptance, seven-year-old Willy's superior piety, and even Agnes's own acquiescence, he turned on himself as the source of all that was wrong. 'Everyone behaves well but me', he declares in a miserable journal entry. 'I have a covetous desire for the life of our Agnes', he adds, after reminding himself of all the biblical injunctions to bear whatever God sends, however mysterious its purpose.[47] Whenever his children's lives were in danger Gladstone essentially blamed himself: not as Darwin did, for faulty genes, but for his own failed relationship with God. To modern readers there seems nothing unreasonable about his desperate pleading for his child's life, but for Gladstone his 'desire' and 'covetousness' as a father (words that suggest extremes of need, normally applied to sex or wealth) were in direct conflict with the will of God, the whole underlying purpose of his life. Another forbidden thought for him, equally alien to today's culture, was his awareness of the disturbing beauty of a sick child, as with Archibald Tait watching his daughters succumb to scarlet fever. 'For the eye her beauty in this illness has been a striking and touching sight', he confesses in his journal, instantly censoring himself with 'but that at such a time we must scarcely speak or think of' (Vol. III, p. 652). What was even more mysterious was the exact coincidence between the dates of his mother's illness and death in 1835, and Agnes's near death and recovery from the same illness. Even his sight of the 'cold clear autumnal moon', as a warning symbol, was the same. 'Was it for nothing that God thus drew the lines of two events each piercing inwards to the dividing of soul and body?' (Vol. III, p. 653). Baffled by the interplay of superstition with reason and religion, and his own powerlessness in prayer and science, as well as the doctors', all he could conclude was that 'these things are sent to temper us'.

Gladstone's spiritual interrogations are mixed in his journal entries with physical descriptions of Agnes's inflamed thigh, the 'tympanitic [*sic*] appearance of the bowels' (p. 654), the bathing of her limbs, moving her in bed, and other details that show that he was fully involved in the intimate care of his child: indeed he was brought out of a chapel service on St Matthew's Day (22 September) to move her, and recorded his belief that God had heard his prayers and answered them. Catherine is pictured in the background of his self-absorption, 'on her child's bed soothing her under the guidance of the wonderful instincts of a mother' (p. 654). Apparently without comparable fatherly instincts, Gladstone could only bargain with God for his child's life: he hastily assembled the words of a thanksgiving inscription for a stained glass window in the chapel at Fasque.

With his second daughter, Catherine Jessy, born in 1845, Gladstone was less fortunate. By 1850, when she became ill with meningitis, his sense of personal guilt had intensified. He had begun scourging himself the previous year with a small whip, and his diary entries refer to his 'besetting sin, impurity'. These were thoughts triggered partly by his evening discussions with prostitutes, but also by an awareness of his susceptibility to pornographic literature, which caught his eye in booksellers' shops.[48] Despite a countervailing appetite for religious books, he was still ripe for spiritual despair when Jessy sickened at the end of March. Once again, he asked himself the dreaded question: 'And now O Father can we readily yield her up to Thee?' (Vol. IV, p. 198). Given the total inadequacy of medicine to cure Jessy, he could only watch by her bedside and hope for another miracle like the one that had saved Agnes. Two days before her death on 9 April he felt sufficiently constrained by his journal to begin a fuller narrative of the illness, which developed into 'a few recollections of her little life' (p. 200). Over the next few days, this became one of several urgent strategies to possess Jessy and have her to himself, the most extreme being his inability to part with her dead body. Leaving Catherine at home with the children, he took Willy by train to prep school on the way to Fasque, with the 'dear remains' (p. 201), then 'Closed my blind to have no other company than the thought of her who seems incessantly to beckon me & say "Come Pappy Come": & of the land whither she is gone' (p. 201). In the memoir he wrote of her afterwards he states quite clearly: 'She & I were alone all the way. It was a great privilege.'[49] Even when she was buried in the family vault, he kept the key, 'and was able to visit my Jessy there' (p. 202), and as he prepared to return home, he wished he could carry away with him 'the seal of that Chamber' (p. 202). His diaries record that whenever he was at Fasque over the next year until his father's death, he made frequent visits to the vault; twenty-three years later, in 1874, when it was reopened for the burial of his elder brother Tom's daughter Ida, he snatched another look at Jessy's coffin.[50]

For a devout Christian like Gladstone, this attachment to his child's remains goes against everything he was meant to believe about the separation of body and spirit and the existence of an afterlife. In this respect, his response is totally different from Edward Benson's. Drawn as he was to Martin's tomb at Winchester, Benson was from the first convinced that his son had entered a physical heaven and that, twelve years later, Nellie had gone to join him. Does this mean that Gladstone's faith wavered at this – probably the worst crisis of his family life? Or should his attempt to come to terms with Jessy's loss by writing about her be seen mainly as a means of persuading himself that she is safely with God: indeed that the child uncorrupted by sin has now become morally superior to the parent? The explanation of his behaviour seems to be not so much that his faith was in question, as that his strong consciousness of the child's physicality, revealed in the memoir, meant that he missed being able to see and touch her. As with Tait's memoir of his daughters, there was a physical bond between father and daughter that, innocent of any sense of sin, thrived on affectionate interaction. Gladstone recalls how Jessy would kiss the stump of his finger (lost in a shooting accident as a young man), and he would stand her and Stephen (at their request) on the chimney piece, one over each pillar. Only on her deathbed did she seem reluctant to kiss him, though when he asked a second time, he 'heard & felt her little lips close & part, with what I now fear was an effort to the dying child' (fo. 137). In fact the child had said 'I want Mammy', and Gladstone had pushed Jessy to give him an equal token of affection at a point when she was scarcely able to form her lips into a kiss.

Afterwards, Gladstone was determined to fit Jessy into a memorial framework he had designed for her. If it was harder to portray her as pious and patient like Agnes, or lively and funny like 'little Mary' (for the benefit of whose poor eyesight the family spent five months in Italy from 1850 to 1851), he could depict her as made for love, including the love of God. 'Love was by far the most powerful instrument of control over her', he reports (fo.134), noting occasions when Jessy had seemed fearful and lethargic – hence his conversion of her into the image of a little girl giving kisses and calling for 'Pappy'. If we return for a moment to the debate about sentimentality in literature that was discussed at the end of the

Introduction, the characterisation of Jessy as the embodiment of 'Love', contrasting with his own dramatic sense of sin, fits almost too neatly the ideological framework of the Victorian idealisation of little girls, which we saw in the Tait case. There is also the issue of the moral or ethical effect of writing and reading her story, and whether the writing of a memorial piece for a four-year-old child can be anything other than a mawkish piece of self-indulgence, even the creation and enjoyment of a decadent type of emotion. Michael Tanner objects to sentimentality precisely because of its self-indulgent quality, because it 'doesn't lead anywhere'.[51] This is especially so in the case of a death, because no action is possible to bring the person back and relieve the mourner's grief. Robert Solomon, on the other hand, explores the relationship between spirituality and sentimentality, and defends grief from the charge of unmanliness (dating back to Hamlet's apparently excessive mourning for his murdered father), by arguing that it 'puts us in touch with our mortality. It also puts us in closer touch with love.' Having once, in his earlier work, *The Passions* (1976), seen grief as a 'a kind of degenerate emotion, a *breakdown* of emotion rather than an emotion itself', Solomon offers several more positive interpretations, including the idea that grief is a 'continuation rather than a cessation of love', an appeal to the imagination in reconstructing memories of the loved one, and indeed 'lost possibilities'.[52]

Gladstone was writing largely for his own consolation, but as he later allowed his daughter Mary to copy his manuscript, he clearly did not intend it to be as private as a diary. Mary herself saw it both as a form of self-discipline and a work of aesthetic beauty, recalling in her biography of her mother that when Jessy died 'it has been related that for some hours after her death . . . her father was in a state of such violent grief as almost to frighten those around him'. When 'suddenly his sense of duty got the upper hand', he composed a record of her life that, in Mary's view, 'might rank with the immortal description written by De Quincey when death first touched his house'.[53] All the evidence suggests that he wanted to construct some shape and purpose for her life, within the framework of a traditional Anglican understanding of death, but that this was not just a selfless memorial; as a father he needed to recover some-thing of his own manly self-discipline, via reassurance that the connec-tion between Jessy and himself had been meaningful, and that he had fully atoned for his faults. 'It is for this cause that the record of her may do us good', he decides near the beginning of his narrative, 'when we peruse it in a world where love is so sorely nipped & blighted, not by sorrow, which waters & feeds it, but by the sharp & biting blast of Sin' (fo. 131).

This need becomes all the more poignant when his memories are compared with his wife's, interleaved on the facing page. Like Mary Benson's, her language is warmer, more fluid and natural, as she recalls the loving relationship she had with Jessy: 'how would she follow me, sweet lamb, to my bedroom, & sit happy in the armchair, living as it were, upon a word or a look of mine' (facing fo. 128). Compared with Gladstone's agonised plea for a kiss, this has a flowing reciprocity about it, which makes the account of Jessy's short life something of an emotional battleground between the Gladstone parents for possession of their daughter's heart.

With the death of their eldest son Willy of a brain tumour at the age of fifty-one in 1891, as with Benson's loss of Nellie, the tone of Gladstone's response is more measured. He is less anxious to prove that his son loved him (best), but stresses the child's early curiosity about God, his pliability and self-effacement. He had three times nearly run away from Eton, testifying to his love of home – and indeed he had told his parents of this only when it would no longer look like a complaint or disturb their peace of mind. Like Benson's disappointment with Martin's school record, however, Gladstone's regrets over his eldest son's lack of academic distinction soon surface in the memoir. It was easy enough to tell quaint anecdotes of Willy's childhood (for example his running naked about the upper gallery of Fasque, or asking whether God rode on the morning clouds). Once his adult life begins, Gladstone finds himself dealing with less tractable material, for which he has to make excuses: 'He took only a good, not an extraordinary, place' at Eton, and though Willy got a first in 'Mods' ('Honour Moderations', the first round of exams at Oxford), he managed only a second in his Finals, which his father admits was a 'sore disappointment'.[54] Just as Benson tried to persuade himself on occasion that Martin had really come first, Gladstone complained about the way these things were managed in Oxford: 'the unhappy change which has I believe virtually excluded scholarships, properly so called, from the final schools at Oxford, & has thereby heavily handicapped in the race for honours men of the stamp of W. Fox, W. Canning & Ld Wellesley' (fo. 145). Worse still, Willy went on to scrape a third in the Law and History Schools, followed (unsurprisingly) by failure to win an All Souls fellowship. Gladstone had invested heavily in teaching Willy himself while he was a young child, however busy he was with matters of state;

thirty years after the Oxford failure, he was still looking for someone to blame, while admitting that perhaps his son had not, as he put it, been 'a sufficiently violent worker'. The second half of the memoir therefore focuses on Willy's 'dutiful' rather than ambitious conduct of his career, which he was 'quite willing to place . . . at the disposal of his parents'. The diary records that by 1865 Gladstone was beginning to appreciate his eldest son's auxiliary usefulness – 'Willy is most satisfactory as a helper' – even if his brief political career was undistinguished.[55] The loyal memoir lapses only when academic failure is recalled: by the end of it, Gladstone has convinced himself that 'it is more than enough that I can have been the parent of such a son' (fo. 151).

AFTERMATHS

How did the deaths of two children apiece change each of these fathers? It might indeed be more pertinent to ask whether there *was* any significant change in their demeanour towards their remaining children, and whether the shared experience of bereavement altered the dynamics of each family as a whole. Both Gladstone and Benson took the loss of their children, at least partly, as a personal chastisement from God for their own sinfulness. While Gladstone's interest in prostitutes and pornography is well known, Benson seemed like 'a stern Puritan' to Arthur, but he was certainly inclined towards black depressions caused by a sense of inadequacy, hypersensitivity to his own troubles and what he called 'strenuous idleness'.[56] Arthur Benson recalls his father a year after Martin's death tearfully confessing to him in the Swiss Alps 'his lifelong struggles with temper, which he had regarded in youth as the easiest method of getting his own way'. So far as Arthur was concerned this confession humanised his father in a way that had been concealed by his previous 'effortless dominance and superiority to all human weakness'.[57] As he worked on the biography, Arthur's views of his father softened. It was typical of the Benson family's bookishness that it was largely through reading their father's diaries that they came at last to understand how passionately he cared about them. Arthur further responded with a poem, 'To my Father', which conceded that he became "Mid pomp and policy divine, / A fonder, gentler father too'.[58]

   Neither man ever really came to terms with what he regarded as his own ingrained vices, heightened by experience of fatherhood, but as their children grew up, the fathers began to engage in a new kind of dialogue with them. It might be argued that this is an inevitable change in the nature of a father's relationship with his young adult children, but Benson and Gladstone were conscious of a stronger degree of guilt and shame than was the case with most of the other fathers in this study. Benson was particularly liable to troubled dreams that included bizarre images of his children. Perhaps the oddest of these, confided to the pages of his 1879 diary and not published in the official biography, was a dream that a doctor had recommended the amputation of Fred's hand, to which his son quietly submitted,

> & the doctor hacked it off with two or three cuts. It did not bleed. I put the hand into my pocket handkerchief and carried it about very pitifully. I stroked the little hand, and bent the fingers, quite flexible and warm – They were slightly dirty; . . . but I could perceive no sign of anything having been the matter with the hand. I then said 'would it not have been better for him to have borne the pain for a time than to get rid of it in this way? What <u>have</u> we done?'[59]

Written before the advent of psychoanalysis, this violent, naively narrated dream of a father watching the maiming of his son reads too obviously as a castration fantasy; but it can also be seen as a symbolic narrative of irrevocable damage done to a child on the advice of a professional that the father accepts and then regrets. Benson's gestures of affection (stroking the still warm severed hand) come too late to serve any purpose. As an ambitious father who placed all his sons in the care of professional educators, Benson – a former Wellington Headmaster – was forced by the circumstances of Martin's death to rethink his ambitious plans for their success. Even then, such ambitions as he had produced disappointing results. Hugh, as the youngest son, was indulged more than Martin had been, and not driven as hard; his father opposed his applying for the Indian Civil Service, noting in his diary (1889): 'I always reckoned on this one to be my great friend as I grew old'.[60] This was more usually the role of a youngest daughter, but Benson came increasingly to depend on all his surviving children as friends and companions. One of his greatest pleasures was riding out on horseback at Addington with two or three sons and daughters and engaging in a vigorous debate with them, while the recollections of clergy colleagues mention the whole family's enjoyment of arguments about grammar and word derivation. Outwardly, the Bensons still presented the appearance of a happy united family, despite their repressed homoerotic sympathies; only Benson himself was unequivocally and strongly heterosexual. Their mother escaped the earlier sexual pressures of her marriage by living in a same-sex relationship with Lucy Tait, daughter of the previous Archbishop, while Arthur, though genial and lively in company, was unable to form close physical relationships, either with men or women. His diaries reveal an aesthetic yearning for beautiful young men and boys, alternating with dreams about his father looming up at social gatherings, and greeting him as if still alive. Although less bizarre than his father's dreams of Fred, they suggest a continuous haunting by a figure usually smiling and offering the blessings or kisses Arthur could have from no one else, but still in some way making claims on him. Frequently mentioning his need for 'liberty', Arthur confessed in his diary that he had never been 'in vital touch with anyone'; he did not want to 'claim or be claimed – I want nothing but a cordial camaraderie' – this perhaps in clear contradistinction to his father's own very virile brand of heterosexuality, which made him choose his bride at twelve and then wait impatiently for her to grow up.[61]

All the Benson children acknowledged that their father had cared deeply about them but, by their own evidence, they grew up emotionally damaged, unable to marry or form lasting relationships and, above all, unable to shake off the memory of their childhood and home life, long after the original domestic circle had been disbanded. What was it exactly that had been so terrible about him? Mary Benson's letters from the early days of their marriage portray an uninhibited family circle who apparently missed their father when he was away on business and consulted about how best to send demonstrations of their love. Martin wanted seventy-seven kisses sending in one letter, and according to another, 'blew you last night not only a kiss according to my suggestion but an embrace, which was quite his own idea'. Even 'Baby' (Nellie) was heard saying '"dear Papa" over & over again as clearly as possible'.[62] Yet from the various testimonies assembled by the Benson autobiographers, it is clear that their father was to most of them a crushing presence whose love was more suffocating than sustaining. His black depressions scared them, as did his overreaction to trifles. 'I understood neither him nor any part of him', Fred claimed, while lavishly, like his brothers and sisters, praising their mother's warmth and humour.[63] Arthur describes him in his biography as 'the eager, anxious, masterful, fatherly man at Lambeth' (Vol. II, p. 680): indeed the terms, 'masterful', 'fatherly' and 'purposeful' reverberate through reminiscences of him, suggesting that they were the most prominent features of his personality; while in dialogue with Fred, Arthur characterised him as 'sentimental rather than loving'.[64] Ultimately, what caused the tragedy of the Benson story was the father's failure to understand and connect with his children, who all belonged emotionally to their mother. Arthur was the only one with any fatherly instincts, and they were directed away from family structures to all-male institutions, where he yearned for romantic companionship with younger men on a more equal basis. Self-doubt, depression and his own high office (for example as Master of Magdalene College, Cambridge) made this increasingly unlikely.

Of the two formidable *fin-de-siècle* fathers discussed in this chapter, Gladstone ought to have been the more daunting, judging by his diaries and letters; yet unlike the Benson children, the Gladstones had nothing but positive recollections of his demeanour at home and towards them individually. His papers tell a story of constant watchfulness over their development and intervention when it was necessary to reprimand them, though with a consciousness of his own shortcomings being more severe than theirs. One of the most striking passages in his diary occurs on 1 January 1848, when he reviews the personalities of his five children in a 'memorandum'. Innocent of the future, he writes of Jessy that she has 'a strong will which has yet to be broken'; Stephen is 'beginning to obey: but is only broken in part'.[65] 'I had to speak most seriously to little Lena', he admits of Helen when she is only five: 'in more things than one she has been tempted & overcome. It seems so hollow to speak to her of her sins & pray with her, & then think of my own.' He often felt the same about Willy, the child he once forced himself to whip for inattention to lessons; the boy's continuing indolence and inertia bothered him, but were usually managed by earnest dialogue, his preferred way of bringing children into line.[66] Stacks of letters in the Flintshire Record Office testify to his willingness to spend hours writing out precise instructions as to the proper way of conducting spiritual exercise and self-examination, nor were secular examples neglected. 'I hope you will always do your work just as you would wish to manage your innings at cricket', he urges Willy at fifteen, having at seven recommended the Duke of Wellington as a role model.[67]

Overall, however, Gladstone felt contented with the natures of his children, and they reciprocated with loyal admiration of him. His second surviving daughter Mary was the most openly approving. 'I think Papa is rather like Shakespeare', she confided to her diary at the age of twenty-two. 'Helen and I nearly died of excitement', she said a few years earlier, after watching him speak in the House of Commons. Each of his speeches seemed to be the greatest he had ever made, until the next one; at her most smitten, she declared him 'the fountain head and origin, and I am a blind follower'.[68] As she grew older, however, she was unafraid of confronting him with some of the more difficult issues of the day, including female suffrage, birth-control and the 'Maiden Tribute of Modern Babylon' affair – a Victorian example of investigative journalism by W. T. Stead in the *Pall Mall Gazette* of July 1885, exposing the scandal of child prostitution. The previous year she had tackled him on female suffrage and nationalisation of land. There is no evidence in her memoirs that he seemed obsessed with sin and gloom; wholly at ease in his company, she refers to him, when out of office, as the 'X', and describes her parents with their arms around each other's waists, or clomping up the stairs singing their favourite 'A ragamuffin husband and a rantipolling wife'.[69] Even Agnes at twelve could address him as 'Dearest old Fatherbird', while Herbert's memoirs support what Mary says of their lack of awe or fear of their father.[70] If access was limited when he was busy in his study, this only made the social times more rewarding: 'He showed us things, told us stories, measured and recorded our heights. But the supreme moment came when he carried four of us at a time – two of my sisters, Henry, and myself – on his back' (p. 7).

In her recent study of Gladstone and women, Anne Isba wonders whether the ageing Prime Minister held his children back, especially his daughters. 'Personal devotion to the patriarch', she argues, 'combined with the thrill of operating at the heart of perhaps the most exciting political family of the nineteenth century, made it difficult for sons and daughters to break away'.[71] All the evidence suggests that Mary Gladstone at least benefited from access to the famous men of the day and a more invigorating social and political life than she might otherwise have enjoyed. In fact each of Gladstone's three daughters chose a way of life that differed from her sisters' and entailed some degree of independence, albeit tempered, in the case of the younger two, by expectations that they would drop their other concerns to look after their elderly parents, nicknamed by the children 'the Grand Old People'.

While the Gladstone children worked hard to recover his posthumous reputation as a father whose happy domestic life was the clue to understanding him, the Bensons in effect did the opposite with theirs, steadily exposing the misery of their relationship in an effort to understand and forgive. On the face of it, Gladstone had been a worse father, preoccupied with the burdens of office, and deserting his family to counsel prostitutes or pursue political ambitions in the House of Commons; in reality, the strait-laced Benson, who was never too busy to write an exhortatory letter to a son at boarding school, had been the more forbidding in his immediate domestic circle. It was Gladstone's children who clustered permanently around Hawarden, while Benson's fled family domesticity in favour of all-male institutions, such as schools, priestly lodgings and colleges. In neither case, however, is it fair to dismiss them as the forbidding patriarch with which this study began. The thundering Victorian father, whose image has persisted despite so much contrary evidence, never carried four children on his back, like Gladstone, or stood them on the mantelpiece for fun; nor did his children plan, like Benson's, to send him seventy-seven kisses in a letter. Both were essentially 'over-anxious fathers', a type John Tosh has identified as missing from the popular categorisation of different modes of fathering.[72] As lifelong diarists, both found, in writing about their children in relation to their work and other concerns, that their anxieties about them were inextricably a part of the way they viewed themselves as men and Christians. Their sense of their own moral shortcomings never eased. In constantly exhorting their children to do better, they wrote with a demoralising sense of their own unfitness to offer advice of any kind. At the heart of Victorian patriarchy, embodied in these two traditional fathers who represented church and Government, lay a fundamental consciousness of unease and failure that was less far removed from the mood of *fin de siècle* than the wider culture and its next generation entirely realised.

Conclusion

You can't manage without the *idea* of a father.[1]

In 1824, the essayist Thomas Carlyle was appalled by his friend Edward Irving's descent into doting fatherhood of a three-month-old son. The worst of it was Irving's constant *talk* about his baby: 'Visit him at any time', he told his wife Jane, 'you find him dry-nursing his offspring'; while to his mother he complained: 'He speculates on the progressive development of *his* senses, on the state of his bowels, on his hours of rest, his pap-spoons and his *hippings* [nappies].'[2] Possibly he overlooked the irony of signing himself off with 'I am ever, My dear Mother's boy', but Carlyle, now celebrated for his impotence, was clearly happier being an adult son than a potential father, and preferred to assert his masculinity as a hero man of letters.[3] Not all great Victorians were great fathers – or fathers at all – but the cult of fatherhood, assisted by fashionable Romanticism, had certainly begun well before Victoria ascended the throne in 1837.

Nevertheless, the Victorians had an uneasy relationship with the 'idea of the father' as well as the reality, and never entirely established agreed parameters. It functioned ultimately as a cultural symbol, a concept of authority, in dialogue with contemporary notions of masculinity. In the nineteenth century, this meant its association with Christianity and manliness; for the middle classes, specifically, *gentle*manliness. Some of the fathers discussed in this study, such as Gladstone and Dr Arnold, fitted the definition perfectly, and were partly responsible for perpetuating it; others, such as the agnostic Huxley and Darwin, or those whose class credentials were somewhat uncertain, such as Huxley again, Macready and Dickens, implicitly challenged it. Material provision for children was another key requirement, again immaculately embodied in Gladstone, who enjoined on his eldest son the serious responsibilities of managing the Hawarden estate for the country and succeeding generations. Victorian fathers were supposed both to provide for their children and ensure that they knew how to provide for themselves. Even those who felt horrified by the birth of one son after another (Dickens and Darwin especially) roused themselves to suggest a career or course of action to each in turn. All the fathers I have discussed in this study were acutely aware of their responsibilities, even if they were not always able to carry them out. Whether or not they helped to improve the negative image of the Victorian patriarch is another matter.

'The idea of a father, especially the idea of rejecting a father, powers the modern world', Howard Jacobson argues in *The Making of Henry* (2004).[4] The notion of the father as an enemy to be overcome on the way to adult maturity – though originating in Oedipus's father Laius – is perhaps most typically embodied in the burly person of the Victorian paterfamilias. Victorian fathers have had a long history of being that enemy. They exist in fiction to be escaped, humiliated or vanquished, and in autobiography to represent the attitudes of a past generation. They are the bogeymen of a period that seems to have experienced more stereo-typing than any other, at least as far as images of the family are concerned. For whatever reason, our culture has cherished the notion of the tyran-nical Victorian father, much as it does the aspidistra, antimacassar and crinoline as evidence of the ugliness and repression of Victorian domestic life – and he did in some ways exist. In fact, as this study has shown, the Victorian 'heavy father', validated as he was by the law of the land, did not gradually disappear as the century progressed and the law became more sympathetic to mothers' rights. Some of the most formidable patriarchs, such as Leslie Stephen, Philip Gosse, W. E. Gladstone and Edward White Benson, belonged to the fin de siècle – at least in their children's memoirs – while milder fathers such as Matthew Arnold, Charles Darwin and William Charles Macready flourished slightly earlier in the century. On the other hand, more relaxed names for the head of the family, such as 'Dad' (used by Huxley, as well as 'Pater'), 'Papsy' (used by G. H. Lewes), Jessy Gladstone's 'Pappy', Agnes Gladstone's 'Fatherbird', Mary Gladstone's 'the X' and Emma Darwin's 'F', all indicate an increasing freedom of address without loss of respect. The father may have remained formidable, but children themselves were challenging the image, and all the fathers in this study were responding.

The aim of this book has to been to examine Victorian fatherhood from the inside, from the fathers' own perspective, and to see what new insights emerge from the subjective viewpoint. By extrapolating from the rest of their biography the most challenging moments of their experience of fatherhood, I have hoped to restore their domestic life to a more central place in their work, and recapture a sense of its effect on the turning points of their careers. Although much hinges on the degree of self-awareness to be found in Victorian men, the examples selected for this study were all articulate fathers who never stopped measuring themselves against both internal and external standards and expectations. If two or three themes emerge as the most urgent, they are the fathers' anxiety about providing for their children materially, their sense of shame at passing on their own weaknesses (moral and physical), and being unable to save their children from life-threatening illness. These concerns reverberate through this study and become part of a general fear of external contingency. However carefully a Victorian father planned his sons' futures, his daughters' marriages or his own work, unexpected events were liable to overturn everything, and leave his ambitions in ruins.

Most of my selected fathers had first to reject the example of their own father, or at the very least create a distinctive and alternative identity for themselves. There often followed an intermediate stage in their lives before they were married, when they belonged to a pseudo-, all-male family, a professional group of fellow undergraduates, churchmen or schoolmasters, men of science, or men of letters who lived and worked in close association. This professional grouping, particularly important to the scientists and churchmen, continued to act as an alternative to the domestic family, in terms of dining, socialising, brotherhood and mentorship. In Dickens's case it provided him with a home-based the-atrical troupe, which gradually absorbed his older children alongside his friends, but excluded his wife. These (semi-) professional associations had the potential to absorb the next generation into their ranks, but it was perhaps only Darwin's sons who followed their father at all closely into this structure. When it came to preparing their own children for a career, most of my chosen fathers were disappointed by their sons' lack of energy and ambition. As Martin Danahay has argued, desk-bound fathers were conscious of appearing effeminate in a muscular culture of physical labour, where 'inactive contemplation' seemed valueless.[5] Darwin, Hooker and Huxley had all been vigorous travellers and researchers before they married, but by the time their children knew them, they were thinkers, rather than active doers. It may have seemed a good idea to reassert more masculine values in the next generation, but there is also almost an acceptance of evolutionary decline in the decision to send them away to dig, farm or fight in distant wars, rather than to write books, or initiate ideas. Charles Darwin, comparing unmotivated sons with Joseph Hooker in 1862, suggested that in demanding conditions, hereditary talent might eventually emerge. He cited the story of 'a son of very able parents' who was thought a dunce until he became an Australian settler, whereupon he 'exhibited his inherited genius'.[6]

No such signs of delayed inherited genius emerged in Dickens's exiled sons, whom he expected to fend for themselves in the world of ultra-masculine employment. Of the seven, Walter and Francis both served in India, Walter with the army and Francis with the Bengal Mounted Police (later joining Canada's Northwest Mounted Police); Alfred and Edward spent much of their lives in Australia; and Sydney entered a navy cadetship at the age of thirteen. Only Charley and Henry stayed at home; Henry as a lawyer, and Charley following his father into a career of literary journalism (via bankruptcy). Kingsley's two sons Maurice and Grenville, the younger Thomas Arnold and his brother William Dela-field, Matthew Arnold's son Richard, Hooker's son Brian, and Lewes's Thornton and Herbert all worked in tough conditions in New Zealand, India, South America, Australia, Mexico or South Africa, Maurice Kingsley as a railway engineer, Brian Hooker in gold mining. Even the more stay-at-home sons were encouraged to do something physical. Gladstone engaged his eldest son Willy in tree felling exercises at Hawarden, while Benson liked to take his children horse riding around the countryside. By contrast, the daughters were expected to stay close at hand; their education was normally provided by governesses at home (the Benson daughters unusually went to Truro High School and Lady Margaret Hall, Oxford); and active careers were discouraged (Helen Gladstone a notable exception). Despite these inequalities, though, several daughters became writers or artists, and Maggie Benson an Egypt-ologist. The adulatory prose of Mary Gladstone Drew and Mamie Dickens testifies to the existence of other compensations: pleasure in following their father's success, and an intense emotional bond that the culture more openly fostered in daughters than it did demonstrative relations between fathers and sons. 'I can see him now, through the mist of years, with a child nearly always on his knee', recalls Mamie Dickens in a deeply feminised memory of her father as a kind of male Madonna.[7] Because her mother is so markedly absent from her memoirs, there is a danger of Dickens subverting gender roles and becoming a hybrid mother and father, at least in her representation.

Whether these men can now be judged as influential fathers who left a permanent mark on the practice and definition of fatherhood is harder to gauge. Prince Albert was the first high-profile father in a position to influence the nation at the start of the Victorian period proper. Not without some controversy and criticism he asserted a father's right to involve himself in the daily domestic details of his children's upbringing. In terms of gendered activity, many fathers, both working- and middle-class, implicitly queried the traditional demarcations between male and female employment. Most of those discussed in this study worked at home, or in a workplace (such as a school or church) that adjoined the family base. For Hood and Darwin, as chronic invalids, a housebound lifestyle obviously compromised their ability to perform physical masculine work, while others, such as Dickens, Macready, Gladstone and Arnold, who nursed their children in illness, crossed another traditional gender boundary. Tait's domesticity during the Carlisle tragedy of 1856 went unquestioned and commiserated; indeed his family values, like Benson's, and Dr Arnold's, were seen as completing and sanctifying his character as a Christian leader. Dickens's image as an instigator of children's entertainments, as witnessed by his household, enhanced his reputation as a family author, while Charles Kingsley's known love of children was reflected in his authorship of *The Water-Babies* and *Madam How and Lady Why*. Thomas Arnold, as the country's best-known headmaster-father embodied a version of masculinity that combined vigorous physical activity with leadership and care of the young. The evidence of memoirs and periodicals indeed confirms that for many mid-Victorians Arnold was the supreme father figure whose early death plunged a nation of ex-schoolboys into symbolic orphanhood. In validating the worth of strong manly feeling associated with the care of children, all these father figures made Christian sentimentality compatible with Christian muscularity. Gladstone, Tait, Benson and the agnostic Darwin all found ways of expressing their love and yearning for their dead children in private 'memorials' testifying to their sense of each child's unique importance.

Where the paternal image was less obviously congruent with a man's sterner public reputation, as with Gladstone, Benson and Huxley, public curiosity about his private life encouraged a spate of memoirs and informal family photographs, especially with grandchildren. 'Among the wavering, inconsequent recollections of childhood he seems to stand as the ultimate pillar of the house', Leonard Huxley testified of his father in 1925. Nevertheless, even a loving and modern-sounding father like Huxley was remembered as rather different from the twentieth-century version: 'The companionship between parent and child, so prevalent to-day, was unknown a century ago and rare fifty years since.'[8] The most informal of the father figures discussed earlier still commanded silence and respect for strictly observed working hours, and while some men (such as Tait and Dickens) welcomed children into their studies, these male domestic workspaces remained sacrosanct for several generations of Victorian children. Iconic memories – of drawings, lion games or orange-peel carvings – took on a lasting symbolic importance as the essence of a father's style of play, however infrequent.

Ultimately the homes of Victorian writers and intellectuals revolved around the father's needs, more than the mother's or children's. This was especially true of Darwin, whose hours of rest and work drove the routines of Down House, but most of the fathers discussed in the preceding chapters were supreme controllers of their households. Though Darwin's was an exceptional case, a similar priority was given to the father's work in all the other examples I have discussed, especially Thomas Arnold's, Gladstone's and Benson's. Men have worked at home throughout history, but what was significant about these examples is their merging of the business of fatherhood, work and home in ways that made it hard to determine where one function began and another ended. Darwin finalising his species theory while two children were ill upstairs, Gladstone working at his papers with a new baby in the room, Kingsley and Dickens writing alongside playing children, Matthew Arnold composing his Preface to *Culture and Anarchy* while a child lay dying: all these images of fatherhood, conducted in fluctuating domestic conditions, suggest a cultural acceptance of permeable boundaries between gender-specific work and home-based activity. In adapting their own personal circumstances to their requirements as intellectual workers and fathers, these high-profile fathers helped change the perception of fatherhood as something detached from the home, and lacking home values. All the men I have discussed saw themselves as entitled to be involved in their children's upbringing. By appropriating the role of adviser on all issues related to education and career choice, they removed themselves from suggestions of effeminacy. Even their attendance on sickbeds often acquired a stronger professional or spiritual dimension than the mother's. In the process of proving themselves 'man enough' (in Victor Seidler's words) for the challenge of being a father, they confronted the underlying tragedy of Victorian fatherhood, which was the impossibility of being the all-powerful protector against the chance contingencies of modern life.

Notes

INTRODUCTION. LOOKING FOR THE VICTORIAN FATHER

1 Lewis Carroll, *The Rectory Magazine*, ed. Jerome Bump (Austin and London: University of Texas Press, 1975), p. 7.
2 F. Anstey, *Vice Versa; or, A Lesson to Fathers* [1882] (London: John Murray, 1969), p. 136.
3 Samuel Butler, *The Way of All Flesh* [1903] (Harmondsworth: Penguin, 1966), p. 57.
4 Leonore Davidoff and Catherine Hall, *Family Fortunes: Men and Women of the English Middle Class, 1780–1850* (University of Chicago Press, 1987).
5 John Tosh, *A Man's Place: Masculinity and the Middle-Class Home in Victorian England* (New Haven and London: Yale University Press, 1999) includes a chapter called 'The Decline of Deference', pp. 145–69.
6 Anon., 'Fathers', *All the Year Round* (2 September 1865), 133–5.
7 Henry Sumner Maine, 'The Patriarchal Theory', *Quarterly Review* 162 (January 1886), 181–209 (p. 186).
8 Nancy E. Dowd, *Redefining Fatherhood* (New York and London: New York University Press, 2000), pp. 1–2.
9 John R. Gillis, *A World of Their Own Making: Myth, Ritual, and the Quest for Family Values* (Cambridge, MA: Harvard University Press, 1996), p. 180.
10 David Roberts, 'The Paterfamilias of the Victorian Governing Classes', in *The Victorian Family: Structure and Stresses*, ed. Anthony S. Wohl (London: Croom Helm, 1978), pp. 59–81 (pp. 59, 77).
11 Tosh, *A Man's Place*, pp. 95–9, 79.
12 Stuart C. Aitken, 'The Awkward Spaces of Fathering', in *Spaces of Masculinities*, ed. Bettina van Hoven and Kathrin Hörschelmann (London and New York: Routledge, 2005), pp. 222–36 (pp. 223, 231).
13 Matthew Sweet, *Inventing the Victorians* (London: Faber and Faber, 2002), p. 183.
14 Sally Shuttleworth, 'Demonic Mothers: Ideologies of Bourgeois Motherhood in the Mid-Victorian Era', in *Rewriting the Victorians: Theory, History and the Politics of Gender*, ed. Linda M. Shires (London and New York: Routledge, 1992), pp. 31–51 (p. 32).

15 William Frederick Poole, *An Index to Periodical Literature* (London and Boston: James R. Osgood and Trübner and Co., 1882), pp. 446, 457.

16 Sarah Stickney Ellis (1812–72), best known of the early-Victorian advice book authors, followed *The Women of England* (1839) with *The Daughters of England* (1842), *The Mothers of England* (1843) and *The Wives of England* (1843).

17 Natalie J. McKnight, *Suffering Mothers in Mid-Victorian Novels* (New York: St Martin's Press, 1997), p. 3.

18 Steven Mintz summarises his findings in 'Mothers and Fathers in America: Looking Backward, Looking Forward'. Retrieved on 19 December 2007 from www.digitalhistory.uh.edu/historyonline/mothersfathers.cfm.

19 William Cobbett, *Advice to Young Men* [1830] (Oxford University Press, 1980), p. 235.

20 Agnes Strickland, 'The Cottage Fire', *The Home* 1:2 (12 July 1851), inside cover.

21 Anon., 'The Question as to the Legal Custody of Infants', *The Times* (4 April 1864), p. 8; Frances Elizabeth Hoggan M.D., *The Position of the Mother in the Family* (Manchester: A. Ireland & Co., 1884), p. 8.

22 Sonya O. Rose, *Limited Livelihoods: Gender and Class in Nineteenth-Century England* (London: Routledge, 1992), p. 56.

23 In a long speech objecting to Clause 55 of the Bill, the Bishop of Exeter, Henry Philpotts, claimed that 'the law of God imposes on the father of a bastard child the duty of maintaining that child, as much as the duty of maintaining his legitimate child'. *Hansard* 25 (8 August 1834), 1065, 1080.

24 See for example Mary Poovey, *Uneven Developments: The Ideological Work of Gender in Mid-Victorian England* (London: Virago, 1989), or Alan Chedzoy, *A Scandalous Woman: The Story of Caroline Norton* (London: Allison and Busby, 1992).

25 *Chetwynd* v. *Chetwynd*, *The Times* (29 November 1865), 11.

26 William Blackstone, *Commentaries on the Laws of England*, 4 vols. (Oxford: Clarendon Press, 1765–9), Vol. 1, pp. 435–6.

27 *Hansard* 39 (14 December 1837), 1083.

28 Allen Horstman, *Victorian Divorce* (London and Sydney: Croom Helm, 1985), p. 104. In 1871, he claims, '40% of the suits involved childless couples'.

29 Leonore Davidoff, Megan Doolittle, Janet Fink and Katherine Holden (eds.), *The Family Story: Blood, Contract and Intimacy, 1830–1960* (London and New York: Longman, 1999), p. 140. The Agar Ellis case concerned a Catholic mother and a Protestant father, whose daughters' religious upbringing as Catholics offended their father. The judges involved in the case found in favour of the father's right to raise his children in his own faith.

30 *The Times* (25 November 1878), p. 9; *ibid.* (7 August 1878), p. 9.

31 *Ibid.* (25 November 1878), p. 9.

32 Ben Griffin, 'The Parliamentary Politics of Domestic Authority', conference paper given at King's College, Cambridge, for *The Politics of Domestic Authority in Britain* (27 July 2006).

33 *Hansard* 286 (3rd series) (26 March 1884), 818, 823–4, 827.

34 The paintings mentioned in this section can be found in Christopher Wood, *Victorian Panorama* (London: Faber & Faber, 1976).

35 Tim Barringer discusses this picture in his *Men at Work: Art and Labour in Victorian Britain* (New Haven and London: Yale University Press, 2005), p. 32.

36 Both pictures are reproduced in Wood, *Victorian Panorama*, Figs. 1A (Cope) and 52 (Bowkett). Bowkett's picture no longer exists.

37 Martineau's picture (widely discussed) is reproduced in Christopher Wood, *The Pre-Raphaelites* (London: Weidenfeld and Nicolson, 1981), p. 72.

38 Frith's *The Road to Ruin* series is discussed by Aubrey Noakes in *William Frith: Extraordinary Victorian Painter. A Biographical and Critical Essay* (London: Jupiter, 1978), pp. 119–26.

39 Davidoff and Hall, *Family Fortunes*, p. 335.

40 Joseph A. Kestner, *Masculinities in Victorian Painting* (Aldershot: Scolar Press, 1995), p. 39.

41 These paintings were shown in the recent Millais exhibition and are discussed in the catalogue: Jason Rosenfeld and Alison Smith, *Millais* (London: Tate Publishing, 2007).

42 Fildes's *The Doctor*, in Wood, *Victorian Panorama*, p. 101. The painting is discussed by Fildes's son, L. V. Fildes, in his *Luke Fildes R.A.: A Victorian Painter* (London: Michael Joseph, 1968), pp. 116–28.

43 For example, Archibald Tait, discussed in the next chapter, or Matthew Arnold, who had a photograph taken of his dead son Basil in 1868.

44 Charles Dickens, *Great Expectations* [1861] (Harmondsworth: Penguin, 1965), p. 337.

45 George Eliot, *Daniel Deronda* [1876] (Harmondsworth: Penguin, 1967), p. 697.

46 Thomas Hardy, *The Mayor of Casterbridge* [1886] (Harmondsworth: Penguin, 1978), p. 199.

47 John Stuart Mill, *Autobiography* [1873], ed. Jack Stillinger (Oxford University Press, 1971), p. 157.

48 According to Morton Cohen, 'No conclusive evidence exists about the rupture', though a rupture clearly existed: Morton N. Cohen, *Lewis Carroll: A Biography* (London: Macmillan Papermac, 1995), p. 100.

49 Kerry J. Daly, 'Reshaping Fatherhood: Finding the Models', in *Fatherhood: Contemporary Theory, Research, and Social Policy*, ed. William Marsiglio (London: Sage, 1995), pp. 21–40 (p. 40).

50 Sir John Everett Millais, *The Life and Letters of Sir John Everett Millais*, ed. John Guille Millais, 2 vols. (London: Methuen, 1902), Vol. II, pp. 217–63. Herbert Gladstone regretted John Morley's scant details of Gladstone's family life in his official biography of 1903: see this volume, Chapter 6, p. 169. Chapter 17 of Leonard Huxley's *Thomas Henry Huxley: A Character Sketch*, Life Stories of Famous Men series (London: Watts & Co., 1920), pp. 111–16, cites Leonard Huxley's repeated anecdotes of his father's domestic behaviour.

51 Pat Jalland, *Death in the Victorian Family* (Oxford University Press, 1996); Laurence Lerner, *Angels and Absences: Child Deaths in the Nineteenth Century* (Nashville and London: Vanderbilt University Press, 1997).

52 Randal Keynes, *Annie's Box: Charles Darwin, His Daughter, and Human Evolution* (London: Fourth Estate, 2001).

53 Victor Jeleniewski Seidler, *Man Enough: Embodying Masculinities* (London, Thousand Oaks, CA and New Delhi: Sage, 1997), pp. 5, 106–7; Damon Syson, 'Daddy's Home', *Observer Magazine* (24 February 2008), pp 42–49.

54 Michael E. Lamb, *The Father's Role: Applied Perspectives* (New York: John Wiley & Sons, 1986), pp. xi, 7, 11.

55 Robert Southey, *New Letters of Robert Southey*, ed. Kenneth Curry, 2 vols. (New York and London: Columbia University Press, 1965), Vol. 1, p. 212.

56 David C. Hanson, 'Precocity and the Economy of the Evangelical Self in John Ruskin's Juvenilia', in *The Child Writer from Austen to Woolf*, ed. Christine Alexander and Juliet McMaster (Cambridge University Press, 2005), pp. 200–21 (p. 203).

57 John James Ruskin *et al.*, *The Ruskin Family Letters*, ed. Van Akin Burd, 2 vols. (Ithaca, NY and London: Cornell University Press, 1973), Vol. 1, pp. 231–2.

58 Miriam Bailin, ' "Dismal Pleasure": Victorian Sentimentality and the Pathos of the Parvenu', *ELH* 66:4 (1999), 1015–32 (pp. 1015–16).

59 Julie-Marie Strange, ' "Speechless with Grief": Bereavement and the Working-Class Father, *c.* 1880–1914', in *Gender and Fatherhood in the Nineteenth Century*, eds. Trev Lynn Broughton and Helen Rogers (Basingstoke: Palgrave Macmillan, 2007), pp. 138–49 (p. 140).

60 Southey, *New Letters*, Vol. 1, p. 325.

1 THE FAILURE OF FATHERHOOD AT MID-CENTURY: FOUR CASE HISTORIES

1 Roger Fulford (ed.), *Dearest Child: Letters between Queen Victoria and the Princess Royal 1858–1861* (London: Evans Brothers Ltd, 1964), p. 124

2 Philip Magnus, *King Edward the Seventh* (London: John Murray, 1964), p. 17.

3 The lithographs are reprinted in Helmut and Alison Gernsheim, *Queen Victoria: A Biography in Word and Picture* (London: Longmans, Green & Co., 1959), pp. 72, 77.

4 John Leech, 'A Royal Nursery Rhyme for 1860', *Punch* 7 (1844), p. 79.

5 The lithograph can be found in Gernsheim and Gernsheim, *Queen Victoria: A Biography*, p. 79; for *A Book of English Song*, see Dorothy Thompson, *Queen Victoria: Gender and Power* (London: Virago, 1990), p. 45. Pictures of the Royal Family at Osborne, taken in 1857, best exemplify this image of Albert with his family.

6 Anon., 'The Royal Nursery', *The Times* (18 November 1841), 4.

7 Robert Rhodes James, *Albert, Prince Consort: A Biography* (London: Hamish Hamilton, 1983), p. 126.

8 Fulford (ed.), *Dearest Child*, p. 205.

9 Nina Epton, *Victoria and Her Daughters* (London: Weidenfeld and Nicolson, 1971), p. 115.

10 Fulford (ed.), *Dearest Child*, p. 112.

11 Roger Fulford (ed.), *Dearest Mama: Letters between Queen Victoria and the Crown Princess of Prussia 1861–1864* (London: Evans Brothers Ltd, 1968), p. 26.

12 *The Saturday Review* 12 (21 December 1861), p. 631.

13 Anon., 'The Close of 1861', *Fraser's Magazine* 65 (January 1862), 123–34 (p. 126).

14 Albert, Prince Consort of Victoria, Queen of Great Britain, *Letters of the Prince Consort 1831–1861*, ed. Kurt Jagow (London: John Murray, 1938), p. 83.

15 Charles Darwin, 'A Biographical Sketch of an Infant', *Mind* (July 1877), 285–94 (pp. 285, 291).

16 Theodore Martin, *The Life of His Royal Highness, the Prince Consort*, 5 vols. (London: Smith, Elder & Co., 1879), Vol. IV, pp. 467–8.

17 Prince Albert, *Letters*, p. 291

18 Fulford (ed.), *Dearest Mama*, pp. 198, 267.

19 Fulford (ed.), *Dearest Child*, p. 46.

20 Fulford (ed.), *Dearest Mama*, p. 193.

21 Cited by Hannah Pakula, *An Uncommon Woman: The Empress Frederick* (Phoenix: Giant, 1997), p. 159.

22 Charles Dickens, *The Letters of Charles Dickens*, ed. Madeline House *et al.*, 12 vols. (Oxford: Clarendon Press, 1965–99), Vol. X (1862–4), ed. Graham Storey, p. 54.

23 Anon., 'The Close of 1861', p. 126.

24 Arthur Helps, Review of Theodore Martin, '*The Life of His Royal Highness, the Prince Consort*', *Quarterly Review* 138 (January 1875), 107–38 (p. 138).

25 W. Lucas Collins, Review of Theodore Martin, '*The Life of His Royal Highness*', *the Prince Consort*, *Blackwood's Edinburgh Magazine* 120 (November 1876), 611–31 (p. 631).

26 Mary Elizabeth Braddon, *Aurora Floyd* [1862] (London: Virago, 1984), p. 51.

27 Margaret Oliphant, Review of Theodore Martin, '*The Life of His Royal Highness*', *the Prince Consort*, *Blackwood's Edinburgh Magazine* 117 (January 1875), 114–31 (p. 117).

28 Thomas Hood, *The Letters of Thomas Hood*, ed. Peter F. Morgan (Edinburgh: Oliver and Boyd, 1973) pp. 434–5.

29 *Ibid.*, pp. 274–5.

30 Thomas Hood, 'Copyright and Copywrong', in *The Works of Thomas Hood* [eds. Tom Hood and Frances Broderip], 10 vols. (London: E. Moxon & Co., 1869–73), Vol. VI, pp. 377–413 (p. 380).

31 'Memorials of Thomas Hood', in Hood, *Works*, Vol. X, pp. 1–468 (p. 311).

32 John Clubbe, *Victorian Forerunner: The Later Career of Thomas Hood* (Durham, NC: Duke University Press, 1968), p. 197.

33 Hood, *Letters*, p. 583.

34 J. C. Reid, *Thomas Hood* (London: Routledge & Kegan Paul, 1963), p. 250.

35 Hood, *Letters*, p. 133.

36 Thomas Hood, 'Youth and Age', in *Works*, Vol. IX, p. 17.

37 Thomas Hood, 'A Serenade', in *The Poetical Works of Thomas Hood*, ed. William Michael Rossetti, 2nd edn (London and New York: Ward Lock, n.d.), p. 290.

38 Thomas Hood, 'Parental Ode to My Son, Aged Three Years and Five Months', in *ibid.*, p. 136.

39 Thomas Hood, *Our Family*, in *ibid.*, Vol. IX, pp. 273–459 (p. 411).

40 Hood, 'Copyright and Copywrong', p. 387.

41 Margaret Oliphant, *The Autobiography of Margaret Oliphant*, ed. Elisabeth Jay [1899] (Oxford University Press, 1990), p. 86.

42 *Ibid.*, p. 85.

43 Laurence Lerner, *Angels and Absences: Child Deaths in the Nineteenth Century* (Nashville and London: Vanderbilt University Press, 1997), p. 188.

44 David Hughes, *The Lent Jewels* (London: Arrow Books, 2003), pp. 179, 66.

45 Arnold Dallimore, *The Life of Edward Irving: Fore-runner of the Charismatic Movement* (Edinburgh and Pennsylvania: The Banner of Truth Trust, 1983), p. 109.

46 Canon Fremantle, 'Archbishop Tait', *Good Words* (1883), pp. 88–94 (p. 93).

47 Victoria, Queen of Great Britain, *The Letters of Queen Victoria*, ed. George Earle Buckle, 2nd series, 3 vols. (London: John Murray, 1928), Vol. III, p. 364.

48 Pat Jalland, *Death in the Victorian Family* (Oxford University Press, 1996), p. 128.

49 Mary Gladstone [Drew], *Mary Gladstone (Mrs Drew): Her Diaries and Letters*, ed. Lucy Masterman (London: Methuen & Co., 1930), p. 16.

50 Archibald Campbell Tait, Journal, 14 March–11 July 1856 (Lambeth Palace Library, Tait Papers), Vol. XXXVIII, p. 7. The first entries were written on 14 March, when two children had died, but he was then unable to resume writing until 8 May.

51 William Benham (ed.), *Catharine and Craufurd Tait, Wife and Son of Archibald Campbell, Archbishop of Canterbury: A Memoir* (London: Macmillan, 1879), p. 347.

52 *Ibid.*, p. 265.

53 Elisabeth Bronfen, *Over Her Dead Body: Death, Femininity and the Aesthetic* (Manchester University Press, 1992), p. 13.

54 Tait, Journal, p. 64.

55 *Ibid.*, Vol. XL, p. 6.

56 *Ibid.*, p. 2 ; Benham (ed.), *Catharine and Craufurd Tait*, pp. 391–2.

57 Catherine Robson, *Men in Wonderland: The Lost Girlhood of the Victorian Gentleman* (Princeton and Oxford: Princeton University Press, 2001), p. 5.

58 Bronfen, *Over Her Dead Body*, p. 15.

59 Henry Wace, 'Archbishop Tait and the Primacy', *Quarterly Review* 155 (January 1883), 2–35 (p. 8).

60 P. T. Marsh, *The Victorian Church in Decline: Archbishop Tait and the Church of England 1868–1882* (London: Routledge & Kegan Paul, 1969), p. 16; Elizabeth Longford, *Victoria R. I.* (London: Pan, 1966), p. 452.

61 Kathryn Hughes, *George Eliot: The Last Victorian* (London: Fourth Estate, 1998), p. 139.

62 Rosemary Ashton, *G. H. Lewes: A Life* (Oxford: Clarendon Press, 1991), pp. 9–10.

63 George Eliot, *The George Eliot Letters*, ed. Gordon S. Haight, 9 vols. (New Haven: Yale University Press, 1954–79), Vol. III, p. 116.

64 *Ibid.*, p. 274.

65 Hughes, *George Eliot*, p. 235.

66 'Vivian' [G. H. Lewes], 'Vivian's Review of Fredrika Bremer's *Easter Offering*', *The Leader* (23 September 1854), 69.

67 'Vivian', Review of Coyne, '*The Hope of the Family*', *The Leader* (10 December 1853), 1195.

68 'Vivian', 'How to Make Home Happy', *The Leader* (12 November 1853), 1099.

69 'Vivian', 'Vivian in His Easy Chair', *The Leader* (19 April 1851), 373.

70 'Vivian', 'The Bachelor's Evening', *The Leader* (25 October 1851), 1022–3 (p. 1022).

71 Charles Lamb, 'Dream Children: A Reverie', in *The Essays of Elia* [1823], Everyman Edition (London: J. M. Dent, 1962), 117–21 (p. 117).

72 Ashton, *G. H. Lewes*, p. 224.

73 Eliot, *Letters*, Vol. IV, p. 309.

74 Henry James, *Autobiography*, ed. Frederick W. Dupee (London: W. H. Allen, 1956), pp. 573, 575, 577.

75 Eliot, *Letters*, Vol. V, p. 66.

76 *Ibid.*, Vol. VI, pp. 165, 191.

77 *Ibid.*, Vol. V, p. 4.

78 *Ibid.*, p. 60.

2 THEATRICAL FATHERHOOD: DICKENS AND MACREADY

1 Charles Dickens, *The Letters of Charles Dickens*, ed. Madeline House *et al.*, 12 vols. (Oxford: Clarendon Press, 1965–99), Vol. VIII (1856–8), ed. Graham Storey and Kathleen Tillotson, p. 357.

2 'Tavistock-House Theatre', *The Times* (7 January 1857), 7.

3 Jane Austen, *Mansfield Park* [1814] (Harmondsworth: Penguin, 1966), p. 198. 'The smallest theatre in the world' heads his playbill for Wilkie Collins's *The Lighthouse*.

4 Charles Dickens [the Younger], 'Personal Reminiscences of My Father', Supplement to *Windsor Magazine* (Christmas 1934), 1–31 (p. 11).

5 Dickens, *Letters*, Vol. VII (1853–5), ed. Graham Storey, Kathleen Tillotson and Angus Easson, p. 501.

6 *Ibid.*, pp. 629, 638.

7 *Ibid.*, pp. 497, 638; Vol. VIII, p. 238.

8 *The Illustrated London News* (17 January 1857), p. 51.

9 Dickens, *Letters*, Vol. VIII, pp. 262, 270.

10 *Ibid.*, p. 260.

11 *Saturday Review* (1 August 1857), p. 107.

12 Dickens, *Letters*, Vol. VIII, pp. 432–3.

13 The complete text of *The Frozen Deep* is reprinted in Robert Louis Brannan (ed.), *Under the Management of Mr Charles Dickens: His Production of 'The Frozen Deep'*, ed. Robert Louis Brannan (Ithaca, NY: Cornell University Press, 1966), pp. 93–160. The quotation cited is on p. 106.

14 Brannan (ed.), *The Frozen Deep*, p. 103.

15 Dickens, *Letters*, Vol. VIII, p. 397.

16 Gladys Storey, *Dickens and Daughter* (London: Frederick Muller Ltd, 1939), p. 133.

17 Dickens, *Letters*, Vol. VIII, p. 256.

18 Charles Dickens, 'PERSONAL', *Household Words* (12 June 1858), 601.

19 Vincent Crummles, the theatrical actor-manager of *Nicholas Nickleby*, is the father of Ninetta Crummles, the so-called 'Infant Phenomenon'.

20 Charles Dickens, *Hard Times* [1854] (Harmondsworth: Penguin, 1969), p. 77.

21 Hilary M. Schor, *Dickens and the Daughter of the House* (Cambridge University Press, 1999); Dianne F. Sadoff, *Monsters of Affection: Dickens, Eliot and Brontë on Fatherhood* (Baltimore and London: Johns Hopkins University Press, 1982).

22 Dickens, *Letters*, Vol. IV (1844–6), ed. Kathleen Tillotson, p. 647.

23 *Ibid.*, p. 235.

24 Dickens, *Letters*, Vol. XII (1868–70), ed. Graham Storey, p. 187.

25 Trev Lynn Broughton and Helen Rogers (eds.), *Gender and Fatherhood in the Nineteenth Century* (Basingstoke: Palgrave Macmillan, 2007), p. 14.

26 William Charles Macready, *Diaries of William Charles Macready*, ed. William Toynbee, 2 vols. (London: Chapman & Hall Ltd, 1912), Vol. I, p. 407.

27 *Ibid.*, Vol. II, pp. 205, 397.

28 *Ibid.*, Vol. I, p. 275.

29 *Ibid.*, p. 470.

30 *Ibid.*, pp. 42–3.

31 Edgar and Eleanor Johnson (eds.), *The Dickens Theatrical Reader* (London: Victor Gollancz Ltd, 1964), p. 155. Thomas Betterton (*c.* 1635–1710) was a distinguished Restoration actor.

32 Reviews in *The Times* (16 October 1845), 5; (25 October 1849), 5.

33 William Charles Macready, *Macready's Reminiscences, and Selections from His Diaries and Letters*, ed. Sir Frederick Pollock, 2 vols. (London: Macmillan & Co., 1875), Vol. II, p. 61. This collection contains slightly different material from the later volumes edited by Toynbee.

34 W. B. Donne, review of Macready, *Reminiscences*, *Edinburgh Review* 141 (April 1875), 416–47 (p. 430).

35 Dickens, *Letters*, Vol. I (1820–39), ed. Madeline House and Graham Storey, p. 221.

36 Dickens to George Cruikshank, 9 January 1837, in Dickens, *Letters*, Vol. I, p. 221.

37 Dickens to Thomas Beard, 6 December 1837, in *ibid.*, p. 338; to Samuel Lover, 6 December 1837, in *ibid.*, p. 338; and to William Jerdan, 6 December 1837, in *ibid.*, p. 339. The quotation has proved untraceable.

38 Dickens, *Letters*, Vol. II (1840–1), ed. Madeline House and Graham Storey, p. 117.

39 Macready, *Diaries*, Vol. II, p. 75.

40 Henry's birth: Dickens to William Macready, 2 February 1849, in Dickens, *Letters*, Vol. V (1847–9), ed. Graham Storey and K. J. Fielding, p. 486; Edward's birth: to Mrs Gaskell, 13/14(?) March 1852, *ibid.*, Vol. VI (1850–2), ed. Storey and Fielding, p. 625; 'The Plornishghenter': to Georgina Hogarth, 25 November 1853, *ibid.*, Vol. VII, p. 210.

41 Dickens, *Letters*, Vol. IV, p. 419; cf. p. 418.

42 *Ibid.*, Vol. VI, p. 627.

43 Charles Dickens, *Little Dorrit* [1857] (Harmondsworth: Penguin, 1967), p. 179.

44 Dickens, *Letters*, Vol. IV, p. 659.

45 *Ibid.*, Vol. VI, p. 634; Vol. IV, p. 585.

46 Peter Ackroyd, *Dickens* (London: Minerva, 1991), p. 477.

47 Henry Dickens, *The Recollections of Sir Henry Dickens, KC* (London: William Heinemann Ltd, 1934), p. xviii.

48 Dickens, *Letters*, Vol. VI, pp. 152–3.

49 Ackroyd, *Dickens*, p. 633; Mamie [Mary] Dickens, 'Charles Dickens at Home, with Especial Reference to His Relations with Children, by His Eldest Daughter', *Cornhill Magazine* 4 (1885), 32–51 (p. 48).

50 Macready, *Reminiscences*, Vol. II, p. 342. Macready is here slightly misquoting Shakespeare's Sonnet 110.

51 Macready, *Diaries*, Vol. II, pp. 463, 490.

52 *Ibid.*, p. 99.

53 *Ibid.*, p. 458.

54 *Ibid.*, p. 180.

55 *Ibid.*, p. 116.

56 *Ibid.*

57 Dickens, *Letters*, Vol. II, p. 184.

58 Catherine Robson, *Men in Wonderland: The Lost Girlhood of the Victorian Gentleman* (Princeton and Oxford: Princeton University Press, 2001), p. 49.

59 Charles Dickens, 'A Child's Dream of a Star', *Household Words* (6 April 1850), 25–6.

60 Dickens, *Letters*, Vol. VI, p. 622.

61 *Ibid.*, Vol. X (1862–4), ed. Graham Storey, p. 356.

62 *Ibid.*, Vol. XII, p. 530.

63 Martin A. Danahay, *Gender at Work in Victorian Culture: Literature, Art and Masculinity* (Aldershot: Ashgate, 2005), pp. 4, 7.

64 Dickens, *Letters*, Vol. VII, p. 245.
65 *Ibid.*, Vol. XII, p. 530.
66 *Ibid.*, Vol. XI (1865–7), ed. Graham Storey, p. 93. Henry Fielding Dickens eventually became a High Court judge, and was knighted in 1922.
67 Storey, *Dickens and Daughter*, p. 95.
68 Henry Dickens, *Recollections*, p. 84.
69 Macready, *Diaries*, Vol. II, p. 372.
70 Dickens, *Letters*, Vol. VIII, pp. 741, 575.
71 Helena Michie, 'From Blood to Law: The Embarrassments of Family in Dickens', in *Palgrave Advances in Charles Dickens Studies*, ed. John Bowen and Robert L. Patten (Basingstoke: Palgrave Macmillan, 2006), pp. 131–54.
72 Charles Dickens, *Our Mutual Friend* [1864–5] (Harmondsworth: Penguin, 1971), p. 371.
73 Catherine Waters, *Dickens and the Politics of the Family* (Cambridge University Press, 1997), pp. 193, 205–6.
74 Claudia Nelson, 'Deconstructing the Paterfamilias: British Magazines and the Imagining of the Maternal Father, 1850–1910', *The Journal of Men's Studies* 11:3 (Spring 2003), 293–308 (p. 296).
75 Dickens [the Younger], 'Personal Reminiscences of My Father', p. 25; Storey, *Dickens and Daughter*, p. 93.
76 Storey, *Dickens and Daughter*, pp. 86, 91.
77 Sally Ledger, ' "Don't be so melodramatic!" Dickens and the Affective Mode', *19: Interdisciplinary Studies in the Long Nineteenth Century* 4 (2007), 1–14 (p. 7). Retrieved on 18 March 2008 from www.19.bbk.ac.uk/issue4/SallyDickens.pdf.
78 Dickens, *Letters*, Vol. IV, p. 235.
79 Theodore Martin, Review of Macready, '*Reminiscences*', *Quarterly Review* 138 (April 1875), 305–44 (p. 335).
80 Macready, *Reminiscences*, Vol. II, p. 175.

3 'HOW?' AND 'WHY?': KINGSLEY AS EDUCATING FATHER

1 Charles Kingsley, *Madam How and Lady Why; or, First Lessons in Earth Lore for Children* [1870] (London: Macmillan, 1899), p. 262.
2 *Ibid.*, p. 29.
3 Christopher Hibbert, *Edward VII: A Portrait* (London: Allen Lane, 1976), p. 39.
4 Charles Kingsley, *His Letters and Memories of His Life, Edited by His Wife*, ed. Fanny Kingsley, 2 vols. [1876], 5th edn (London: Henry S. King & Co., 1877), Vol. I, p. 279; Mary Kingsley, Memoir, in George Henry Kingsley, *Notes on Sport and Travel by George Henry Kingsley. With a Memoir by His Daughter Mary H. Kingsley* (London: Macmillan, 1900), p. 47. William Yarrell's *A History of British Fishes* was published in two volumes from 1835 to 1836.

5 Mary Kingsley, Memoir, p. 9.

6 George Kingsley, 'Chamois Hunting', *Fraser's Magazine* 44 (July 1851), 133–48.

7 Kingsley, *Letters*, Vol. I, p. 293.

8 Frederick Dolman, '"Lucas Malet at Home": A Chat with the Daughter of Charles Kingsley', *The Young Woman: A Monthly Journal and Review* 4 (1896), 145–9 (p. 148).

9 Maria and R. L. Edgeworth, *Practical Education*, 3 vols. [1798], 2nd edn (London: J. Johnson, 1801), Vol. III, pp. 357, 332.

10 Jean-Jacques Rousseau, *Émile* [1762], trans. Barbara Foxley (London : J. M. Dent, 1974), p. 5.

11 Richmal Mangnall, *Historical and Miscellaneous Questions for the Use of Young People* [1800], new edn (London: Fisher, Son & Co., 1840), p. 392.

12 Charles Kingsley, *The Water-Babies* [1863], ed. Brian Alderson (Oxford and New York: Oxford World's Classics, 1995), p. 165. Further references are given in the text.

13 Maria Edgeworth, *Rosamond Part i, by the Author of the Parent's Assistant* (Boston, MA: Cummings and Hilliard, 1813), p. 22; Edgeworth, *Harry and Lucy Concluded: Being the Last Part of Early Lessons* [1825], 3 vols., 4th edn (London: Simpkin, Marshall, & Co., 1846) Vol. I, p. 62.

14 Mrs [Jane] Marcet, *Conversations for Children: On Land and Water* (London: Longman, Orme, Brown, Green & Longmans, 1838), pp. 176–7.

15 Alan Rauch, *Useful Knowledge: The Victorians, Morality, and the March of Intellect* (Durham, NC and London: Duke University Press, 2001), p. 52.

16 B. H. Draper, *Conversations of a Father with His Son, on Some Leading Points in Natural Philosophy* (London: Wightman & Cramp, [1825]), pp. 83, 145.

17 William Pinnock, *Pinnock's Catechism of Geology*, 8th edn (London: G. B. Whittaker & Co., [1840?]), p. 67.

18 Charles Kingsley, 'How to Study Natural History', in *Scientific Lectures and Essays* (London: Macmillan and Co., 1890), pp. 289–310 (p. 304).

19 J. Hillis Miller, 'Reading *The Swiss Family Robinson* as Virtual Reality', in *Children's Literature: New Approaches*, ed. Karen Lesnik-Oberstein (Basingstoke: Palgrave, 2004), pp. 78–92 (p. 84).

20 *Ibid.*, p. 80.

21 Johann Rudolf Wyss, *The Swiss Family Robinson* [1812] (Ware: Wordsworth Classics, 1993), p. 119. Further references are included in the text.

22 Hillis Miller, p. 82, 'Reading *The Swiss Family Robinson*', p. 82.

23 Mary Martha Sherwood, *The History of the Fairchild Family; or, The Child's Manual* [1818–47], 3 vols., 24th edn (London: Hatchards, 1869), Vol. I, pp. 15–16.

24 Humphrey Carpenter and Mari Prichard (eds.), *The Oxford Companion to Children's Literature* (Oxford and New York: Oxford University Press, 1999), p. 407.

25 Kingsley, *Madam How*, p. ix.

26 J. K. Laughton, Review of '*Charles Kingsley: His Letters and Memories*', *Edinburgh Review* 145 (April 1877), 415–46 (p. 433).

27 Charles Kingsley, 'The Wonders of the Shore', *North British Review* 22 (November 1854), 1–56 (p. 43). In *Glaucus* this passage reappears with 'father's' changed to 'parents": Kingsley, *Glaucus* [1855], rept. *The Water-Babies and Glaucus* (New York: J. M. Dent, 1908), p. 282.

28 Kingsley, 'The Wonders of the Shore', p. 17.

29 Kingsley, *The Water-Babies and Glaucus*, p. 248.

30 Brendan A. Rapple, 'The Educational Thought of Charles Kingsley', *Historical Studies in Education* 9:1 (Spring 1997), 46–64.

31 Charles Kingsley, 'Thrift', in *Sanitary and Social Lectures and Essays* (London: Macmillan, 1880), pp. 77–104 (p. 103).

32 John C. Hawley, SJ, 'The Muscular Christian as Schoolmarm', in *Victorian Scandals: Representations of Gender and Class*, ed. Kristine Ottesen Garrigan (Athens, OH: Ohio University Press, 1992), pp. 134–56 (p. 135).

33 David Rosen, 'The Volcano and the Cathedral: Muscular Christianity and the Origins of Primal Manliness', in *Muscular Christianity: Embodying the Victorian Age*, ed. Donald E. Hall (Cambridge University Press, 1994), pp. 17–44 (pp. 19, 29).

34 Claudia Nelson, *Boys Will Be Girls: The Feminine Ethic and British Children's Fiction 1857–1917* (New Brunswick, NJ and London: Rutgers University Press, 1991), p. 152.

35 Laura Fasick, 'The Failure of Fatherhood: Maleness and Its Discontents in Charles Kingsley', *Children's Literature Association Quarterly* 18:3 (1993), 91–113 (p. 107).

36 Charles Kingsley, *The Water-Babies*, *Macmillan's Magazine* 7 (November 1862–April 1863), p. 100. This omission is pointed out by Larry K. Uffelman and Patrick Scott in 'Kingsley's Serial Novels II: *The Water-Babies*', *Victorian Periodicals Review* 19:4 (Winter 1986), 122–31 (p. 125).

37 Kingsley, Preface to 'Town Geology', in *Scientific Lectures and Essays*, pp. 3–151 (p. 18).

38 Kingsley, 'The Air-Mothers', in *ibid.*, pp. 131–63 (p. 135).

39 Kingsley, 'Heroism', in *ibid.*, pp. 225–54 (pp. 247–8).

40 I am grateful to Trev Broughton for coining this term during discussion of the paper I gave on Kingsley at the *Father Figures* conference held at Liverpool John Moores University in July 2003.

41 Kingsley, 'The Air Mothers', p. 138.

42 Charles Kingsley, 'The Science of Health', in *Sanitary and Social Lectures and Essays*, pp. 21–45 (p. 37).

43 Fasick, 'The Failure of Fatherhood', p. 109.

44 Susan Chitty, *The Beast and the Monk: A Life of Charles Kingsley* (London: Hodder & Stoughton, 1974), p. 255.

45 Rose G. Kingsley, *South by West; or, Winter in the Rocky Mountains and Spring in Mexico*, ed. and Pref. Charles Kingsley (London: W. Isbister & Co., 1874), pp. 129, 50.

46 Rose G. Kingsley, Preface to Kingsley, *The Water-Babies and Glaucus* (1908), pp. vii–ix (p. viii).

47 Rose G. Kingsley, *Eversley Gardens and Others* (London: George Allen, 1907), pp. 257, 18.

48 Dolman, 'Lucas Malet at Home', p. 147.

49 'Lucas Malet' [Mary Kingsley], *The Tutor's Story: An Unpublished Novel by the Late Charles Kingsley, Revised and Completed by His Daughter Lucas Malet . . .* (London: Smith, Elder & Co., 1916), p. vii.

50 Anon., 'A Posthumous Legacy', *Times Literary Supplement* (5 October 1916), 474.

51 Janet E. Hogarth, 'Lucas Malet's Novels', *Fortnightly Review* 71 (1902), 532–40 (p. 533); Janet Courtney, 'A Novelist of the 'Nineties'', *Fortnightly Review* 131 (1932), 230–41 (p. 238).

52 Patricia Srebrnik, 'The Re-subjection of "Lucas Malet": Charles Kingsley's Daughter and the Response to Muscular Christianity', in *Muscular Christianity: Embodying the Victorian Age*, ed. Hall, pp. 194–214 (p. 194).

53 'Lucas Malet' [Mary Kingsley], 'The Threatened Re-Subjection of Woman', *Fortnightly Review* 77 (1905), 806–19 (p. 818).

54 Kingsley, *His Letters and Memories of His Life*, Vol. 1, p. 299.

55 Anon., 'Miss Mary Kingsley' (obituary), *The Athenaeum* (23 June 1900), 784–5 (p. 785).

56 Katherine Frank, *A Voyager Out: The Life of Mary Kingsley* (London: Hamish Hamilton, 1986), p. xv.

57 Frank, *A Voyager Out*, pp. 15, 35, 58.

58 George Henry Kingsley, *Notes on Sport and Travel*, p. 202.

59 Both obituaries were headed 'Miss Mary Kingsley': the first on 16 June 1900 (750–1), the second on 23 June 1900 (784–5).

4 MATTHEW AND SON (AND FATHER): THE ARNOLDS

1 Matthew Arnold, *The Letters of Matthew Arnold*, ed. Cecil Y. Lang, 6 vols. (Charlottesville and London: University of Virginia Press, 1996–2001), Vol. 1, p. 351.

2 *Ibid.*, Vol. 11, p. 145.

3 *Ibid.*, Vol. 1v, p. 220.

4 A. C. Swinburne, 'Matthew Arnold's New Poems' (1867), in *The Complete Works of Algernon Charles Swinburne*, ed. Sir Edmund Gosse and Thomas James Wise, 20 vols. (London and New York: William Heinemann Ltd, 1926–7), Vol. xv, p. 84; Arnold, *The Letters of Matthew Arnold*, Vol. vi, p. 72.

5 Arnold Whitridge, *Dr Arnold of Rugby* (London: Constable & Co., 1928), p. 206.

6 Katharine Lake (ed.), *Memorials of William Charles Lake* (London: Edward Arnold, 1901), p. 164.

7 Terence Copley, *Black Tom: Arnold of Rugby. The Myth and the Man* (London and New York: Continuum, 2002), p. 266.

8 Thomas Hughes, *Tom Brown's Schooldays* [1857] (Harmondsworth: Puffin, 1971), p. 287.

9 Ian Hamilton, *A Gift Imprisoned: The Poetic Life of Matthew Arnold* (London: Basic Books, 1998), p. 34.

10 A. P. Stanley, 'Arnold and Rugby', *Macmillan's Magazine* 30 (July 1874), 279–80 (p. 280).

11 T. Mozley, *Reminiscences Chiefly of Oriel College and the Oxford Movement*, 2 vols. (London: Longmans, Green & Co., 1882), Vol. 11, pp. 48–54.

12 Frances J. Woodward, *The Doctor's Disciples. A Study of Four Pupils of Arnold of Rugby: Stanley, Gell, Clough, William Arnold* (London: Oxford University Press, 1954).

13 Whitridge, *Dr Arnold of Rugby*, p. 211.

14 James Fitzjames Stephen, Review of Hughes, '*Tom Brown's Schooldays*', *Edinburgh Review* 107 (January 1858), 172–93 (pp. 183, 189).

15 Mozley, *Reminiscences*, Vol. 11, p. 54.

16 Charlotte Brontë, *The Letters of Charlotte Brontë*, ed. Margaret Smith, 3 vols. (Oxford: Clarendon Press, 2000), Vol. 11, pp. 495, 554.

17 W. H. Auden, 'Matthew Arnold', in Auden, *Collected Shorter Poems 1927–1957* (London: Faber and Faber, 1966), p. 73.

18 Park Honan, *Matthew Arnold: A Life* (London: Weidenfeld and Nicolson, 1981); Nicholas Murray, *A Life of Matthew Arnold* (London: Hodder and Stoughton, 1996); Hamilton, *A Gift Imprisoned*.

19 Arnold, *Letters*, Vol. 11, pp. 379, 407.

20 *Ibid.*, pp. 86, 421, 479; Vol. 111, p. 207.

21 *Ibid.*, Vol. 111, p. 51.

22 Thomas Arnold, Letters of Thomas Arnold: 107 letters to family members and friends. Leeds University Library, Brotherton Collection MS 19c Arnold (Arnold Family Letters, Series 1), 4 April 1823.

23 *Ibid.*, 29 December 1823.

24 *Ibid.*, 17 August 1827; 15 June 1828.

25 *Ibid.*, 17 May 1830; Mary Arnold, Records of Thomas Arnold's conversations (1829). Leeds University Library, Brotherton Collection, MS 19c Arnold 27, fo. 53.

26 Mary Arnold, 'Records, Reminiscences for Her Children', 2 vols., Vol. 1 (1822–33). Leeds University Library, Brotherton Collection, MS 19c Arnold 11–12, fo. 34. Nine of the Arnold children lived to adulthood; two baby daughters died, in 1824 and 1832.

27 *Ibid.*, fo. 49.

28 Christine Alexander, 'Play and Apprenticeship: The Culture of Family Magazines', in *The Child Writer from Austen to Woolf*, ed. Christine Alexander and Juliet McMaster (Cambridge University Press, 2005), pp. 31–50. Gillian E. Boughton's essay in the same collection, 'Dr Arnold's Granddaughter: Mary Ward', pp. 237–53, includes some illustrations from the *Fox How Magazine*.

29 Mary Arnold, 'Notebook of Poems etc., by Family', 1836. Leeds University, Brotherton Collection, MS 19c Arnold 6, fo. 72.

30 Thomas Arnold *et al.*, *Fox How Magazine* (1838–42), unpublished manuscript. Jerwood Library, Dove Cottage, Grasmere (1 January 1839), fo. 50.

31 *Ibid.* (1 January 1840), fo. 104; (1 January 1841), fo. 6.

32 Thomas Arnold [the Younger], *Passages in a Wandering Life* (London: Edward Arnold, 1900), p. 9.

33 Arnold, *Letters*, Vol. 1, p. 5.

34 Quoted in Copley, *Black Tom*, p. 79.

35 Arnold, *Letters*, Vol. 1, pp. 5–6.

36 Mary Arnold, 'Notebook of Poems'.

37 A. P. Stanley, *The Life and Correspondence of Thomas Arnold, D.D.* [1844], 2 vols., 8th edn (London: T. Fellows, 1858), Vol. 1, p. 189.

38 Norman Wymer, *Dr Arnold of Rugby* (London: Robert Hale Ltd, 1953), p. 113.

39 Thomas Arnold, *Christian Life, Its Hopes, Its Fears, and Its Close: Sermons, Preached Mostly in the Chapel of Rugby School by the Late Thomas Arnold, D. D.* (London: B. Fellowes, 1849), pp. 115, 95.

40 Harriet Martineau, *The Collected Letters of Harriet Martineau*, ed. Deborah A. Logan, 5 vols. (London: Pickering & Chatto, 2007), Vol. IV, p. 31.

41 Lionel Trilling, *Matthew Arnold* (New York and London: Columbia University Press and George Allen and Unwin, 1949), p. 33.

42 Carl Dawson (ed.), *Matthew Arnold: The Poetry*, Critical Heritage series (London and Boston, MA: Routledge and Kegan Paul, 1973), p. 96.

43 *Ibid.*, p. 114.

44 Rowland Prothero, 'The Poetry of Matthew Arnold', *Edinburgh Review* 168 (October 1888), 337–73 (p. 344); R. H. Hutton, 'The Poetry of Matthew Arnold', in *Literary Essays* (London: Macmillan, 1896), p. 312.

45 Matthew Arnold, 'Thirty-five Years of School Inspecting: Mr Matthew Arnold's Farewell', in *The Complete Prose Works of Matthew Arnold*, ed. R. H. Super, 11 vols. (Ann Arbor: University of Michigan Press, 1990), Vol. XI, *The Last Word*, pp. 374–9 (pp. 376–7).

46 Matthew Arnold, 'Rugby Chapel. November 1857', in *The Poems of Matthew Arnold* [ed. Kenneth Allott, 1965], 2nd edn, ed. Miriam Allott (London and New York: Longman, 1979), p. 482. All further references will be to this edition.

47 W. B. Yeats, *Poems of W. B. Yeats: A New Selection*, ed. A. Norman Jeffares (London and Basingstoke: Macmillan, 1984), p. 246, lines 7–8.

48 Honan, *Matthew Arnold*, p. 69.

49 Arnold, 'Cromwell', in *Poems*, pp. 221–2, lines 221–2.

50 Cited in the *Times* review of Stanley's *Life* (28 October 1844) p. 7.

51 Honan, *Matthew Arnold*, p. 296.

52 *The Times* (28 October 1844) p. 7.

53 Arnold, 'Sohrab and Rustum', in *Poems*, pp. 319–55.

54 Honan, *Matthew Arnold*, p. 281; Murray, *A Life of Matthew Arnold*, p. 139.

55 Arnold, 'A Picture at Newstead', in *Poems*, p. 521, line 5.

56 Arnold, 'Mycerinus', in *ibid.*, pp. 26–32, lines 13–14.

57 Arnold, *Letters*, Vol. 1, p. 239.

58 *Ibid.*, p. 482.
59 'From my little study I can hear all that passes': *ibid.*, p. 411.
60 Matthew Arnold, 'Preface', in *Culture and Anarchy* [1869], ed. J. Dover Wilson (Cambridge University Press, 1981), p. 8.
61 Arnold, 'Preface' (1853), in *Poems*, p. 663.
62 *Punch* (10 November 1883), p. 221.
63 Arnold, *Letters*, Vol. v, p. 211.
64 Murray, *A Life of Matthew Arnold*, p. 328; Arnold, *Letters*, Vol. v, p. 249.
65 W. H. Mallock, *The New Republic* [1877] (London: Chatto & Windus, 1908), p. 34.
66 Thomas Arnold [the Younger], *Passages in a Working Life*, p. 9.

5 'A FINE DEGREE OF PATERNAL FERVOUR': SCIENTIFIC FATHERING

1 Charles Darwin, *The Correspondence of Charles Darwin*, ed. Frederick Burkhardt and Sydney Smith, 15 vols. (Cambridge University Press, 1983–2005), Vol. x (1862), p. 330.
2 Darwin, *Correspondence*, Vol. 11 (1837–42), Appendix iv, pp. 444–5.
3 Paul White argues that the term 'man of science', used by Huxley in preference to the new term 'scientist', was marked by specific conventions of class and profession, as well as gender (compared with 'man of letters', for example). See Paul White, *Thomas Huxley: Making the 'Man of Science'* (Cambridge University Press, 2003).
4 Beatrice Webb, *The Diary of Beatrice Webb*, ed. Norman and Jeanne Mackenzie, 2 vols. (London: Virago, 1986), Vol. 1, pp. 202–3.
5 Cited by Adrian Desmond in his *Huxley: The Devil's Disciple* (London: Michael Joseph, 1994), p. 309. This is the same Catharine Tait discussed in my 'Case Histories' chapter, wife of Archibald Tait.
6 Darwin's religious position is harder to explain than Huxley's agnosticism, not least because he did not talk at length about it. Religious belief never seems to have been particularly important to him. The Darwin Correspondence Project website, www.darwinproject.ac.uk/, has a useful section on his religious belief, suggesting he shifted gradually towards deism and agnosticism, but was genuinely uncertain about religious questions (accessed 17 April 2008).
7 Paul White, 'Genius in Public and Private', in *Thomas Henry Huxley's Place in Science and Letters: Centenary Essays*, ed. Alan P. Barr (Athens, GA and London: University of Georgia Press, 1997), p. 215.
8 For example in his essay 'Emancipation – Black and White' (1865), reproduced in Thomas Henry Huxley, *Science and Education* (London: Macmillan, 1925), pp. 66–75.
9 White, 'Genius in Public and Private', p. 252.
10 Eve Kosofsky Sedgwick, *Between Men: English Literature and Male Homosexual Desire* (New York: Columbia University Press, 1985), p. 1.

11 Sara Ahmed, *The Cultural Politics of Emotion* (Edinburgh University Press, 2004), p. 3.

12 Charles Darwin, *Charles Darwin's Notebooks, 1836–1844*, ed. Paul H. Barrett *et al.* (Cambridge University Press and the British Museum, 1987), pp. 520, 536.

13 Charles Darwin and Thomas Henry Huxley, *Charles Darwin, Thomas Henry Huxley: Autobiographies*, ed. Gavin de Beer (London, New York and Toronto: Oxford University Press, 1974), p. 22.

14 Leonard Huxley (ed.), *Life and Letters of Sir Joseph Dalton Hooker*, 2 vols. (London: John Murray, 1918), Vol. ii, p. 199.

15 James A. Secord, 'The Geological Survey of Great Britain as a Research School, 1839–1855', *History of Science* 24 (1986), 233–75 (pp. 240, 251).

16 Leonard Huxley (ed.), *Life and Letters of Thomas Henry Huxley*, 2 vols. (London: Macmillan & Co. Ltd, 1900); *Life and Letters of Sir Joseph Dalton Hooker*. Both Darwin and Hooker were his godfathers.

17 Francis Darwin edited *The Life and Letters of Charles Darwin*, 3 vols. (London: John Murray, 1887), which includes a chapter entitled 'Reminiscences of My Father's Everyday Life' (Vol. i, pp. 108–60); and, with A. C. Seward, *More Letters of Charles Darwin*, 2 vols. (Cambridge University Press, 2004). Henrietta Litchfield edited *Emma Darwin: Wife of Charles Darwin: A Century of Family Letters, by Her Daughter H. E. Litchfield*, 2 vols. (Cambridge University Press, 1904); George Darwin's reminiscences are in Cambridge University Library, ms DAR 112. See also Gwen Raverat, *Period Piece: A Cambridge Childhood* (London: Faber & Faber, 1952). Aldous Huxley's 'T. H. Huxley as a Literary Man' (the Huxley Memorial Lecture for 1932) is reprinted in *The Olive Tree and Other Essays* (London: Chatto & Windus, 1947), pp. 46–81.

18 Michael Shortland and Richard Yeo (eds.), *Telling Lives in Science: Essays on Scientific Biography* (Oxford University Press, 1996), p. 2. The modern Huxley biographies are Adrian Desmond's two-part *Huxley: The Devil's Disciple* (1994) and *Huxley: Evolution's High Priest* (London: Michael Joseph, 1997).

19 Anon., review of *The Life and Letters of Charles Darwin*, ed. Francis Darwin, *Saturday Review* 64 (19 November 1887), p. 701.

20 Adrian Desmond and James Moore, *Darwin* (Harmondsworth: Penguin, 1992), pp. 314, 406.

21 Darwin and T. H. Huxley, *Autobiographies*.

22 Darwin, *Correspondence*, Vol. ii, p. 250.

23 *Ibid.*, Vol. iii (1844–6), p. 216.

24 *Ibid.*, Vol. vii (1858–9), p. 33.

25 *Ibid.*, Vol. ii, p. 255; L. Huxley (ed.), *Life and Letters of Thomas Henry Huxley*, Vol. i, pp. 265, 425; Darwin, *Correspondence*, Vol. vii, p. 365; unpublished letter to Asa Gray, 8 May 1868, Darwin Correspondence Project, letter 6167.

26 Darwin, *Correspondence*, Vol. vi (1856–7), p. 334.

27 Claudia Nelson, *Invisible Men: Fatherhood in Victorian Periodicals 1850– 1910* (Athens, GA and London: University of Georgia Press, 1995), pp. 105, 205.

28 Thomas Henry Huxley, 'Owen's Position in the History of Anatomical Science', in *The Scientific Memoirs of Thomas Henry Huxley*, ed. Michael Foster and E. Ray Lankester (London: Macmillan, 1902), pp. 683, 685.

29 Leonard Huxley, 'Scenes from Huxley's Home Life, by His Son Leonard Huxley', *The Century Magazine* 33 (1897), 355–62 (p. 358); similar stories appear in Leonard Huxley's 'Home Memories', Supplement to *Nature* 150 (9 May 1925), 698–702.

30 L. Huxley (ed.), *Life and Letters of Thomas Henry Huxley*, Vol. 1, p. 305; Vol. 11, p. 431 – a point repeated in his *Thomas Henry Huxley*, Life Stories of Famous Men series (London: Watts & Co., 1920), p. 112, and 'Scenes from Huxley's Home Life', p. 355.

31 Jessie Oriana Waller, 'Mental and Physical Training of Children', *The Nineteenth Century* 26 (October 1889), 659–67 (pp. 660–1).

32 James Sully, 'The New Study of Children', *Fortnightly Review* 64 (November 1895), 723–37.

33 Darwin's 'Observations on Children' are reprinted as Appendix 111 in Darwin, *Correspondence*, Vol. 1v (1847–50), pp. 410, 411.

34 *Ibid.*, p. 413.

35 *Ibid.*, p. 415.

36 'The Death of Charles Waring Darwin', in *ibid.*, Vol. v11, p. 521.

37 Charles Darwin, 'A Biographical Sketch of an Infant', *Mind* (July 1877), 285–94 (pp. 294, 288).

38 Darwin, *Correspondence*, Vol. 11, p. 293.

39 *Ibid.*, Vol. v (1851–5), p. 14. In 1840 Darwin had been ill at the Wedgwood family home, Maer in Staffordshire, for over three months.

40 Darwin's memorial is reproduced as Appendix 11, in *Ibid.*, pp. 540–2.

41 *Ibid.*, Vol. x11 (1864), p. 325.

42 L. Huxley, *Life and Letters of Thomas Henry Huxley*, Vol. 1, p. 151.

43 Pat Jalland, *Death in the Victorian Family* (Oxford University Press, 1996), p. 355; L. Huxley, *Life and Letters of Thomas Henry Huxley*, Vol. 1, p. 241.

44 H. A. Huxley, 'Reminiscences by Mrs Huxley of Early Married Life', Huxley Papers, Vol. xxx1, Imperial College London, fos. 91–2.

45 L. Huxley, *Life and Letters of Thomas Henry Huxley*, Vol. 1, p. 152.

46 Darwin, *Correspondence*, Vol. v111 (1860), pp. 365–6.

47 *Ibid.*, Vol. x1 (1863), pp. 640, 644–6.

48 Thomas Henry Huxley, 'The Romanes Lecture', in *Evolution and Ethics* (London and New York: Macmillan, 1893), pp. 46–116 (pp. 52–3).

49 Thomas Henry Huxley, 'Prolegomena' (1894) to 'Evolution and Ethics' (1893), in *'Evolution and Ethics' and Other Essays* (London and New York: Macmillan, 1925), p. 39.

50 Webb, *Diary*, Vol. 1, p. 203.

51 L. Huxley, 'Scenes from Huxley's Home Life', p. 356.

52 This is a favourite Huxley anecdote from 1878, recounted fully here by Aldous Huxley in 'T. H. Huxley as a Literary Man', in *The Olive Tree*, pp. 46–81 (p. 49).

53 Thomas Henry Huxley, 'Address to the Royal Academy', *Medical Times and Gazette* (May 1871), extract available on the Huxley File website, created by Charles Blinderman. Retrieved on 20 April 2008 from http://alepho.clarku.edu/huxley/UnColl/Gazettes/RoyAc71.html.

54 White, *Thomas Huxley*, p. 97.

55 Thomas H. Huxley, 'The Connection between Science and Art and Literature', *Nature* 36 (5 May 1887), 14.

56 Charles S. Blinderman, 'T. H. Huxley's Theory of Aesthetics: Unity in Diversity', *Journal of Aesthetics and Art Criticism* 21 (1962), 49–55 (pp. 51, 54).

57 Thomas H. Huxley, 'The Struggle for Existence in Human Society' (1888), in '*Evolution and Ethics*', pp. 185–236 (p. 220); 'On Science and Art in Relation to Education' (1882), in *Science and Education: Essays by Thomas H. Huxley* (London: Macmillan and Co. Ltd, 1925), pp. 160–88 (p. 183).

58 T. H. Huxley, 'Emancipation – Black and White' (1865), in *Science and Education*, p. 71.

59 Adrian Desmond, *Huxley: Evolution's High Priest*, p. 197.

60 Cited by Janet Browne in *Charles Darwin: The Power of Place* (London: Pimlico, 2003), p. 488.

61 This picture, called *The Artist at Work*, is owned by the National Portrait Gallery, and was briefly exhibited there in 2008.

62 Anon., 'Exhibition of the Royal Academy', *The Times* (28 June 1880), 5.

63 'Professor Huxley's Homes, by a friend', *The Illustrated London News* (6 July 1895), 3.

64 Elaine Showalter, *The Female Malady: Women, Madness, and English Culture, 1830–1980* (London: Virago, 1985), p. 147.

65 Thomas H. Huxley, 'The Value of Witness to the Miraculous' (1889), in *Science and Christian Tradition*, pp. 160–91 (pp. 168–9).

66 *Ibid.*, pp. 189, 183.

67 Josef Breuer and Sigmund Freud, *Studies on Hysteria*, Standard Edition of the Complete Psychological Works of Sigmund Freud, ed. James Strachey, 2 vols. (London: Hogarth Press, 1955), Vol. II, p. 22.

68 Francis Galton, *Hereditary Genius: An Inquiry into Its Laws and Consequences* (1869) and *English Men of Science: Their Nature and Nurture* (1874). The latter was based on a study of 180 distinguished men, to whom he sent a questionnaire about their families.

69 Darwin, *Correspondence*, Vol. x, pp. 618–19, 26.

70 L. Huxley (ed.), *Life and Letters of Sir Joseph Dalton Hooker*, Vol II, p. 366.

71 Desmond, *Evolution's High Priest*, p. 197.

72 Aldous, Huxley, *Letters of Aldous Huxley*, ed. Grover Smith (London: Chatto & Windus, 1969), pp. 208–9.

73 George Howard Darwin, 'Marriages between First Cousins', *Fortnightly Review* 27, new series (July 1875), 22–41 (p. 41).

74 Darwin, *Correspondence*, Vol. VII, p. 38

75 *Ibid.*, Vol. VIII, p. 89.

76 *Ibid.*, Vol. VII, p. 302.

77 *Ibid.*, Vol. XI, p. 403.

78 T. H. Huxley, *Life and Letters of Sir Joseph Dalton Hooker*, Vol. II, p. 367.

79 J. D. Hooker to Joseph Hooker, 'Lion Letters', Royal Botanic Gardens, Kew JDH/2/7; 1887 (hypocaust); 1 July 1888 (rainfall); July 10 1888 (elm tree). Typed transcripts of unpublished letters.

80 G. H. Darwin, Reminiscences, Cambridge University Library, MS DAR 112, fo. 11.

81 Philip Gosse obviously does not fit this pattern, his religious fanaticism making him a harsh disciplinarian, as his son Edmund records in *Father and Son* [1907] (Harmondsworth: Penguin, 1983).

82 Cyril Bibby (ed.), *The Essence of T. H. Huxley* (London: Macmillan/St Martin's Press, 1967), p. 10.

6 DEATH COMES FOR THE ARCHBISHOP (AND PRIME MINISTER)

1 W. E. Gladstone, *The Gladstone Diaries*, ed. M. R. D. Foot and H. C. G. Matthew, 14 vols. (Oxford: Clarendon Press, 1968–94), Vol. VIII, ed. H. C. G. Matthew, p. 262.

2 *Ibid.*, Vol. X, ed. H. C. G. Matthew, p. clxxvii; A. C. Benson (ed.), *The Life of Edward White Benson*, 2 vols. (London: Macmillan, 1899), Vol. I, p. 643.

3 St Deiniol's Library, Hawarden, Glynne–Gladstone MS 603 (28 December 1857), accessed at Flintshire Record Office.

4 A. C. Benson, *Memories and Friends* (London: John Murray, 1924), p. 29.

5 Robert Hugh Benson, *Confessions of a Convert* (London: Longmans, Green & Co., 1913), pp. 15–16.

6 Ethel Smyth, *The Memoirs of Ethel Smyth*, abridged and ed. Ronald Crichton (London: Viking, 1987), p. 145.

7 Roy Jenkins, *Gladstone* (London and Basingstoke: Macmillan, 1995), pp. 114–15; Jenny West, 'Gladstone and Laura Thistlethwayte, 1865–75', *Historical Research* 80 (August 2007), 368–92.

8 Gladstone, *The Gladstone Diaries*, Vol. IX, ed. H. C. G. Matthew, p. 471.

9 A. C. Benson, *Life of E. W. Benson*, Vol. I, p. 592.

10 Mary Drew [Gladstone], *Catherine Gladstone, by Her Daughter Mary Drew* [1919] (London: Nisbet and Co., 1928), Introduction, n. p.

11 Gladstone, *The Gladstone Diaries*, Vol. XIII, ed. H. C. G. Matthew, pp. 222–3.

12 Mary published a sketch of her mother in the *Cornhill Magazine* in 1916, expanded into a full biography, *Catherine Gladstone*, in 1919; some material on her father appeared in *Acton, Gladstone and Others* (1924), and her own diaries and letters were edited and published by Lucy Masterman in 1930: Mary Gladstone [Drew], *Mary Gladstone (Mrs Drew): Her Diaries and Letters*, ed. Lucy Masterman (London: Methuen & Co., 1930). Herbert Gladstone

published a defence of his father's reputation in 1928: Herbert Gladstone, *After Thirty Years* (London: Macmillan, 1928). For a full account of Herbert and Henry Gladstone's efforts on their father's behalf, see John P. Gardiner, 'Gladstone, Gossip and the Post-War Generation', *Historical Research* 74 (November 2001), 409–24.

13 George W. E. Russell, *William Ewart Gladstone* (London: Sampson Low, Marston and Co., 1891), pp. 281–2.

14 Cited by J. Ewing Ritchie, *The Real Gladstone: An Anecdotal Biography* (London and New York: T. Fisher Unwin, 1898), p. 278.

15 Sir Wemyss Reid (ed.), *The Life of William Ewart Gladstone* (London: Cassell and Co., 1899), pp. 591ff.

16 Benson, *Life of Edward White Benson*, Vol. I, p. 589; A. C. Benson, *The Trefoil: Wellington College, Lincoln and Truro* (London: John Murray, 1923), p. 170.

17 John Tosh, 'Domesticity and Manliness in the Victorian Middle Class: The Family of Edward White Benson', in *Manful Assertions: Masculinities in Britain since 1800*, ed. Michael Roper and John Tosh (London and New York: Routledge 1991), pp. 44–73 (pp. 61–2).

18 Stuart C. Aitken, 'The Awkward Spaces of Fathering', in *Spaces of Masculinities*, ed. Bettina van Hoven and Kathrin Hörschelmann (London and New York: Routledge, 2005), pp. 222–36 (pp. 222–3). As recently as March 2008, Cole Moreton, in *The Independent on Sunday*, commented that Gordon Brown had benefited 'both as a politician and a man' from having a wife and children, and cited David Cameron as saying 'People want to know who you are and what you are like and what makes you tick': Cole Moreton, 'Politics for Breakfast: Will Cameron Regret Placing Tots in the Frontline?', *Independent on Sunday* (16 March 2008), 43.

19 David Williamson, *Gladstone the Man* (London: James Bowden, 1898), p. 25.

20 H. Gladstone, *After Thirty Years*, pp. xiii, xv.

21 Aitken, 'The Awkward Spaces of Fathering', p. 222.

22 Thomas Laqueur, 'The Facts of Fatherhood', in *Rethinking the Family: Some Feminist Questions*, ed. Barrie Thorne and Marilyn Yalom (Boston, MA: Northeastern University Press, 1992), pp. 155–75.

23 Jenkins, *Gladstone*, p. 66. John Morley was Gladstone's first biographer (1903).

24 Gladstone, *The Gladstone Diaries*, Vol. III, ed. M. R. D. Foot and H. C. G. Matthew, p. 65.

25 Glynne–Gladstone MS 835, fos. 1–2.

26 Gladstone, *Diaries*, Vol. IV, ed. M. R. D. Foot and H. C. G. Matthew, p. 389.

27 *Ibid*., p. 372.

28 E. W. Benson, *Boy-Life: Its Trial. Its Strength. Its Fulness* (London: Macmillan & Co./Wellington College: George Bishop, 1874), pp. 356–7.

29 A. C. Benson, *Life of Edward White Benson*, Vol. I, p. 82; undated letter to Mary Benson, Bodleian Library, Oxford, MS Benson 3/15, fo. 142 .

30 Leonore Davidoff, 'Kinship as a Categorical Concept: A Case Study', *Journal of Social History* 39:2 (2005), 411–28.

31 W. T. Stead, 'Mr Gladstone', Part 11, *Review of Reviews* (May 1892), 461–3 (p. 466).

32 Anon., review of A. C. Benson, *The Life of Edward White Benson*, *The Saturday Review* 89 (13 January 1900), 50–1 (p. 51); F. W. Farrar, 'Two Archbishops', *Contemporary Review* 70 (December 1896), 623–35 (p. 633).

33 Glynne–Gladstone MS 984, fo. 31.

34 Glynne–Gladstone MS 835, fo. 22.

35 Margaret Oliphant, *The Autobiography of Margaret Oliphant*, ed. Elisabeth Jay [1899] (Oxford University Press, 1990).

36 E. W. Benson, unpublished manuscript diary. Trinity College, Cambridge, MS EWB A3, fo. 97.

37 Thomas Hughes, *Tom Brown's Schooldays* [1857] (Harmondsworth: Puffin, 1971), pp. 243–5.

38 David Newsome, *Godliness and Good Learning: Four Studies on a Victorian Ideal* (London: John Murray. 1961). Since the publication of Newsome's book, Martin's half of the correspondence with his parents seems to have disappeared from the Bodleian archive.

39 Unpublished letter from Mary Benson to Martin Benson, 20 September 1870. Bodleian Library, Oxford, MS Benson 3/43–4, fo. 5.

40 A. C. Benson, *Life of Edward White Benson*, Vol. 11, p. 317.

41 Unsigned memoir by A. C. Benson, in S. R. Holman, 'New Introduction' to Nellie [Mary Eleanor] Benson, *Lambeth Women Speak* (originally *Streets and Lanes of the City*, 1890). Retrieved on 18 October 2008 from www.povertystudies.org/NellieBenson/01-Introduction.htm.

42 E. W. Benson, 'Brief Memoir', in Mary Eleanor Benson, *Streets and Lanes of the City: With a Brief Memoir by Her Father* (London and Bungay: Richard Clay and Sons Ltd, 1891), pp. xvii, xii.

43 A. C. Benson, *Life of Edward White Benson*, Vol. 11, p. 413.

44 *Ibid.*, p. 535.

45 Gladstone, *The Gladstone Diaries*, Vol. 111, p. 33.

46 *Ibid.*, p. 366.

47 *Ibid.*, pp. 650–1.

48 For example, *ibid.*, Vol. 1V, pp. 51, 55.

49 W. E. Gladstone, 'Some account of our second daughter Catherine Jessy Gladstone', unpublished manuscript. British Library, Add. MS 46269, fos. 131–41 (fo. 141). This is a more legible version of Add. MS 44738, fos. 122–46, copied by Mary Drew.

50 Gladstone, *The Gladstone Diaries*, Vol. V111, p. 507.

51 Michael Tanner, 'Sentimentality', *Proceedings of the Aristotelian Society* 77 (1976–7), 127–47 (p. 130).

52 Robert C. Solomon, *In Defence of Sentimentality* (Oxford University Press, 2004), pp. 79–81.

53 Drew, *Catherine Gladstone*, p. 73. She is probably referring to De Quincey's response to his favourite sister Elizabeth's death in 1792, described in 'The Affliction of Childhood' (1845).

54 Gladstone's unpublished manuscript, headed 'For the Sacred Memory of William Henry Gladstone', is in the British Library, Add. MS 46269, fo. 144.

55 Gladstone, *The Gladstone Diaries*, Vol. VI, p. 325.

56 A. C. Benson, *Life of Edward White Benson*, Vol. II, pp. 680, 267.

57 A. C. Benson, *The Trefoil*, pp. 251–2.

58 A. C. Benson, *The Poems of A. C. Benson* (London: John Lane, The Bodley Head, 1909), p. 129.

59 E. W. Benson, diary, fos. 301–2.

60 A. C. Benson, *Life of Edward White Benson*, Vol. II, p. 260.

61 A. C. Benson, *The Diary of Arthur Christopher Benson*, ed. Percy Lubbock (London: Hutchinson & Co., 1926), pp. 169, 255; David Newsome, *On the Edge of Paradise. A. C. Benson: The Diarist* (London: John Murray, 1980), p. 333.

62 E. F. Benson, miscellaneous literary papers. Bodleian Library, Oxford, MS 3/3, fos. 20, 43.

63 E. F. Benson, *Our Family Affairs 1867–1896* (London: Cassell and Co., 1920), p. 101.

64 David Newsome, *On the Edge of Paradise. A. C. Benson: The Diarist* (London: John Murray, 1980), p. 15.

65 Gladstone, *The Gladstone Diaries*, Vol. IV, p. 1.

66 *Ibid.*, Vol. V, ed. H. C. G. Matthew, pp. 119; Vol. III, p. 65.

67 Glynne–Gladstone MS 835, fos. 51, 9.

68 Mary Gladstone, *Diaries and Letters*, pp. 51, 24, 146.

69 *Ibid.*, p. 304.

70 Glynne–Gladstone MS 693 (17 June 1855).

71 Anne Isba, *Gladstone and Women* (London: Continuum, 2006), p. 125.

72 John Tosh, 'Authority and Nurture in Middle-Class Fatherhood: The Case of Early and Mid-Victorian England', *Gender and History* 8:1 (April 1996), 48–64 (p. 54).

CONCLUSION

1 Howard Jacobson, *The Making of Henry* [2004] (London: Vintage, 2005), p. 6.

2 Thomas and Jane Welsh Carlyle, *The Collected Letters of Thomas and Jane Welsh Carlyle*, ed. Charles Richard Sanders *et al.*, 34 vols. to date (Durham, NC: Duke University Press, 1970–), Vol. III, ed. Sanders, pp. 200, 195.

3 The fifth of Carlyle's series of lectures, 'On Heroes, Hero-Worship, and the Heroic in History' (1840), was 'The Hero as a Man of Letters: Johnson, Rousseau, Burns'. It provided a more masculine image of authorship than that contrasted elsewhere with the hard physical labour of the navvy. Thomas

Carlyle, 'The Hero as Man of Letters', in *Sartor Resartus: On Heroes and Hero Worship* (London: Dent, 1973), pp. 383–422.

4 Jacobson, *The Making of Henry*, p. 6.

5 Martin A. Danahay, *Gender at Work in Victorian Culture: Literature, Art and Masculinity* (Aldershot: Ashgate, 2005), p. 7.

6 Charles Darwin, *The Correspondence of Charles Darwin*, ed. Frederick H. Burkhardt, Sydney Smith *et al.*, 15 vols. (Cambridge University Press, 1983–2005), Vol. x (1862), p. 26.

7 Mamie [Mary] Dickens, 'Charles Dickens at Home, with Especial Reference to His Relations with Children, by His Eldest Daughter', *Cornhill Magazine* 4 (1885), 32–51 (p. 34).

8 Leonard Huxley, 'Home Memories', Supplement to *Nature* 115 (9 May 1925), 698–702 (p. 698).

Bibliography

MANUSCRIPTS

Arnold, Mary, 'Notebook of Poems etc., by Family', 1836. Leeds University Library, Brotherton Collection, MS 19c Arnold 6.

'Records, Reminiscences for Her Children', 2 vols., 1822–33 and 1834–40. Leeds University Library, Brotherton Collection, MS 19c Arnold 11–12.

Records of Thomas Arnold's conversations. Leeds University Library, Brotherton Collection, MS 19c Arnold 27.

Arnold, Thomas, Letters of Thomas Arnold: 107 letters to family members and friends. Leeds University Library, Brotherton Collection, MS 19c Arnold (Arnold Family Letters, Series 1).

Journal Notebook: 'Diary Rugby Fox How 1837–1839'. Leeds University Library, Brotherton Collection, MS 19c Arnold 8.

Journal Notebook: 'Diary Rugby School 1839–February 1840'. Leeds University Library, Brotherton Collection, MS 19c Arnold 9.

Journals, Vol. VIII (1830, 1831, 1837). Leeds University Library, Brotherton Collection, MS 19c Arnold 3.

Arnold, Thomas *et al.*, *Fox How Magazine* (1838–42). Unpublished manuscript, Jerwood Library, Dove Cottage, Grasmere.

Benson, A. C., Letters from A. C. Benson to his parents. Bodleian Library, Oxford, MSS Benson 3/48–9.

Benson, A. C. *et al.*, Miscellaneous correspondence, 1845–1918, n.d. Bodleian Library, Oxford, MSS Benson 3/16–40.

Benson, E. F., Miscellaneous literary papers. Bodleian Library, Oxford, MSS Benson 3/1–4.

Benson, E. W., Diary, Trinity College, Cambridge, MS EWB A3.

Benson, M. W., Letters from his father and mother, 1868–77, n.d. Bodleian Library, Oxford, MSS Benson 3/43–4.

Benson, Mary, Correspondence of Mary Benson: letters from her husband, E. W. Benson, 1852–96. Bodleian Library, Oxford, MSS Benson 3/14–15.

Darwin, George Howard, Reminiscences of his father. Cambridge University Library, Darwin Papers, MS DAR112.

Gladstone, W. E., 'For the Sacred Memory of William Henry Gladstone'. British Library, Add. MS 46269, fo. 144.

'Some account of our second daughter Catherine Jessy Gladstone'. Unpublished manuscript, British Library, Add. MS 46269, fos. 131–41.

Glynne–Gladstone MSS. St Deiniol's Library, Hawarden.

Hooker, J. D. to Joseph Hooker, 'Lion Letters'. Royal Botanic Gardens, Kew JDH/2/7.

Huxley, H. A., 'Reminiscences by Mrs Huxley of Early Married Life'. Huxley Papers, Vol. XXXI, Imperial College London.

Huxley, Thomas Henry, 'Scientific and General Correspondence', 2 vols. Huxley Papers, Vol. II, Imperial College London.

Tait, Archibald Campbell, Journal, 14 March–11 July 1856. Lambeth Palace Library, Tait Papers.

PRIMARY SOURCES

Albert, Prince Consort of Victoria, Queen of Great Britain, *Letters of the Prince Consort 1831–1861*, ed. Kurt Jagow. London: John Murray, 1938.

Allott, Miriam, and Super, R. H. (eds.), *Matthew Arnold*, Oxford Authors series. Oxford: Oxford University Press, 1986.

Anon., *Austin Hall; or, After Dinner Conversations between a Father and His Children on Subjects of Amusement and Instruction*. London: Baldwin & Cradock, 1831.

Anstey, F., *Vice Versa; or, A Lesson to Fathers* [1882]. London: John Murray, 1969.

Arnold, Matthew, *Culture and Anarchy* [1869], ed. John Dover Wilson. Cambridge University Press, 1981.

   The Letters of Matthew Arnold, ed. Cecil Y. Lang, 6 vols. Charlottesville and London: University of Virginia Press, 1996–2001.

   Letters of Matthew Arnold 1848–1888, ed. G. W. E. Russell 2 vols. New York and London: Macmillan, 1895.

   The Poems of Matthew Arnold [ed. Kenneth Allott, 1965], 2nd edn, ed. Miriam Allott. London and New York: Longman, 1979.

   'Thirty-five Years of School Inspecting: Mr Matthew Arnold's Farewell', in *The Complete Prose Works of Matthew Arnold*, ed. R. H. Super, 11 vols., Vol. XI, *The Last Word*, pp. 374–9. Ann Arbor: University of Michigan Press, 1990.

Arnold, Thomas, *Christian Life, Its Hopes, Its Fears, and Its Close: Sermons, Preached Mostly in the Chapel of Rugby School by the Late Thomas Arnold, D. D.* London: B. Fellowes, 1849.

Arnold, Thomas [the Younger], *Passages in a Wandering Life*. London: Edward Arnold, 1900.

Auden, W. H., *Collected Shorter Poems 1927–1957*. London: Faber, 1966.

Austen, Jane, *Mansfield Park* [1814]. Harmondsworth: Penguin, 1966.

Benson, A. C., *The Diary of Arthur Christopher Benson*, ed. Percy Lubbock. London: Hutchinson & Co., 1926.

   Hugh: Memoirs of a Brother. London: Smith, Elder & Co., 1915.

   Life and Letters of Maggie Benson. London: John Murray, 1917.

(ed.), *The Life of Edward White Benson*, 2 vols. London: Macmillan, 1899.

Memories and Friends. London: John Murray, 1924.

The Poems of A. C. Benson. London: John Lane, The Bodley Head, 1909.

The Trefoil: Wellington College, Lincoln and Truro. London: John Murray, 1923.

Benson, E. F., *Final Edition*. London: The Hogarth Press, 1940.

Mother. London: Hodder & Stoughton, 1925.

Our Family Affairs, 1867–1896. London: Cassell & Co., 1920.

Benson, E. W. *Boy-Life: Its Trial. Its Strength. Its Fulness*. London: Macmillan & Co./Wellington College: George Bishop, 1874.

Benson, Mary Eleanor, *At Sundry Times and in Divers Manners*, 2 vols. London: Kegan Paul, Trench, Trübner & Co., 1891.

Streets and Lanes of the City: With a Brief Memoir by Her Father. London and Bungay: Richard Clay and Sons Ltd, 1891.

Benson, Robert Hugh, *Confessions of a Convert*. London: Longmans, Green & Co., 1913.

Braddon, Mary Elizabeth, *Aurora Floyd* [1862]. London: Virago, 1984.

Breuer, Josef and Sigmund Freud, *Studies on Hysteria*, Standard Edition of the Complete Psychological Works of Sigmund Freud, ed. James Strachey, 2 vols., Vol. II. London: The Hogarth Press, 1955.

Brontë, Charlotte, *The Letters of Charlotte Brontë*, ed. Margaret Smith, 3 vols. Oxford: Clarendon Press, 2000.

Browning, Elizabeth Barrett *et al.*, *Letters of the Brownings to George Barrett*, eds. Paul Landis and Ronald E. Freeman. Urbana: University of Illinois Press, 1958.

Butler, Samuel, *The Way of All Flesh* [1903]. Harmondsworth: Penguin, 1966.

Carlyle, Thomas, 'The Hero as Man of Letters', in *Sartor Resartus: On Heroes and Hero Worship*. London: Dent, 1973, pp. 383–422.

Carlyle, Thomas and Jane Welsh Carlyle, *The Collected Letters of Thomas and Jane Welsh Carlyle*, ed. Charles Richard Sanders *et al.*, 34 vols. to date. Durham, NC: Duke University Press, 1970–.

Carroll, Lewis, *The Rectory Magazine*, ed. Jerome Bump. Austin and London: University of Texas Press, 1975.

Chavasse, Pye Henry, *Advice to a Mother on the Management of her Children*, 11th edn. London: J. & A. Churchill, 1873.

Cobbett, William, *Advice to Young Men* [1830]. Oxford University Press, 1980.

Darwin, Charles, 'A Biographical Sketch of an Infant', *Mind* (July 1877), 285–94.

Charles Darwin's Notebooks, 1836–1844, ed. Paul H. Barrett *et al.* Cambridge University Press and the British Museum, 1987.

The Correspondence of Charles Darwin, eds. Frederick H. Burkhardt, Sydney Smith *et al.*, 15 vols. Cambridge University Press, 1983–2005.

The Life and Letters of Charles Darwin, including an Autobiographical Chapter, Edited by his Son Francis Darwin, ed. Francis Darwin, 3 vols. London: John Murray, 1887.

More Letters of Charles Darwin, ed. Francis Darwin and A. C. Seward, 2 vols. Cambridge University Press, 2004.

The Origin of Species [1859]. Harmondsworth: Penguin, 1968.

Darwin, Charles and Thomas Henry Huxley, *Charles Darwin, Thomas Henry Huxley: Autobiographies*, ed. Gavin de Beer. London, New York and Toronto: Oxford University Press, 1974.

Darwin, George Howard, 'Marriages between First Cousins', *Fortnightly Review* 27, new series (July 1875), 22–41.

Dickens, A. Tennyson, 'My Father and His Friends', *Nash's Magazine* (September 1911), 627–41.

Dickens, Charles, 'A Child's Dream of a Star', *Household Words* (6 April 1850), 25–6.

Dombey and Son [1848]. Harmondsworth: Penguin, 1970.

Great Expectations [1861]. Harmondsworth: Penguin, 1965.

Hard Times [1854]. Harmondsworth: Penguin, 1969.

The Letters of Charles Dickens, ed. Madeline House *et al.*, 12 vols. Oxford: Clarendon Press, 1965–99.

Little Dorrit [1857]. Harmondsworth: Penguin, 1967.

Our Mutual Friend [1864–5]. Harmondsworth: Penguin, 1971.

'PERSONAL', *Household Words* (12 June 1858), 601.

Dickens, Charles [the Younger], 'Personal Reminiscences of My Father', Supplement to *Windsor Magazine* (Christmas 1934), 1–31.

Dickens, Henry, *Memories of My Father*. London: Victor Gollancz, 1928.

The Recollections of Sir Henry Dickens, KC. London: William Heinemann Ltd, 1934.

Dickens, Mamie [Mary], 'Charles Dickens at Home, with Especial Reference to His Relations with Children, by His Eldest Daughter', *Cornhill Magazine* 4 (1885), 32–51.

My Father as I Recall Him. Westminster: Roxburghe Press, 1897.

Draper, B. H., *Conversations of a Father with His Son, on Some Leading Points in Natural Philosophy*. London: Wightman & Cramp, 1825.

Edgeworth, Maria, *Harry and Lucy Concluded: Being the Last Part of Early Lessons [1825]*, 3 vols. London: Simpkin, Marshall & Co., 1846.

Rosamond Part I, by the Author of the Parent's Assistant. Boston, MA: Cummings and Hilliard, 1813.

Edgeworth, Maria and R. L. Edgeworth, *Practical Education*, 3 vols. [1798], 2nd edn. London: J. Johnson, 1801.

Eliot, George, *Daniel Deronda* [1876]. Harmondsworth: Penguin, 1967.

Fulford, Roger (ed.), *Dearest Child: Letters between Queen Victoria and the Princess Royal 1858–1861*. London: Evans Brothers Ltd, 1964.

(ed.), *Dearest Mama: Letters between Queen Victoria and the Crown Princess of Prussia 1861–1864*. London: Evans Brothers Ltd, 1968.

Galton, Francis, *English Men of Sciences: Their Nature and Nurture*. London: Macmillan, 1874.

Hereditary Genius: An Inquiry into Its Laws and Consequences. London: Macmillan, 1869.

Gladstone, Herbert, *After Thirty Years*. London: Macmillan, 1928.

Gladstone, W. E., *The Gladstone Diaries*, ed. M. R. D. Foot and H. C. G. Matthew, 14 vols. Oxford: Clarendon Press, 1968–94.

Gosse, Edmund, *Father and Son* [1907]. Harmondsworth: Penguin, 1983.

Haight, Gordon S. (ed.), *The George Eliot Letters*, 9 vols. New Haven: Yale University Press, 1954–79.

Hardy, Thomas, *The Mayor of Casterbridge* [1886]. Harmondsworth: Penguin, 1978.

Hood, Thomas, *The Letters of Thomas Hood*, ed. Peter F. Morgan. Edinburgh: Oliver and Boyd, 1973.

  The Poetical Works of Thomas Hood, ed. William Michael Rossetti, 2nd edn. London and New York: Ward Lock, n.d.

  The Works of Thomas Hood, eds. Tom Hood and Frances Broderip, 10 vols. London: E. Moxon & Co., 1869–73.

Hooker, Joseph Dalton, *A Sketch of the Life and Labours of Sir William Jackson Hooker, K. H. by His Son Joseph Dalton Hooker*. Oxford: Clarendon Press, 1903.

Hughes, David, *The Lent Jewels*. London: Arrow Books, 2003.

Hughes, Thomas, *Tom Brown's Schooldays* [1857]. Harmondsworth: Puffin, 1971.

Hunt, Leigh, *The Autobiography of Leigh Hunt*, ed. J. E. Morpurgo. London: The Cresset Press, 1948.

Huxley, Aldous, *Letters of Aldous Huxley*, ed. Grover Smith. London: Chatto & Windus, 1969.

  The Olive Tree and Other Essays. London: Chatto & Windus, 1947.

Huxley, Leonard, 'Home Memories', Supplement to *Nature* CXV (9 May 1925), 698–702.

  (ed.), *Life and Letters of Sir Joseph Dalton Hooker*, 2 vols. London: John Murray, 1918.

  (ed.), *Life and Letters of Thomas Henry Huxley, by His Son Leonard Huxley*, 2 vols. London: Macmillan & Co., 1900.

  'Scenes from Huxley's Home Life, by His Son Leonard Huxley', *The Century Magazine* 33 (1897), 355–62.

  Thomas Henry Huxley, Life Stories of Famous Men series. London: Watts & Co., 1920.

Huxley, Thomas Henry, 'Address to the Royal Academy', *Medical Times and Gazette* (May 1871). Retrieved on 20 April 2008 from http://alepho.clarku.edu/huxley/UnColl/Gazettes/RoyAc71.html.

  'The Connection between Science and Art and Literature', *Nature* 35 (5 May 1887), 14.

  'Evolution and Ethics' and Other Essays. London and New York: Macmillan, 1925.

  'A Liberal Education; and Where to Find It: An Inaugural Address', *Macmillan's Magazine 17* (March 1868), 367–78.

  Science and Christian Tradition: Essays. London: Macmillan, 1893.

Science and Education: Essays by Thomas H. Huxley. London: Macmillan and Co. Ltd, 1925.

The Scientific Memoirs of Thomas Henry Huxley, eds. Michael Foster and E. Ray Lankester. London: Macmillan, 1902.

Jacobson, Howard, *The Making of Henry* [2004]. London: Vintage, 2005.

James, Henry, *Autobiography*, ed. Frederick W. Dupee. London: W. H. Allen, 1956.

Kingsley, Charles, *Alton Locke: Tailor and Poet. An Autobiography* [1850], ed. Elizabeth A. Cripps. Oxford and New York: Oxford World's Classics, 1983.

Charles Kingsley: His Letters and Memories of His Life, Edited by His Wife, ed. Fanny Kingsley, 2 vols. [1876], 5th edn. London: Henry S. King & Co., 1877.

Glaucus [1855], rept. *The Water-Babies and Glaucus*. New York: J. M. Dent, 1908.

The Heroes; or, Greek Fairy Tales for My Children [1856]. London: Macmillan, 1892.

Madam How and Lady Why; or, First Lessons in Earth Lore for Children [1870]. London: Macmillan, 1899.

Sanitary and Social Lectures and Essays (London: Macmillan, 1880)

Scientific Lectures and Essays. London: Macmillan, and Co., 1890.

The Water-Babies [1863], ed. Brian Alderson. Oxford and New York: Oxford World's Classics, 1995.

The Water-Babies, Macmillan's Magazine 6 (May–October 1862), 7 (November 1862–April 1863).

'The Wonders of the Shore', *North British Review* 22 (November 1854), 1–56.

The Works of Charles Kingsley, 28 vols. London: Macmillan, 1888.

Kingsley, George, 'Chamois Hunting', *Fraser's Magazine* 44 (July 1851), 133–48.

Kingsley, George Henry, *Notes on Sport and Travel by George Henry Kingsley. With a Memoir by His Daughter Mary H. Kingsley*. London: Macmillan, 1900.

Kingsley, Rose G., *Eversley Gardens and Others*. London: George Allen, 1907.

South by West; or, Winter in the Rocky Mountains and Spring in Mexico, ed. and Pref. Charles Kingsley. London: W. Isbister & Co., 1874.

Lamb, Charles, 'Dream Children: A Reverie', in *The Essays of Elia* [1823], Everyman Edition. London: J. M. Dent, 1962, pp. 117–21.

Litchfield, Henrietta E., *Emma Darwin: Wife of Charles Darwin. A Century of Family Letters, by Her Daughter H. E. Litchfield*, 2 vols. Cambridge University Press, 1904.

Macready, William Charles, *Diaries of William Charles Macready*, ed. William Toynbee, 2 vols. London: Chapman & Hall Ltd, 1912.

Macready's Reminiscences, and Selections from His Diaries and Letters, ed. Sir Frederick Pollock, 2 vols. London: Macmillan & Co., 1875.

'Malet, Lucas' [Mary Kingsley], 'The Threatened Re-Subjection of Woman', *Fortnightly Review* 77 (1905), 806–19.

The Tutor's Story: An Unpublished Novel by the Late Charles Kingsley, Revised and Completed by His Daughter Lucas Malet . . . London: Smith, Elder & Co., 1916.

Mallock, W. H., *The New Republic* [1877]. London: Chatto & Windus, 1908.

Mangnall, Richmal, *Historical and Miscellaneous Questions for the Use of Young People, new edn.* London: Fisher, Son & Co., [1840].

Marcet, Mrs [Jane], *Conversations for Children: On Land and Water.* London: Longman, Orme, Brown, Green & Longmans, 1838.

Martineau, Harriet, *The Collected Letters of Harriet Martineau,* ed. Deborah A. Logan, 5 vols. London: Pickering & Chatto, 2007.

Meredith, George, *The Ordeal of Richard Feverel* [1859], Standard Edition. London: Constable & Co., 1914.

Mill, John Stuart, *Autobiography* [1873], ed. Jack Stillinger. Oxford University Press, 1971.

Millais, Sir John Everett, *The Life and Letters of Sir John Everett Millais,* ed. John Guille Millais, 2 vols. London: Methuen, 1902.

Oastler, Richard (ed.), *The Home.* London: Tatham, 1851–5.

Oliphant, Margaret, *The Autobiography of Margaret Oliphant,* ed. Elisabeth Jay [1899]. Oxford University Press, 1990.

Pinnock, William, *Pinnock's Catechism of Chemistry,* 8th edn. London: G. B. Whittaker, 1823.

   Pinnock's Catechism of Geology, 8th edn. London: G. B. Whittaker & Co., [1840?].

Raverat, Gwen, *Period Piece: A Cambridge Childhood.* London: Faber & Faber, 1952.

Rousseau, Jean-Jacques, *Émile* [1762], trans. Barbara Foxley. London: J. M. Dent, 1974.

Ruskin, John James *et al.,* *The Ruskin Family Letters,* ed. Van Akin Bird, 2 vols. Ithaca, NY and London: Cornell University Press, 1973.

Sherwood, Mary Martha, *The History of the Fairchild Family; or, The Child's Manual* [1818–47], 3 vols., 24th edn. London: Hatchards, 1869.

Smyth, Ethel, *The Memoirs of Ethel Smyth,* abridged and ed. Ronald Crichton. London: Viking, 1987.

Southey, Robert, *New Letters of Robert Southey,* ed. Kenneth Curry, 2 vols. New York and London: Columbia University Press, 1965.

Strickland, Agnes, 'The Cottage Fire', *The Home* 1:2 (12 July 1851), inside cover.

Swinburne, A. C., *The Complete Works of Algernon Charles Swinburne,* ed. Sir Edmund Gosse and Thomas James Wise, 20 vols. London and New York: William Heinemann Ltd, 1926.

Tennyson, Alfred Lord, *The Letters of Alfred Lord Tennyson,* ed. Cecil Y. Lang and Edgar F. Shannon, 3 vols. Oxford: Clarendon Press, 1982–90.

Tennyson, Lady Emily, *The Letters of Emily, Lady Tennyson,* ed. James O. Hoge. University Park and London: Pennsylvania State University Press, 1974.

Thackeray, William Makepeace, *The Letters and Private Papers of William Makepeace Thackeray,* ed. Gordon N. Ray, 4 vols. London: Oxford University Press, 1945.

Trollope, Anthony, *The Way We Live Now* [1875]. Oxford: World's Classics, 1982.

Victoria, Queen of Great Britain, *The Letters of Queen Victoria*, ed. George Earle Buckle, 2nd series, 3 vols. London: John Murray, 1928.

'Vivian' [G. H. Lewes], 'The Bachelor's Evening', *The Leader* (25 October 1851), 1022–3.

'How to Make Home Happy', *The Leader* (12 November 1853), 1099.

'Review of Coyne, *The Hope of the Family*', *The Leader* (10 December 1853), 1195.

'Vivian in His Easy Chair', *The Leader* (19 April 1851), 373.

'Vivian's Review of Fredrika Bremer's *Easter Offering*', *The Leader* (23 September 1854), 69.

Webb, Beatrice, *The Diary of Beatrice Webb*, ed. Norman and Jeanne Mackenzie, 2 vols., Vol. 1. London: Virago, 1986.

Wyss, Johann Rudolf, *The Swiss Family Robinson* [1812]. Ware: Wordsworth Classics, 1993.

Yeats, W. B., *Poems of W. B. Yeats: A New Selection*, ed. A. Norman Jeffares. London and Basingstoke: Macmillan, 1984.

SECONDARY SOURCES

Ackroyd, Peter, *Dickens*. London: Minerva, 1991.

Ahmed, Sara, *The Cultural Politics of Emotion*. Edinburgh University Press, 2004.

Aitken, Stuart C., 'The Awkward Spaces of Fathering', in Bettina van Hoven and Kathrin Hörschelmann (eds.), *Spaces of Masculinities*. Abingdon, London and New York: Routledge, 2005, pp. 222–36.

Alexander, Christine, 'Play and Apprenticeship: The Culture of Family Magazines', in Alexander and McMaster (eds.), *The Child Writer from Austen to Woolf*, pp. 31–50.

Alexander, Christine and Juliet McMaster (eds.), *The Child Writer from Austen to Woolf*. Cambridge University Press, 2005.

Amigoni, David (ed.), *Life Writing and Victorian Culture*. Aldershot: Ashgate, 2006.

Anon., 'The Close of 1861', *Fraser's Magazine* 65 (December 1861), 123–34.

'Exhibition of the Royal Academy', *The Times* (28 June 1880), 5.

'Fathers', *All the Year Round* (2 September 1865), 133–5.

'The Judicial Separation of Mother and Child', *Westminster Review* 67 (1885), 430–59.

'Miss Mary Kingsley' (obituary), *The Athenaeum* (16 June 1900), 750–1.

'Miss Mary Kingsley' (obituary), *The Athenaeum* (23 June 1900), 784–5.

'A Posthumous Legacy', *Times Literary Supplement* (5 October 1916), 474.

'Professor Huxley's Homes', *Illustrated London News* (6 July 1895), 3.

'The Question as to the Legal Custody of Infants', *The Times* (4 April 1864), 8.

'Review of A. C. Benson, The Life of Edward White Benson', *The Saturday Review* 89 (13 January 1900), 50–1.

'Review of A. P. Stanley, *The Life and Correspondence of Thomas Arnold*', *The Times* (28 October 1844), 7.

'Review of *The Life and Letters of Charles Darwin*', ed. Francis Darwin, *Saturday Review* 64 (19 November 1887), 701–2.

'The Royal Nursery', *The Times* (18 November 1841), 4.

'Tavistock-House Theatre', *The Times* (7 January 1857), 7.

Ashton, Rosemary, *G. H. Lewes: A Life*. Oxford: Clarendon Press, 1991.

Bailin, Miriam, '"Dismal Pleasure": Victorian Sentimentality and the Pathos of the Parvenu', *ELH* 66:4 (1999), 1015–32.

Barringer, Tim, *Men at Work: Art and Labour in Victorian Britain*. New Haven and London: Yale University Press, 2005.

Bell, Alan (ed.), *Sir Leslie Stephen's Mausoleum Book*. Oxford: Clarendon Press, 1977.

Benham, William (ed.), *Catharine and Craufurd Tait, Wife and Son of Archibald Campbell, Archbishop of Canterbury: A Memoir*. London: Macmillan, 1879.

Bergonzi, Bernard, *A Victorian Wanderer: The Life of Thomas Arnold the Younger*. Oxford University Press, 2003.

Bibby, Cyril, (ed.), *The Essence of T. H. Huxley*. London and New York: Macmillan/St Martin's Press, 1967.

Scientist Extraordinary: The Life and Scientific Work of Thomas Henry Huxley 1825–1895. Oxford: Pergamon Press, 1972.

Blackstone, William, *Commentaries on the Laws of England*, 4 vols. Oxford: Clarendon Press, 1765–9.

Blinderman, Charles S., 'T. H. Huxley's Theory of Aesthetics: Unity in Diversity', *Journal of Aesthetics and Art Criticism* 21 (1962), 49–55.

Boughton, Gillian E., 'Dr Arnold's Granddaughter: Mary Ward', in Alexander, and McMaster (eds.), *The Child Writer from Austen to Woolf*, pp. 237–53.

Bown, Nicola, 'Introduction: Crying over Little Nell', *19: Interdisciplinary Studies in the Long Nineteenth Century* 4 (2007), 1–13. Retrieved on 18 March 2008 from www.19.bbk.ac.uk/issue4/BownIntroduction.pdf.

Brannan, Robert Louis (ed.), *Under the Management of Mr Charles Dickens: His Production of 'The Frozen Deep'*. Ithaca, NY: Cornell University Press, 1966.

Bronfen, Elisabeth, *Over Her Dead Body: Death, Femininity and the Aesthetic*. Manchester University Press, 1992.

Broughton, Trev Lynn, *Men of Letters, Writing Lives: Masculinity and Literary Auto/Biography in the Late Victorian Period*. London: Routledge, 1999.

Broughton, Trev Lynn and Helen Rogers (eds.), *Gender and Fatherhood in the Nineteenth Century*. Basingstoke: Palgrave Macmillan, 2007.

Browne, Janet, *Charles Darwin: The Power of Place*. London: Pimlico, 2003

Charles Darwin: Voyaging. Princeton University Press, 1996.

Burgess, Adrienne, *Fatherhood Reclaimed: The Making of the Modern Father*. London: Vermilion, 1997.

Carpenter, Humphrey and Mari Prichard (eds.), *The Oxford Companion to Children's Literature*. Oxford and New York: Oxford University Press, 1999.

Chase, Karen and Michael Levenson, *The Spectacle of Intimacy: A Public Life for the Victorian Family*. Princeton University Press, 2000.

Chedzoy, Alan, *A Scandalous Woman: The Story of Caroline Norton*. London: Allison and Busby, 1992.

'*Chetwynd* v. *Chetwynd*', *The Times* (29 November 1865), 11.

Chitty, Susan, *The Beast and the Monk: A Life of Charles Kingsley*. London: Hodder & Stoughton, 1974.

Clark, Anna, *The Struggle for the Breeches: Gender and the Making of the British Working Class*. London: Rivers Oram Press, 1995.

Clubbe, John, *Victorian Forerunner: The Later Career of Thomas Hood*. Durham, NC: Duke University Press, 1968.

Codell, Julie F., *The Victorian Artist: Artists' Life-Writings in Britain, ca. 1870–1910*. Cambridge University Press, 2003.

Cohen, Morton N., *Lewis Carroll: A Biography*. London: Macmillan Papermac, 1995.

Collini, Stefan, *Arnold*. Oxford University Press, 1988.

Collins, W. Lucas, Review of Theodore Martin, '*The Life of His Royal Highness, the Prince Consort*', *Blackwood's Edinburgh Magazine* 120 (November 1876), 611–31.

Colp, Ralph, *To Be an Invalid: The Illness of Charles Darwin*. Chicago and London: The University of Chicago Press, 1977.

Copley, Terence, *Black Tom: Arnold of Rugby. The Myth and the Man*. London and New York: Continuum, 2002.

Courtney, Janet, 'A Novelist of the 'Nineties', *Fortnightly Review* 131 (1932), 230–41.

Crichton, Ronald (ed.), *The Memoirs of Ethel Smyth* (abridged). London: Viking, 1987.

Dallimore, Arnold, *The Life of Edward Irving: Fore-runner of the Charismatic Movement*. Edinburgh and Pennsylvania: The Banner of Truth Trust, 1983.

Daly, Kerry J., 'Reshaping Fatherhood: Finding the Models', in William Marsiglio (ed.), *Fatherhood: Contemporary Theory, Research, and Social Policy*. London: Sage, 1995, pp. 21–40.

Danahay, Martin A., *Gender at Work in Victorian Culture: Literature, Art and Masculinity*. Aldershot: Ashgate, 2005.

Dangerfield, George, *Victoria's Heir: The Education of a Prince*. London: Constable & Co., 1941.

Davidoff, Leonore, 'Kinship as a Categorical Concept: A Case Study', *Journal of Social History* 39:2 (2005), 411–28.

Davidoff, Leonore, Megan Doolittle, Janet Fink and Katherine Holden (eds.), *The Family Story: Blood, Contract and Intimacy, 1830–1960*. London and New York: Longman, 1999.

Davidoff, Leonore and Catherine Hall, *Family Fortunes: Men and Women of the English Middle Class, 1780–1850*. University of Chicago Press, 1987.

Davidson, Randall Thomas (ed.), *Life of Archibald Campbell Tait, Archbishop of Canterbury*, 2 vols. London: Macmillan & Co., 1891.

Dawson, Carl (ed.), *Matthew Arnold: The Poetry*, Critical Heritage series. London and Boston, MA: Routledge and Kegan Paul, 1973.

Desmond, Adrian, *Huxley: The Devil's Disciple*. London: Michael Joseph, 1994.
  Huxley: Evolution's High Priest. London: Michael Joseph, 1997.
Desmond, Adrian and James Moore, *Darwin*. Harmondsworth: Penguin, 1992.
Dever, Carolyn, *Death and the Mother from Dickens to Freud: Victorian Fiction and the Anxiety of Origins*. Cambridge University Press, 1998.
Dolman, Frederick, '"Lucas Malet at Home": A Chat with the Daughter of Charles Kingsley', *The Young Woman: A Monthly Journal and Review* 4 (1896), 145–9.
[Donne, W. B.], 'The Late Prince Consort', *Westminster Review* 21, new series (January 1862), 225–30.
  'Review of Macready, *Reminiscences*', *Edinburgh Review* 141 (April 1875), 416–47.
Dowd, Nancy E., *Redefining Fatherhood*. New York and London: New York University Press, 2000.
Drew, Mary [Gladstone], *Catherine Gladstone, by Her Daughter Mary Drew* [1919]. London: Nisbet & Co., 1928.
Drew, Mary [Gladstone], *Mary Gladstone (Mrs Drew): Her Diaries and Letters*, ed. Lucy Masterman. London: Methuen & Co., 1930.
Easley, Alexis, 'Ebenezer Elliott and the Reconstruction of Working-Class Masculinity', *Victorian Poetry* 39:2 (2001), 303–18.
Epton, Nina, *Victoria and Her Daughters*. London: Weidenfeld and Nicolson, 1971.
Farrar, F. W., 'Two Archbishops', *Contemporary Review* 70 (December 1896), 623–35.
Fasick, Laura, 'Charles Kingsley's Scientific Treatment of Gender', in Donald E. Hall (ed.), *Muscular Christianity: Embodying the Victorian Age*. Cambridge University Press, 1994, 91–113.
  'The Failure of Fatherhood: Madness and Its Discontents in Charles Kingsley', *Children's Literature Association Quarterly* 18:3 (1993), 106–11.
Fildes, L. V., *Luke Fildes R.A.: A Victorian Painter*. London: Michael Joseph, 1968.
Forrester, David W. F., 'Dr Pusey's Marriage', in Perry Butler (ed.), *Pusey Revisited*. London: SPCK, 1983, pp. 119–38.
Frank, Katherine, *A Voyager Out: The Life of Mary Kingsley*. London: Hamish Hamilton, 1986.
Fremantle, Canon, 'Archbishop Tait', *Good Words* (1883), 88–94.
Gardiner, John P., 'Gladstone, Gossip and the Post-War Generation', *Historical Research* 74 (November 2001), 409–24.
Gernsheim, Helmut and Alison Gernsheim, *Queen Victoria: A Biography in Word and Picture*. London: Longmans, Green & Co., 1959.
Gillis, John R., *A World of Their Own Making: Myth, Ritual, and the Quest for Family Values*. Cambridge, MA: Harvard University Press, 1996.
[Greg, W. R.], 'Dr Arnold', *Westminster Review* 39 (1843), 1–33.
Griffin, Ben, 'The Parliamentary Politics of Domestic Authority', conference paper given at King's College Cambridge for *The Politics of Domestic Authority in Britain* (27 July 2006).

Hall, Donald E. (ed.), *Muscular Christianity: Embodying the Victorian Age*. Cambridge University Press, 1994.

Hamilton, Ian, *A Gift Imprisoned: The Poetic Life of Matthew Arnold*. London: Basic Books, 1998.

Hammerton, A. James, *Cruelty and Companionship: Conflict in Nineteenth-Century Married Life*. Routledge: London and New York, 1992.

Hanson, David C., 'Precocity, and the Economy of the Evangelical Self in John Ruskin's Juvenilia', in Alexander and McMaster (eds.), *The Child Writer from Austen to Woolf*, pp. 200–21.

Hawley, John C., SJ, 'The Muscular Christian as Schoolmarm', in Kristine Otteson Garrigan (ed.), *Victorian Scandals: Representations of Gender and Class*. Athens, OH: Ohio University Press, 1992, pp. 134–56.

Helps, Arthur, Review of Theodore Martin, '*The Life of His Royal Highness, the Prince Consort*', *Quarterly Review* 138 (January 1875), 107–38.

Hibbert, Christopher, *Edward VII: A Portrait*. London: Allen Lane, 1976.

Hillis Miller, J., 'Reading *The Swiss Family Robinson* as Virtual Reality', in Karen Lesnik-Oberstein (ed.), *Children's Literature: New Approaches*. Basingstoke: Palgrave, 2004, pp. 78–92.

Hogarth, Janet E., 'Lucas Malet's Novels', *Fortnightly Review* 71 (1902), 532–40.

Hoggan, Frances Elizabeth, M. D., *The Position of the Mother in the Family*. Manchester: A. Ireland & Co., 1884.

Holman, S. R., 'New Introduction' to Nellie [Mary Eleanor] Benson, *Lambeth Women Speak*. Retrieved on 18 October 2008 from www.povertystudies.org/NellieBenson/01-Introduction.htm.

Honan, Park, *Matthew Arnold: A Life*. London: Weidenfeld and Nicolson, 1981.

Horstman, Allen, *Victorian Divorce*. London and Sydney: Croom Helm, 1985.

Hughes, Kathryn, *George Eliot: The Last Victorian*. London: Fourth Estate, 1998.

Hunt, Peter, *Children's Literature*, Blackwell Guides to Literature. Oxford: Blackwell, 2001.

Hutton, R. H., 'The Poetry of Matthew Arnold', in *Literary Essays*. London: Macmillan, 1896.

Huxley, Elspeth, *The Kingsleys: A Biographical Anthology*. London: George Allen & Unwin Ltd, 1973.

Isba, Anne, *Gladstone and Women*. London: Continuum, 2006.

Jalland, Pat, *Death in the Victorian Family*. Oxford University Press, 1996.
  Women, Marriage and Politics 1860–1914. Oxford: Clarendon Press, 1986.

Jenkins, Roy, *Gladstone*. London and Basingstoke: Macmillan, 1995.

Johnson, Edgar and Eleanor (eds.), *The Dickens Theatrical Reader*. London: Victor Gollancz Ltd, 1964.

Kestner, Joseph A., *Masculinities in Victorian Painting*. Aldershot: Scolar Press, 1995.

Keynes, Randal, *Annie's Box: Charles Darwin, His Daughter, and Human Evolution*. London: Fourth Estate, 2001.

Kollar, Rene, 'A Death in the Family: Bishop Archibald Campbell Tait, the Rights of Parents, and Anglican Sisterhoods in the Diocese of London', *Journal of Religious History* 27:2 (June 2003), 198–214.

Lake, Katharine (ed.), *Memorials of William Charles Lake*. London: Edward Arnold, 1901.

Lake, W. C., 'The Life and Correspondence of T. Arnold, D.D.', *Quarterly Review* 74 (October 1844), 467–508.

Lamb, Michael E., *The Father's Role: Applied Perspectives*. New York: John Wiley & Sons, 1986.

Laqueur, Thomas, 'The Facts of Fatherhood', in Barrie Thorne and Marilyn Yalom (eds.), *Rethinking the Family: Some Feminist Questions*. Boston, MA: Northeastern University Press, 1992, pp. 155–75.

Laughton, J. K., 'Review of *Charles Kingsley: His Letters and Memories*', *Edinburgh Review* 145 (April 1877), 415–46.

Ledger, Sally, '"Don't be so melodramatic!" Dickens and the Affective Mode', *19: Interdisciplinary Studies in the Long Nineteenth Century* 4 (2007), 1–14. Retrieved online on 18 March 2008 from www.19.bbk.ac.uk/issue4/Sally-Dickens.pdf.

Lerner, Laurence, *Angels and Absences: Child Deaths in the Nineteenth Century*. Nashville and London: Vanderbilt University Press, 1997.

Liddon, Henry Parry (ed.), *Life of Edward Bouverie Pusey*, 4 vols., 4th edn. London and New York: Longmans, Green & Co., 1894.

Loftus, Donna, 'The Self in Society: Middle-Class Men and Autobiography', in Amigoni, David (ed.), *Life-Writing and Victorian Culture*. London: Ashgate, 2006.

Longford, Elizabeth, *Victoria R. I.* London: Pan, 1966.

Machann, Clinton, *Matthew Arnold: A Literary Life*. Basingstoke: Macmillan, 1998.

McKee, Lorna and Margaret O'Brien (eds.), *The Father Figure*. London: Tavistock Publications, 1982.

McKnight, Natalie J., *Suffering Mothers in Mid-Victorian Novels*. New York: St Martin's Press, 1997.

Magnus, Philip, *King Edward the Seventh*. London: John Murray, 1964.

Maidment, Susan, *Child Custody and Divorce*. London and Sydney: Croom Helm, 1984.

Maine, Henry Sumner, 'The Patriarchal Theory', *Quarterly Review* 162 (January 1886), 181–209.

Marsh, P. T., *The Victorian Church in Decline: Archbishop Tait and the Church of England, 1868–1882*. London: Routledge & Kegan Paul, 1969.

Marsiglio, William (ed.), *Fatherhood: Contemporary Theory, Research, and Social Policy*. London: Sage, 1995.

Martin, Theodore, *The Life of His Royal Highness, the Prince Consort*, 5 vols. London: Smith, Elder & Co., 1879.

'Review of Macready, *Reminiscences*', *Quarterly Review* 138 (April 1875), 305–44.

Michie, Helena, 'From Blood to Law: The Embarrassments of Family in Dickens', in John Bowen and Robert L. Patten (eds.), *Palgrave Advances in Charles Dickens Studies*. Basingstoke: Palgrave Macmillan, 2006.

Mintz, Steven, 'Mothers and Fathers in America: Looking Backward, Looking Forward'. Retrieved on 19 December 2007 from www.digitalhistory.uh. edu/historyonline/mothersfathers.cfm.

Moreton, Cole, 'Politics for Breakfast: Will Cameron Regret Placing Tots in the Frontline?', *Independent on Sunday* (16 March 2008), 43.

Mozley, T., *Reminiscences Chiefly of Oriel College and the Oxford Movement*, 2 vols. London: Longmans, Green & Co., 1882.

Murray, Nicholas, *A Life of Matthew Arnold*. London: Hodder and Stoughton, 1996.

Nelson, Claudia, *Boys Will Be Girls: The Feminine Ethic and British Children's Fiction 1857–1917*. New Brunswick, NJ and London: Rutgers University Press, 1991.

'Deconstructing the Paterfamilias: British Magazines and the Imagining of the Maternal Father, 1850–1910', *The Journal of Men's Studies* 11:3 (Spring 2003), 293–308.

Invisible Men: Fatherhood in Victorian Periodicals 1850–1910. Athens, GA and London: University of Georgia Press, 1995.

Newsome, David, *Godliness and Good Learning: Four Studies on a Victorian Ideal*. London: John Murray, 1961.

On the Edge of Paradise. A. C. Benson: The Diarist. London: John Murray, 1980.

Noakes, Aubrey, *William Frith: Extraordinary Victorian Painter. A Biographical and Critical Essay*. London: Jupiter, 1978.

Nunn, Pamela Gerrish, *Victorian Women Artists*. London: The Women's Press, 1987.

Oliphant, Margaret, 'Review of Theodore Martin, *The Life of His Royal Highness, the Prince Consort*', *Blackwood's Edinburgh Magazine* 117 (January 1875), 114–31.

Pakula, Hannah, *An Uncommon Woman: The Empress Frederick*. Phoenix: Giant, 1997.

Pollock, Griselda, *Differencing the Canon: Feminist Desire and the Writing of Art Histories*. London and New York: Routledge, 1999.

Poole, William Frederick, *An Index to Periodical Literature*. London and Boston: James R. Osgood and Trübner and Co., 1882.

Poovey, Mary, *Uneven Developments: The Ideological Work of Gender in Mid-Victorian England*. London: Virago, 1989.

Prothero, Rowland, 'The Poetry of Matthew Arnold', *Edinburgh Review* 168 (October 1888), 337–73.

Rapple, Brendan A., 'The Educational Thought of Charles Kingsley', *Historical Studies in Education* 9:1 (Spring 1997), 46–64.

Rauch, Alan, *Useful Knowledge: The Victorians, Morality, and the March of Intellect*. Durham, NC and London: Duke University Press, 2001.

Reid, J. C., *Thomas Hood*. London: Routledge & Kegan Paul, 1963.

Reid, Sir Wemyss (ed.), *The Life of William Ewart Gladstone*. London: Cassell and Co., 1899.

Rhodes James, Robert, *Albert, Prince Consort: A Biography*. London: Hamish Hamilton, 1983.

Ritchie, J. Ewing, *The Real Gladstone: An Anecdotal Biography*. London and New York: T. Fisher Unwin, 1898.

Roberts, David, 'The Paterfamilias of the Victorian Governing Classes', in Wohl (ed.), *The Victorian Family*, pp. 59–81.

Robson, Catherine, *Men in Wonderland: The Lost Girlhood of the Victorian Gentleman*. Princeton and Oxford: Princeton University Press, 2001.

Rose, Sonya O., *Limited Livelihoods: Gender and Class in Nineteenth-Century England*. London: Routledge, 1992.

Rosen, David, 'The Volcano and the Cathedral: Muscular Christianity and the Origins of Primal Manliness', in Hall (ed.), *Muscular Christianity*, pp. 17–44.

Rosenfeld, Jason and Alison Smith, *Millais*. London: Tate Publishing, 2007.

Russell, George W. E., *William Ewart Gladstone*. London: Sampson, Low, Marston & Co., 1891.

Sadoff, Dianne F., *Monsters of Affection: Dickens, Eliot and Brontë on Fatherhood*. Baltimore and London: Johns Hopkins University Press, 1982.

Schor, Hilary M., *Dickens and the Daughter of the House*. Cambridge University Press, 1999.

Seccombe, Wally, *Weathering the Storm: Working-Class Families from the Industrial Revolution to the Fertility Decline*. London and New York: Verso, 1993.

Secord, James A., 'The Geological Survey of Great Britain as a Research School, 1839–1855', *History of Science* 24 (1986), 223–75.

Sedgwick, Eve Kosofsky, *Between Men: English Literature and Male Homosexual Desire*. New York: Columbia University Press, 1985.

Seidler, Victor, 'Father, Authority and Masculinity', in Rowena Chapman and Jonathan Rutherford (eds.), *Male Order: Unwrapping Masculinity*. London: Lawrence and Wishart, 1988.

Seidler, Victor Jeleniewski, *Man Enough: Embodying Masculinities*. London, Thousand Oaks, CA and New Delhi: Sage, 1997.

Shortland, Michael and Richard Yeo (eds.), *Telling Lives in Science: Essays on Scientific Biography*. Oxford University Press, 1996.

Showalter, Elaine, *The Female Malady: Women, Madness, and English Culture, 1830–1980*. London: Virago, 1985.

Shuttleworth, Sally, 'Demonic Mothers: Ideologies of Bourgeois Motherhood in the Mid-Victorian Era', in Linda M. Shires (ed.), *Rewriting the Victorians: Theory, History and the Politics of Gender*. New York and London: Routledge, 1992, pp. 31–51.

Slater, Michael, *Dickens and Women*. London and Melbourne: J. M. Dent & Sons, 1983.

Solomon, Robert C., *In Defence of Sentimentality*. Oxford University Press, 2004.

Srebrnik, Patricia, 'The Re-subjection of "Lucas Malet": Charles Kingsley's Daughter and the Response to Muscular Christianity', in Hall (ed.), *Muscular Christianity*, pp. 194–214.

Stanley, A. P., 'Arnold and Rugby', *Macmillan's Magazine* 30 (July 1874), 279–80.

The Life and Correspondence of Thomas Arnold, D.D. [1844], 2 vols., 8th edn. London: T. Fellows, 1858.

Stephen, James Fitzjames, 'Review of Hughes, *Tom Brown's Schooldays*', *Edinburgh Review* 107 (January 1858), 172–93.

Storey, Gladys, *Dickens and Daughter*. London: Frederick Muller Ltd, 1939.

Strachey, Lytton, *Eminent Victorians* [1918]. Harmondsworth: Penguin, 1986.

Literary Essays. London: Chatto & Windus, 1948.

Strange, Julie-Marie, ' "Speechless with Grief": Bereavement, and the Working-Class Father, *c. 1880–1914*', in Broughton, and Rogers (eds.), *Gender and Fatherhood in the Nineteenth Century*, pp. 138–49.

Sully, James, 'The New Study of Children', *Fortnightly Review* 64 (November 1895), 723–37.

Sweet, Matthew, *Inventing the Victorians*. London: Faber and Faber, 2002.

Syson, Damon, 'Daddy's Home', *Observer Magazine* (24 February 2008), pp. 42–49.

Tanner, Michael, 'Sentimentality', *Proceedings of the Aristotelian Society* 77 (1976–7), 127–47.

Thompson, Dorothy, *Queen Victoria: Gender and Power*. London: Virago, 1990.

Tosh, John, 'Authority and Nurture in Middle-Class Fatherhood: The Case of Early and Mid-Victorian England', *Gender and History* 8:1 (April 1996), 48–64.

'Domesticity and Manliness in the Victorian Middle Class: The Family of Edward White Benson', in Michael Roper and John Tosh (eds.), *Manful Assertions: Masculinities in Britain since 1800*. London and New York: Routledge 1991, pp. 44–73.

A Man's Place: Masculinity and the Middle-Class Home in Victorian England. New Haven and London: Yale University Press, 1999.

'Masculinities in an Industrializing Society: Britain 1800–1914', *Journal of British Studies* 44:2 (April 2005), 330–42.

Trevor, Meriol, *The Arnolds: Thomas Arnold and His Family*. London: The Bodley Head, 1973.

Trilling, Lionel, *Matthew Arnold*. New York and London: Columbia University Press and George Allen and Unwin, 1949.

Uffelman, Larry K. and Patrick Scott, 'Kingsley's Serial Novels II: *The Water-Babies*', *Victorian Periodicals Review* 19:4 (Winter 1986), 122–31.

Vallone, Lynne, 'Fertility, Childhood, and Death in the Victorian Family', *Victorian Literature and Culture* 28:1 (2000), 217–26.

Wace, Henry, 'Archbishop Tait and the Primacy', *Quarterly Review* 155 (January 1883), 2–35.

Waller, Jessie Oriana, 'Mental and Physical Training of Children', *The Nineteenth Century* 26 (October 1889), 659–67.

Waters, Catherine, *Dickens and the Politics of the Family*. Cambridge University Press, 1997.

Weintraub, Stanley, *Albert: Uncrowned King*. London: John Murray, 1997.

West, Jenny, 'Gladstone and Laura Thistlethwayte, 1865–75', *Historical Research* 80 (August, 2007), 368–92.

White, Paul, 'Genius in Public and Private', in Alan P. Barr (ed.), *Thomas Henry Huxley's Place in Science and Letters: Centenary Essays*. Athens, GA and London: University of Georgia Press, 1997.

　Thomas Huxley: Making the 'Man of Science'. Cambridge University Press, 2003.

Whitridge, Arnold, *Dr Arnold of Rugby*. London: Constable & Co., 1928.

Williamson, David, *Gladstone the Man*. London: James Bowden, 1898.

Wohl, Anthony S., *The Victorian Family: Structure and Stresses*. London: Croom Helm, 1978.

Wood, Christopher, *Victorian Panorama*. London: Faber, and Faber, 1976.

Woodward, Frances J., *The Doctor's Disciples: A Study of Four Pupils of Arnold Rugby: Stanley, Gell, Clough, William Arnold*. London: Oxford University Press, 1954.

Wymer, Norman, *Dr Arnold of Rugby*. London: Robert Hale Ltd, 1953.

Index

CAMBRIDGE STUDIES IN NINETEENTH-CENTURY
LITERATURE AND CULTURE

General Editor

Gillian Beer, *University of Cambridge*

Titles published